Brown Threat

Brown Threat

Identification in the Security State

Kumarini
Silva

University of Minnesota Press
Minneapolis | London

The Introduction is derived, in part, from "Brown: From Identity to Identification," *Cultural Studies* 24, no. 2 (2010): 167–82, available online at http://www.tandfonline.com/doi/full/10.1080/09502380903541597.

Published by the University of Minnesota Press
111 Third Avenue South, Suite 290
Minneapolis, MN 55401-2520
http://www.upress.umn.edu

Printed in the United States of America on acid-free paper

The University of Minnesota is an equal-opportunity educator and employer.

23 22 21 20 19 18 17 16   10 9 8 7 6 5 4 3 2 1

Library of Congress Cataloging-in-Publication Data
Names: Silva, Kumarini, author.
Title: Brown threat : identification in the security state / Kumarini Silva.
Description: Minneapolis : University of Minnesota Press, [2016] | Includes bibliographical references and index.
Identifiers: LCCN 2016003053 | ISBN 978-1-5179-0002-1 (hc) | ISBN 978-1-5179-0003-8 (pb)
Subjects: LCSH: Racism—United States. | Islamophobia—United States. | Group identity—United States. | Citizenship—United States. | Internal security—United States. | Terrorism—United States—Prevention.
Classification: LCC E184.A1 S598 2016 | DDC 305.800973—dc23
LC record available at http://lccn.loc.gov/2016003053

To David and Ruby with much love and thanks
for hearing the music and
for always keeping rhythm with the mad dancer

I will call my children Mestiza
Because they will be called mixed, biracial, multiracial,
racial, racial, racial
I could call them *Sudda,* which we now think is affectionate
Sinhalese for whitey, but fifty years ago we spat
It out onto the tarred roads the British built for us

I could call them "buck and tan" like my uncle does to
anyone who is "half and half" after the dark brown and
Light brown oxford shoes he had as a child

I will call my children Mestiza because their white father
And their brown mother don't believe in categories

—KUMARINI SILVA, EXCERPT FROM "I WILL CALL MY CHILDREN
MESTIZA," IN *IMAGINING OURSELVES: GLOBAL VOICES
FROM A NEW GENERATION OF WOMEN*

Contents

Introduction
America's Move from Identity to Identification

> When you say "September 11" you are already citing, are you not? You are inviting me to speak here by recalling, as if in quotation marks, a date or a dating that has taken over our public space and our private lives.
>
> —JACQUES DERRIDA, *AUTOIMMUNITY: REAL AND SYMBOLIC SUICIDES*

> BROWN is not exactly the color of excitement. To achieve a hint of glamour, brown must adopt more seductive aliases, like chestnut, cocoa or cafe au lait. Unaltered, brown might as well be plain vanilla, the blah-est of moods, the Charlie Brownest of the ordinary. "Brown shoes don't make it," Frank Zappa sang in a more cutting assessment of this most defenseless of colors.
>
> —ERIC ASIMOV

Prologue

On August 5, 2012, as members of the Oak Creek, Wisconsin, *gurdwara* were preparing *langar*, a communal meal, Wade Michael Page, a White supremacist and former weapons specialist for the U.S. military, walked into the temple and opened fire. Within minutes, the founder of the *gurdwara*, Satwant Singh Kaleka, aged sixty-five; assistant priest Prakash Singh, aged thirty-nine; Paramjit Kaur, aged forty-one; Sita Singh, aged forty-one; Ranjit Singh, aged forty-nine; and Suveg Singh, aged eighty-four, were dead. Longer than a decade after the terrorist attacks of September 11, 2001, their deaths were tragic proof of the ongoing hatred toward a composite, unidentifiable brown threat.

On the day of the shootings, President Barack Obama released an official statement offering condolences to the families of the victims and declaring, "As we mourn this loss which took place at a house of worship, we are reminded how much our country has been enriched by Sikhs, who are a part of our broader American family" (Raghavan and Monteiro 2012). Almost three weeks after the deadly event, on August 24, first lady Michelle Obama visited Oak Creek to meet with grieving families, stating, when thanked by community members for her presence, "I'm the one that's honored to be here. This means so much to me" (Du Bois 2012). In addition to these gestures from the White House, other political entities, both in the United States and globally, strongly spoke out against the attack. At that time, Oak Creek was in the district of then Republican vice presidential candidate Paul Ryan, who introduced his first post-nomination bill in Congress, condemning the massacre. During the second session of the 112th Congress, Resolution 775 condemned the

> senseless attack at the Sikh Temple of Wisconsin in Oak Creek, Wisconsin, on Sunday, August 5, 2012; . . . offers condolences to the families, friends, and loved ones who were killed in the attack and expresses hope for the full recovery of those injured in the attack; . . . honors the selfless, dedicated service of—(A) the emergency response teams and law enforcement officials who responded to the attack; and (B) law enforcement officials who continue to investigate the attack; and . . . remains hopeful, as additional details regarding the attack are gathered, that the citizens of this country will come together, united in a shared desire for peace and justice while standing with the Sikh community to grieve the loss of life.[1]

But despite grandiose gestures like these—gestures that sought to reinforce Sikhs as part of the "broader American community," as referenced in the president's statement[2]—and other political fanfare, the story eventually faded from the public eye. Coinciding with the 2012 Summer Olympics, the death of six Sikhs seemed less relevant to the American public than the number of gold medals won at the Olympic Games in London. But, even as the victims and the outcries against this act of "domestic terrorism"[3] disappeared from the public eye, information about the assassin and his motivations slowly emerged.

There seemed to be a *need* to find out where Wade Michael Page had "gone wrong" and a desire to pinpoint a location where or moment when he had made incorrect "choices"[4] rather than attributing the shootings either to the systemic racism within the country or to Page's own long-standing racist views, which were eventually made public. Page's former stepmother described him as a "kind and loving child," and his best friend from the military, Christopher Robillard, called him "a very kind, very smart individual—loved his friends. One of those guys with a soft spot" (CNN Wire Staff 2012). In the same interviews, Robillard also claimed that although Page was indeed very upset by the events of 9/11 and talked of "holy wars," Robillard didn't believe that Page would "act" on his feelings. Whereas those closest to him attempted to represent Page as a misguided patriot who acted out of character, other information suggested that Page had a long history of involvement in White supremacist groups that showed a clear path leading to the murderous rampage (Elias 2012)—especially foregrounded by the hypervigilantism of post-9/11 U.S. society. In fact, as details of Page's life in the military became public, it was clear that such vigilantism harnessed the latent xenophobia and tied it to other historical and contemporary realties (such as slavery and anti-immigration policies) that simmer underneath the overtly jolly sense of multiculturalism in the United States.[5] It also became clear that such xenophobias are used to feed into, and tacitly sanction, actions like Page's at the same time such actions are decried or denounced as "un-American." Essentially, to define Page as "kind" and "loving" is to blame conditions—such as 9/11—outside the control of Page, or even of American society and policy makers at large, and to nullify the deep and explicit racism of his actions. Such an approach redefines the notions of kind and loving and reframes them within a new discourse of misguided patriotism.

In its analysis of the situation (and providing a much broader context for Page's actions), *The Intelligence Report* of the Southern Poverty Law Center noted the significant influence that the military life in Fort Bragg, North Carolina, had in feeding Page's racist ideologies. It notes that "when Page was transferred there, it also served as the home base for a brazen cadre of White supremacist soldiers. Nazi flags flew and party music endorsed the killing of African-Americans and Jews." In addition, "soldiers openly sought recruits for the National Alliance, then the most dangerous and best organized neo-Nazi group in the country. A billboard just outside the base even advertised for the National Alliance" (Elias 2012). Such displays speak to parallel discourses of race converging around Page's actions: (1) White supremacy as a "tool" or "qualification" for military prowess and love of country and (2) deploying such xenophobic powers to war zones in the Middle East to control and neuter terrorism. Essentially, Page's White (anticolored) supremacist thinking was harnessed to the brown bodies that he was simultaneously being trained to fight and "protect" as part of America's global War on Terror. This contradictory message of U.S. foreign policy in the Middle East was perhaps one of the reasons that the albeit brief, public outcries against Page and his deadly rampage focused, for the most part, on issues of "mistaken identity" and a desire to denounce Page as a racist anomaly in a very accepting U.S. society with an engrained sense of tolerance. While the debates about Page, his mental instability (Heim 2012), the impact of his actions on foreign policy (*Huffington Post* 2012; *Newsmax* 2012), and his subsequent trial remained the most visible aspects of that day, the six dead members of the Sikh American community were soon forgotten. Overshadowed by Olympic coverage, and eventually folded into broader discussions of patriotism, post-9/11 violence, and turbaned brown people, their senseless deaths became yet another casualty of the increasingly normalized and violent racism of contemporary post-9/11 society. When Riddhi Shah, questioning the lack of coverage given to the shooting, rhetorically asked, "Shouldn't this attack, with its label of 'domestic terrorism' and possible political agenda, spark off a larger discussion about the dangerous insularity of American society? Shouldn't we be talking about why white-supremacist ideology would find a favorable recruit in a man with a military background?" the amplified silence of the audience seemed to say no (Shah 2012).

Ironically, at the exact moment the events in Oak Creek were unfolding, I was explaining to a fellow academic what my research was. He responded by asking me whether I honestly thought that the racism against "random brown people" was still as bad as it had been in the aftermath of 9/11. In this instance, there is no pleasure in being proven right, but there is validation for continuing our collective efforts to understand how the events of 9/11 have converged with other sociohistorical facts to create a culture where racism continues to thrive.

Although the election of President Obama seemed to briefly (but inaccurately) represent a moment of post-race(ism), such moments are illusionary and deeply ephemeral in the United States. As the United States struggles with the upkeep of multiple military and political engagements in the Middle East; economic dependencies on the Far East; and immigration, health care, and other political struggles within the country, race becomes both increasingly central and increasingly invisible. After 9/11, the shifting of racial hatred onto brown bodies provided a respite, at least in public and popular discourses, from the long history of anti-Black racism. The fear of Blackness, like other historical "perils," such as the "yellow peril" and the "red peril," was put aside to focus on the "Islamic peril" (Rana 2011). Junaid Rana notes "the racial logic that underlies profiling policies and domestic policing" and that "legal scholars have argued the U.S. government was complicit in these vigilante and extralegal attacks" (51). As the language of security and securitization becomes the basic terminology of rights and citizenship, at the same time that representations of multicultural utopias become staples of visual media, the *increased* prevalence and reality of marginalization and coercion of bodies of color as un-American objects that need policing become less obvious.

The rise of Islamophobia was described by the Runnymede Trust in 1997 as "the dread or hatred of Islam and of Muslims [and it] has existed in western countries and cultures for several centuries, but in the last twenty years has become more explicit, extreme and more dangerous. It is an ingredient of all sections of the media, and is prevalent in all sections of the society" (Conway 1997). Especially after September 11, Islamophobia has produced a culture where being brown—an identification that has become increasingly complicated, as I explain later on— whether somatically or imagined, is seen as abject. Although this abjection is seemingly always harnessed, rhetorically and ideologically, to the attacks in 2001, in reality, it comes out of a much deeper institutionalization of racism in the United States that is rooted in the history of slavery, immigration, and economic disparities that produce a form of collective social anxiety about otherness and difference. Gottschalk and Greenberg (2013), for example, map a long and shared history of Islamophobia in the United States and Britain through a historical exploration of literature, starting in 1697. The authors quote from both theologian Humphrey Prideaux's 1697 tome *The True Nature of Imposture Fully Display'd in the Life of Mahomet* and John Locke's 1689 *A Letter Concerning Toleration* to highlight the ways in which Islam was used as a case of "extremity" and, in Locke's case, to articulate how that extremity reflected on the inclusivity of Protestantism in the British Empire (29).

Such strategic uses of Islam as the *most abject* in an effort to highlight the *most exceptional* aspects of the United States and the British Empire were especially ironic considering that "few Muslims lived in North America and those who did—enslaved African Muslims—seldom were recognized by European Americans as such" (Gottschalk and Greenberg 2013, 27). In present discourses, this connection between African slavery and Islam is largely forgotten, as global politics has shifted Islam to "brown spaces" such as the Middle East and South Asia. Now, geopolitical power struggles—made more visible and public by the foreign policy and military actions undertaken by the administrations of George H. W. Bush and George W. Bush over a two-decade period—have become firmly tethered to brown bodies that supposedly emerge out of these brown spaces.

But the fundamental ideological impetus that Locke had for using Muslims as straw men to make a case for British tolerance is the same ideological impetus that animates contemporary antibrown sentiment, *regardless of where that brown may be located.* As Moustafa Bayoumi (2012) writes, "this is an anxiety about the loss of privileges and power, quite likely related though not exclusively driven by downward economic mobility. . . . Whatever the causes, the form that this hatred takes is cultural, and Muslims, Mexicans, non-White immigrants, really anyone who isn't 'American' by the most conservative definition becomes suspect."

Bayoumi's observations on the loss of power—and the ensuing anxieties around that loss—encapsulate the context for this book. In many ways, this work is an excavation into contemporary anxiety—not psychological anxiety or individual anxiety but a social anxiety surrounding identity. While I delve into the notion of identity in more depth in the following sections, for this moment, I approach it as a form of physical representation made up of socially constructed attributes. Brown identities, and the social baggage they carry, produce a culture of anxiety that is pathologized by political discourse and social interactions (violent and otherwise) and that is, in turn, medicated by popular culture in contemporary U.S. society. And it is this pathologized and medicated relationship between the political and the popular, and its subsequent consequences, that are the focus of this inquiry.

Context: Hordes and Tides—Situating the "New Brown"

In *Brown Tide Rising: Metaphors of Latinos in Contemporary American Public Discourse,* published in 2002, Otto Santa Ana briefly characterizes the political context immediately following the mid-1990s—the timeline focus of his book—by writing, "The United States is experiencing a remarkable moment of domestic ease, as the economy surges to its greatest output in thirty years. The country is content, in contrast to the anxious times of the mid-1990s. As a result, nativist anxieties about the brown population of the United States have also subsided" (xvii). Perhaps prophetically, or with the commonsensical knowledge of any thinking person, Santa Ana goes on to warn that the bubble could burst at any time and that this moment of calm in the xenophobic history of the United States could easily be disrupted. And indeed, that moment of disruption was to follow two years later, in the form of the two terrorist attacks on U.S. soil on September 11, 2001. And with those attacks came a different but also remarkably similar form of xenophobic antibrownness. It was different in that, whereas pre-2001 antibrown sentiments were almost exclusively (at least in public) directed against Latino/a populations, following 2001, this virulence was harnessed against a much larger brown population; it was similar in that, regardless of how conditions change, the practices of racism and xenophobia are always harnessed to nationalism and economics.

This "new" brown shifted, groaned, expanded, and settled to include a metaphorical and somatic identity beyond Latino/as to an unidentifiable and amalgamated Global South/Middle Eastern brown that was rooted in discourses of terror. These browns were not, and are not, viewed as "sleeping giants" or mass hordes washing up in "tides"; instead, they are seen as carefully organized, disruptive networks that are a threat to American security, especially following the events of 2001. And the language of security and securitization is a fire that is fueled by the call on both civil and administrative sectors to act as socially sanctioned vigilantes[6] against unidentifiable assailants. Certainly the growing number of facial recognition and body scan technologies that are increasingly a part of travel, work, and even public life are driven by the need to identify the unidentifiable.[7]

Harnessing and building on the nationalist angst following 9/11, today's anxieties about brown continue to be articulated through that lens, even when it is connected to other issues like global economic trends and global politics. Take, for example, the converging sectors that make up the relationship between India and the United States: starting in the mid-1990s, India's rising force in the global economic and labor markets fuels considerable anxiety for the United States, especially as domestic jobs are outsourced to that continent and India begins to demand a larger role in international economic decision-making processes. The economic and labor anxieties felt in the United States are further intensified by the volatile and unstable relationship with Pakistan—a key geographical location in the "war against terror"—over that country's often wavering support for the U.S.-led presence in the Middle East. Such complex transnational relations and configurations fuel historical proclivities toward racism and racist practices.

While some of those racist practices have been and continue to be violent, especially in the decade after 9/11, there is also a corollary (seemingly benign) cultural appropriation and racism that is manifest in U.S. popular culture. A plethora of South Asian (mostly Indian) cultural goods, including films, music, and clothing, begins to flood the U.S. consumer market in the early 2000s. Indeed, American and British popular culture has embraced awkward Indians and their Holi (wars) as cultural commodities that generate income. Sunaina Maira (2007, 223) calls this "Indo-chic," where "Indo-chic," and "Asian cool" more generally, exemplifies a particular set of historical conjunctures and social anxieties about a "late capitalist orientalism."

These caricatures of a particular form of brown have become enormously popular with Western audiences, who consume them with the voracious appetites of armchair anthropologists. While some of these commodities focus on South Asians in the West (*Aliens in America,* 2007–8; *Little Mosque on the Prairie,* 2007–12), others focus on the West in South Asia (*Outsourced,* 2010–11; *Bollywood Hero,* 2009; *Monsoon Wedding,* dir.

Mira Nair, 2001). Falling between these mediated "travel narratives" are the stories of members of the diaspora (*Bend It Like Beckham,* dir. Gurinda Chadha, 2003; *The Namesake,* dir. Mira Nair, 2006; *The Guru,* dir. Daisy von Scherler Mayer, 2002) as perpetual insiders–outsiders. These representations take place against the backdrop of an ongoing slew of stories generated by *Time, Newsweek,* and *The Economist,* among other news publications, about India's growing power and Pakistan's military instability. It is the triangulation between these various sectors—cultural, political, and economic—that is the focus of this book. It maps the various relationships between cultural performance—mediated and non-mediated—and political culture to interrogate how particular notions of racialized identification are naturalized and made "real." In doing so, it does not mean to lay out a definitive cartography linking one condition with the next: causal relationships are near impossible to map in interrogations of culture. Instead, I ask what connections can be made between the political and cultural anxieties emerging out of global socioeconomic shifts—such as migration and immigration, as well as outsourcing—and their corollary cultural performances in the popular, political, and everyday.

In part, my inquiry follows a model of thinking advocated by Paul Gilroy (2004) in *After Empire: Multiculture or Postcolonial Melancholia.* Gilroy notes that historical nodes of power and their repercussions and manipulations have been realigned around more convoluted axes of power and mobility in such a way that we are more and more living in, next to, and with difference. For Gilroy, the planet is "increasingly divided but also convergent" (3). Such differences and convergences, according to Gilroy, produce "anxious people" who need help coping with "the challenges involved in dwelling comfortably in proximity to the unfamiliar without becoming fearful and hostile" (3). Here I take heed of Gilroy's intimation that we need to try to engage and educate. For me, that work and knowledge come from mapping the space between the past and the rapidly changing future, from studying it as a productive location for understanding the relationship between history and the now. This space consists of divergent areas—among them history, geography, politics, media, migration, immigration, entry, and exit—that make up the prophylactic of cultural politics that collectively produces and medicates the pathologies and anxieties. As such, throughout each chapter, I deploy a multisite analysis that includes political discourse, mediated representations, historical documents, interviews, and other cultural texts. Such a diversity of artifacts is necessary for us to understand the threads that link race relations drawn out here and collectively helps us identify the multiple "anxieties" that Gilroy speaks of.

If we are to understand the shift, after 9/11, from *identity* as the nomenclature of race to *identification,* which is grounded in xenophobic notions of security and threat, we must be willing to clearly acknowledge the enduring relationship between political and popular culture. And, much like Albert Brooks in *Looking for Comedy in the Muslim World* (dir. Albert Brooks, 2005), in which popular culture is the ambassador and mediator of contemporary global politics, very little of it is actually humorous.

Method: Locations

I was visiting family in Sri Lanka when 9/11 "happened." I walked into my parents' house that day in September, after visiting a Hindu temple with my sister, to find my mother and father staring at the television with tears streaming down their faces. Their very real grief—at what they saw as the end of a profound and universal belief in the United States as the safest place on earth (especially for people whose own lives were continually impacted by an ongoing civil war)—was oddly juxtaposed against my own experiences upon returning to the United States. From my moment of arrival into the United States, following September 11 (which I share in more detail later) and well into the present time, I have been struck by the contradictions between that image of my grieving South Asian parents and the growing antibrown sentiment in the country. Motivated by my own experiences of being and becoming brown after 9/11, I started amassing an archive of sorts about various incidents, examples, and actions around brownness. At first, I was not consciously archiving for any particular reason but was merely collecting these examples because they were interesting to me. That collection languished for a few years while I finished my dissertation—on a subject wholly unconnected to 9/11 and only tangentially connected to the United States. But I returned to that archive of news stories, films, television programs, personal experiences, conversations, and fiction as a postdissertation project. It was something to mull over, outside the carefully policed disciplinary boundaries of graduate education. It is that project that unfolds here.

I share this origin story as a context of sorts for my theoretical locations and disciplinary borders. Since I collected that archive out of interest on the broader subject of race and racism after 9/11, what I read theoretically was informed by a similar interest rather than a need for a disciplinary home to locate the project. That approach helped me realize that, by its very nature, brown—as an amalgamation of historical and contemporary facts located in multiple spaces, both physical and ideological—is located nowhere and everywhere.

From this perspective, it makes sense, then, to borrow widely from multiple disciplines or fields, acknowledging that "sometimes people travel with you, or near you, or against you; sometimes they help you, or distract you, or interrupt you, or redirect you; sometimes we take a wrong turn, or a detour, or a dead end; sometimes you are 'hijacked' (Hall 1988c) by another position and sometimes we are the 'hijackers'" (Grossberg 1997, 305). Such a description is apt, for many reasons. First, it appositely describes the interdisciplinary convergences and divergences that this project takes as it articulates a relatively unorthodox approach to defining and studying brown in contemporary culture. Because of its unorthodoxy, I am often located firmly within disciplinary boundaries, specifically cultural studies and media studies; yet, at the same time, I travel alongside other theoretical and methodological approaches, such as Asian American studies, Latino/a studies, and American studies. In addition to this particular resonance with the preceding quotation from Grossberg, this project had its genesis in a special issue of the journal *Cultural Studies* (edited by Grossberg) titled "Conjunctures of Brown," which I guest-edited in 2010. In that issue, I laid the early theoretical groundwork for this project by outlining the relationship between the cultural and the political, where brown—in this instance largely metaphorical, but seemingly tied to the somatic—normalized a social order based on security and discourses of securitization following 9/11. Within these discourses of security and securitization, brown becomes an identificatory strategy that connects the somatic to a metaphorical value. Defining brown as an identificatory strategy rather than as an identity—

as it is used within Chicano/a and Latino/a studies—addresses the need to explain the way brown is continuously deployed in, and produced by, cultural, political, and economic events, both past and present, which are also harnessed to color politics in the United States. In addition, the definition of brown emerges in conversation with and against, and contiguous to existing definitions of brown emerging from, ethnic and area studies.

Such an approach represents a form of destabilizing and decolonizing the theoretical language of race to recognize its processes as multidimensional both in practice and in theory. As Lisa Lowe (1996, 150) writes, "what we call the 'subject' takes place in those articulated spaces of continuing contradictions between the ideological imperative to imagine equivalence and the material disruption of that equivalence, always in process of both speaking and speaking against ideologies of imagined identifications."

Asimov's pithy summary of brown that opens this chapter is an excellent metaphor for what brown identities have become in contemporary North America following September 11, 2001. Prior to the events of 9/11, brown was certainly not considered very exciting, nor was it considered important enough to acknowledge in any meaningful way. But in the current sociopolitical climate, where color-blindness is closely tied to state interventions around security, brown is very much the most defenseless of colors as it is newly imagined. Despite this seeming "newness," I do want to acknowledge that the concept of brown, both somatically and metaphorically, is not new or monochrome in its deployment. As Richard Rodriguez (2002) reminds us in the opening lines of *Brown: The Last Discovery of America,* it is a "color that is not a singular color, not a strict recipe, not an expected result, but a color produced by careless desire, even by accident." And, based on "careless desire," tethered to colonialism and neocolonialism, brown manifests in various locations—from Latin America to South Asia to the creolization of brown in the Caribbean (Harewood 2010). This book acknowledges and appreciates the range of brown and its long history. It recognizes that describing and understanding this category of identity has been a deep and lengthy pursuit in the academy, where the engagement with somatic brown, and its political and popular convergences, has been well documented in many fields, including cultural studies, Latino/a studies, ethnic studies, and communication studies (see, e.g., Valdivia 2000; 2008; Molina-Guzmán 2010; Mendible 2007). Therefore the hope here is not only to think about how discourses and representations construct an otherness simply by being representational but also to understand where and how "browning" is a form of othering that can be transferred from body to body based on specific (but always shifting) cultural and political criteria *at any given time*. By harnessing the representational analysis of specific ethnic identities in popular culture, and theorizing the inherent relationship between culture and power in the naturalization of brown as deviance, the goal of this book is to highlight the ways in which brown, as a metaphor and as a somatic marker, is discursively deployed to reproduce and reinforce existing relations of power through "legitimate" means. In other words, its goal is to show how anyone, at any time, could be brown.

At the same time, there is an essential contradiction in this declaration that I must acknowledge. This project remains tethered to racial hierarchies and racialized transnational (dis)locations that make up both contemporary global culture and U.S. culture. This is due, in large part, to the sociohistorical, political, cultural, and economic relationships within the United States as well as between the United States and other nations, along with historical imperialisms and a different postcolonial sensibility that governs and organizes many of the diasporic communities (Maira 2007; Silva 2010). This research follows on a significant body of work that has focused on mapping race through sites of cultural production and historical and contemporary discourses on migration, immigration, and transnational politics (see, e.g., Mukherjee 2006; Paremesweran 2001; Valdivia 2000; Santo 2002; Nakayama and Krizek 1995). Because this book also engages with the complex relationship between ethnic brown and deviant brown as simultaneously convergent and divergent concepts, it also relies on ethnic and Asian American studies, where issues of race, diaspora, and immigration have been central (e.g., Mani 2012; Mannur 2010; Maira 2007; 2009; Kurien 2003). Media studies, ethnic studies, Asian American studies, and postcolonial studies are harnessed together under the rubric of cultural studies to provide support for the broader arguments about identification that are offered here. Certainly the focus of cultural studies on understanding the relationship between culture and power—and the centrality of race and race performance in these negotiations (Gilroy 1993; 2004; Hall 1992a; 2000; Morley and Chen 1996)—is central to teasing out the aforementioned triangulation between cultural products, politics, and power.

Although this book is primarily focused on the contemporary United States, it must, by its very nature, travel between and through the post- and neocolonial spaces that fuel the aforementioned anxieties that, in turn, create these new racialized identifications. As Stuart Hall (2007, 148–58) points out, "this new conjuncture, neoliberal globalisation, is an international phenomenon, and has involved the re-militarisation of relationships between the West and the rest." Reflecting these geographical mappings, the book also relies on a multisite analysis that includes political discourse, mediated representations, interviews, works of fiction, and other cultural texts to interrogate the convergences between the popular and the political. These divergent texts and discourses collectively form a "structure of feeling" (Williams 1961) that differentiates *this* brown from previous articulations of it. I use Raymond Williams's concept here, fully recognizing the criticisms levied against it as slippery and ambiguous, and I acknowledge Williams's own difficulties in "pinning down" a definition for it. However, I argue that Williams's difficulties with pinning down a definition for this "structure of feeling" are congruous with my approach to brown as an ephemeral, ever-shifting, and mutable identificatory strategy. Additionally, the multiple sites of analysis form a living archive that contradicts the traditional notion of an archive as a completed project and instead places value in recognizing the collection as ongoing (Hall 2001).

Many of the cultural artifacts that I refer to and analyze throughout the book emerge in this living archive to be deployed as prophylactics for the collective anxieties around Hall's "conjuncture of neoliberal globalization." These artifacts, and the anxieties they attempt to assuage, rely extensively on historical narratives of racialized otherness. I also want to make it explicit that although I focus on making the somatic–symbolic–geographical connection between South Asia and South Asian brown, the actual theoretical argument I have laid out here can be applied to *any* identity configuration. The browning metaphor should not be understood as only applying to some kinds of brown and not others, or even to some kinds of bodies and not others. As I stated earlier, anyone at any time could be produced as a brown/deviant by (re)aligning various vectors of both the social and the security of a given time. My approach to brown as a series of identificatory strategies and discourses that produce an (unidentifiable but essentialized) identity allows some flexibility in moving the theoretical aspects of brown from race to other kinds of "deviancies" (such as queer identities) as classified by society at large. These strategies and discourses, in turn, naturalize the system of racialized hierarchies that we come to accept as "normal." Essentially, the various identifications of brown produce what brown means as a "real" identity. And the ideologies of disruptive and dangerous unacceptability that marked Blackness are the same tropes used to describe various othered peoples—from ethnicity to immigration status to geographic location to sexual orientation—in contemporary culture. Therefore to approach identification—almost ephemeral in its fluidity and less somatically tied to a particular group—is to recognize that identities are conceptual rather than fact.

When Identity and Identification Equal Subjugated Essentialism

While acknowledging identity as more than merely somatic, I nonetheless—for the purposes of organization and clarity—define identity in the book as a nomenclature of race. Here nomenclature is understood to be the various historical categories of race making that are routinely employed as stable organizational structures, even as the categories continue to be destabilized and broken down. For example, the U.S. Census as well as online solidarity movements like #BlackLivesMatter use stable race markers as a way to organize society under particular modalities of identity.[8] At the same time that identity is evoked as essential for various overt and covert political interventions—especially around rights discourses—its continued deployment around issues of national security and nation building naturalizes socially constructed and managed ways of being (Hall 2000; Bauman [2004] 2008). It is in essence a paradoxical space, where the stability belies the ways in which identity is manipulated and constructed under sociopolitical, economic, and historical constraints and conditions. It is in this paradoxical space that I locate the relationship between identity and identification. If identity deploys race categories strategically for both maintaining and disrupting social order, its value, then, is its inherent malleability. More simply, identity is always produced as if it were stable, even though the processes of identification constantly change. It is these malleable processes, and the ways in which they are manipulated—by both state and nonstate actors—that I call *identification*. Because these processes of identification are based on matching and grouping any number of identificatory vectors—like class, race, ethnic identity, religion, sex, or sexuality—anyone at any time can be produced as either a law-abiding citizen or deviant terrorist. This practice of assembling various vectors to produce a composite of the abject (vs. the subject) in various contexts, including politics, media, and everyday life, I call *subjugated essentialism*.

Through a manipulation of strategic vectors, both the state and those who act in response to the state, or on behalf of the state, have produced an identity of subjugated essentialism, where the brown body is constantly approached and managed as deviant and/or as a threat to the nation-state.

This particular mapping of identity, identification, and subjugated essentialism relies on and extends the work of José Muñoz (1999) and Gayatri Chakravorty Spivak (1987). The former has written extensively and eloquently on (dis)identification and the latter on strategic essentialism. For Muñoz, disidentification is a form of "recycling and rethinking encoded meaning. The process of disidentification scrambles and reconstructs the encoded message of a cultural text in a fashion that both exposes the encoded message's universalizing and exclusionary machinations and recruits its workings to account for, include, and empower minority identities and identifications" (31). Along similar lines, Spivak argues that in contemporary rights politics, marginalized groups can potentially navigate "a strategic use of positivist essentialism" for what she calls "scrupulously visible political interest" (205). For Spivak and Muñoz, universalizing meanings and political managements can be countermanipulated by deliberately misreading and actively rejecting universalizing essentialisms. While I agree with both Muñoz and Spivak that the emancipatory potentials of strategic essentialism and disidentification exist, I also extend this to ask what happens when the disidentification and essentialism are produced outside the individual or collective that seeks emancipation. More simply, what impact do mass-produced (political and cultural), deliberate (mis)identifications (rather than disidentifications) and essentialisms look like? And what are their disciplining practices? Throughout the book, each chapter illuminates an answer to this broader question.

Racial Logic and Racialization

One essential focus of this book is that it engages with ways in which a national obsession with security and nation building after 9/11 effectively circumvented long-standing race struggles in the United States. A clarion call to unite against a common (brown) enemy in the immediate and subsequent aftermath created a fragile, faux esprit de corps that lingered for several years after 2001, eventually erupting in race riots in 2014. When the very public murders of Trayvon Martin, Michael Brown,[9] Eric Garner,[10] and Renisha McBride (among others) collectively added to a percolating anger at the continued overt and covert ostracization of Black bodies in contemporary culture, they eventually led to protests in various parts of the country.

The intensity of the responses and protests, such as those in Ferguson, Missouri, and marches in New York City, highlights the faux post-racial nationalist camaraderie, effectively hiding the ways in which historical racisms continued, and continue, to thrive in the United States. Perhaps more egregiously, it disguised how this obsession with national security was, and continues to be, used strategically in the service of maintaining racial hierarchies both nationally and internationally. Here Blackness was constructed as equally malleable to brown. In "Heteropatriarchy and the Three Pillars of White Supremacy," Andrea Smith[11] (2006) notes that these racial hierarchies differ through historical conditions and constraints but are nonetheless often evoked as an amalgamated universalized minority group that suffers shared and equal discrimination. For Smith, race relations in the United States function along three differing but equally distributed pillars that hold up the normalizing and neutral functions of Whiteness. Slavery and capitalism, genocide and colonialism, and Orientalism and war, Smith tells us, point to the differing structures that are harnessed to shore up a White norm. I extend this framework to show the ways in which these pillars are then used strategically *against each other* to continue racial hierarchies, while seeming to eliminate them. For example, Smith notes that the twin discourses of slavery and capitalism continue to be applied to Black bodies through the prison–industrial complex. But, as I explain in detail in chapter 4, the prison–industrial complex—deployed as it is to produce and discipline Blackness—was effortlessly harnessed to brown through national security in the aftermath of 9/11. Smith points out that Orientalism and war construct certain peoples as "civilizations" that are a threat to the United States and that these people's bodies serve as "anchors" for U.S. military intervention. This is further complicated by the fact, as Alfred López (2005) has noted, that many immigrants to the United States have a complex and contradictory relationship to Whiteness based on their experiences of colonization. For these communities, Whiteness is both a desire and a representation of power that must be adhered to and followed at all costs.

This popular and political discursive shift temporarily relocated Blackness outside slavery/capitalism, but eventually, the deeply embedded and historically naturalized anti-Black sentiments erupted publicly and violently, recentering long-held antagonisms. This is especially visible in the ways welfare reform laws have been harnessed to the Illegal Immigration Reform and Immigrant Responsibility Act of 1996 and powers have been granted to local authorities to act on behalf of identifying and determining illegality and poverty through race. Here brown illegality is connected to discourses of Black (willful and amoral) poverty and is articulated as a drain on "American" resources. This notion of draining resources has become a mantra for political autocrats, including presidential candidates Donald Trump and Jeb Bush. On June 16, 2015, Trump announced his bid for the office of president and, in that speech, noted that "when Mexico sends its people, they're not sending their best. They're not sending you. They're not sending you. They're sending people that have lots of problems, and they're bringing those problems with us [sic]. They're bringing drugs. They're bringing crime. They're rapists. And some, I assume, are good people" (Lee 2015). Despite considerable backlash, Trump has stood by the statement, declaring that he does "not have a racist bone" in his body but is merely stating "the truth."

Reading This Book

I am, by nature, a storyteller. By profession, I like to think I am a sociocultural cartographer. This book combines these two narratives that represent my self to tell stories about race and otherness in contemporary culture. But these are not the fairy tales of a perfect life; they are the real events that expose the underbelly of an imagined perfection—one that comes at enormous cost to those whose selves are imagined as dangerous and without value. Each chapter deals with a particular theme that emerges out of visual culture and asks how these particular representations serve to create a contemporary understanding of brown, both dependent on and, at the same time, separated from the past. It combines popular visual texts, including film and television, contemporary fiction, online and historical documents, and political and public discourses, as multiple sites that speak collectively to they ways brown is produced as simultaneously coherent and malleable. The chapters juxtapose visual spectacle against and by way of the historical patterns of immigration, migration, and movement as well as broader discourses about race and race relationships in the United States to articulate the compelling and productive relationship between popular culture and political culture as they coproduce various identities and categories of identification.

Starting with a simple question, "What Is Brown?," I map my theoretical approach to this category that I call both somatic and metaphorical in chapter 1. Foregrounded by the way arrivals and departures to the United States are structured following 9/11, and tying that to the political implications of immigration, in this opening chapter, I lay out the foundations of brown as both deeply historical and newly established. Through specific examples of detention and interrogation that are tethered to archival invisibility, I articulate the fluidity of brown as something that moves from body to body, simultaneously marked as brown and yet disconnected from the way we popularly understand the identity.

In chapter 2, I move to connect this concept of brown to how "belonging" is positioned under new forms of patriotism and homeland. Following September 11, 2001, one of the most contested and complicated concepts was *home*. In this instance, home, both as constructed nation-state and excessively romanticized belonging, converged under both governmental and social spheres. The way to demarcate belonging was based on identifying and producing those *who did not belong*. Such a demarcation happened on two levels. On the state level, the U.S. Department of Homeland Security (DHS) and the Uniting and Strengthening America by Providing Appropriate Tools Required to Intercept and Obstruct Terrorism

Act of 2001 (USA PATRIOT Act) were put into effect to secure the geographically marked homeland from external perpetrators. The popular and visual culture translation of this state-mandated "homeland" facilitated the recategorization of all of America—ostensibly united and strengthened under the act—into two populations: those who belonged and those who did not. It is here that I begin my discussion. I approach this concept of belonging (or not) by focusing in chapter 2 on how the state and popular and political discourses produced and act(ed) on this notion of belonging.

I first look at the way "home" was produced by the state in the immediate aftermath of 9/11 through the consolidation of the DHS, interrogating how such a demarcation creates an identification of patriot versus terrorist—essentially the formalized production of subjugated essentialism described earlier. I then look at how the legal/state establishment of a "homeland" translates this notion of subjugated essentialism to society at large. This latter section has two foci: one is the way that identities are produced as part of the discourses of securitization; the other is how the sense of alienation becomes part of diasporic communities in the United States.

Although the government, and the administration of George W. Bush in particular, repeatedly stated that the changes in law and the convergence of various governmental departments—including the Immigration and Naturalization Service—under the newly created DHS were meant as protection, the governmental restructuring validated the fears of "unidentifiable others" that were heightened after 9/11. Indeed, two months after the attacks, on November 8, President Bush cautioned the American public that the citizenry had "new responsibilities," which included being vigilant—"inspect our mail, stay informed on public health matters"—even while he cautioned against "exaggerated fears or passing rumors" (Bush 2001b). The President urged Americans to have "good judgment and good old common sense. We will care for those who've lost loved ones and comfort those who might, at times, feel afraid. We will not judge fellow Americans by appearance, ethnic background or religious faith" (Bush 2001b).

The contradictory demands of this message—we must be vigilant but not exaggerate our fears; we must inspect our mail but not judge fellow Americans by appearance; and where good old common sense was essentially the same as good judgment, though neither is explained or identified—are exemplary of the ways in which the concepts of "home" and "belonging" translated to American citizenry. The collective "we" included in this message are clearly those whose appearance couldn't be judged because of their ethnic backgrounds and religious faiths. Essentially, language like this, coupled with the policies around immigration, produced a normative, baseline American citizen against whom everyone else was/could/should be judged: a White, Judeo-Christian avatar of wholesome Americanness.

Such a validation of Whiteness by the state empowered much of the citizenry to act on these notions of otherness, building on existing racial hierarchies in the United States. A form of citizen-vigilante emerged that took on the "burden" of protecting the homeland from deviant brown bodies. In the second half of chapter 2, I look at the impact of this state–citizen corollary that results in a form of alienation for the diasporic community.

In chapter 3, I look at the corollary of who belongs. If the "we" who do belong are tethered to a construction of the citizen as a vigilante, then how do those "we" recognize who does not belong? The chapter looks at various examples of how nonbelonging is produced through the framework of brown as an identification of deviance—especially as either funny or as terror suspect. Extending this argument about belonging and connecting it to the anxieties surrounding shifts in contemporary global politics and economics that I have explained in this introduction, I juxtapose the construction of space and place *outside* the homeland. Here I argue that space and place, as visually represented in the short-lived television series *Outsourced* and the film *Looking for Comedy in the Muslim World* (dir. Albert Brooks, 2005), work to validate the antibrown sentiments in the United States by highlighting their difference from a mythic American "norm" that is largely signified through Whiteness.

I also juxtapose the concepts of Homeland and the Other to look at how these mediated images simultaneously propagandize American exceptionalism while ignoring the hyperracist contexts of post-9/11 American society. I argue that this form of exceptionalism and the construction of U.S. vs. Other help to medicate the pathological anxiety that has pervaded the country since the attacks of September 11. I extend Evelyn Alsultany's (2012) notion of "simplified complex representation" to highlight how a random brown becomes a construction of terror, which is then corralled through either humor or valor.

Chapter 4 looks at how this post-9/11 brown and the shift to identification intersect with historical race policies and politics in the United States. The chapter was initially based on the premise that a prolonged national obsession with brownness and brown identification displaces sustained conversations about Blackness and its history and that—as Blackness becomes subsumed in brown securitizations—it would take an eruption or visible upheaval for Blackness to become a centralized discourse in U.S. race politics after 9/11. Shortly after I finished the chapter, the most extensively publicized act of racism against an African American in recent times took place: the murder of Trayvon Martin at the hands of George Zimmerman. When Zimmerman was acquitted, it seemed inevitable that there would be more public incidents of anti-Black violence. Such blatant dismissal violence against a minority population normalizes and even sanctions that disciplining as an inevitability: a "burden" based on racist stereotypes. Since then, we have been witness to the murders of Michael Brown (2014) and Eric Garner (2014); the massacre of Cynthia Marie Graham Hurd, Susie Jackson, Ethel Lee Lance, DePayne Middleton Doctor, Clementa C. Pinckney, Tywanza Sanders, Daniel Simmons, Sharonda Coleman-Singleton, and Myra Thompson in Charleston, South Carolina (2015);[12] and the suicide of Sandra Bland[13] in police custody (2015), among a host of other violent deaths, some publicly documented, others invisible. Even public protests in Ferguson, Missouri, and the activism of groups like #BlackLivesMatter and #SolidarityIsForWhiteWomen[14] to educate the general public about the ways in which explicit and implicit violence impacts communities across the country have been unable to quell what seems to be a rising tide of increased and systematic violence against African Americans. Instead, their very presence gives rise to countermovements that reinforce White supremacy. I share this here as context for the basic premise of the argument I make in chapter 4: that these realities were/are predicated on the focus on national security and securitization—vis-à-vis brown terror—coupled with the apocryphal cries of a (fictitious) post-race America with the election of Barack Hussein Obama II as the forty-fourth president of the United States.

I conclude the book by revisiting the concept of brown that I started with, broadly summarizing its core value and applying it to some recent examples of brown (mis)identification.

1
What Is Brown?
Theorizing Race in Everyday Life

No doubt there are certain general features to racism. But even more significant are the ways in which these general features are modified and transformed by the historical specificity of the contexts and environments in which they become active. In the analysis of particular historical forms of racism, we would do well to operate at a more concrete, historicized level of abstraction (i.e., not racism in general but racisms).

—STUART HALL, *GRAMSCI'S RELEVANCE TO THE STUDY OF RACE AND ETHNICITY*

I write about race in America in hopes of undermining the notion of race in America.

—RICHARD RODRIGUEZ, *BROWN: THE LAST DISCOVERY OF AMERICA*

In the film *Vijay and I* (dir. Sam Garbarski, 2013), the protagonist Wilhelm Wilder (Moritz Bleibtreu), a curmudgeonly forty-year-old German-Jewish New Yorker who works as a rabbit in a popular children's program, decides to capitalize on a case of "mistaken death" to find out what his friends and family really think of him. With the help of his best friend, Rad (Danni Pudi)—who owns an Indian restaurant where the waiters, all of them Latino, are trained to *act* Indian with lessons in turban wearing, "sounding Indian," and painting brown faces—Wilhelm transforms himself into Vijay Singh, a courtly and sophisticated Indian gentleman who attends Wilhelm's funeral claiming a long-standing friendship with the "deceased." As Vijay Singh, the heretofore rather uninteresting and self-absorbed Wilhelm is considerably more charismatic and likeable, and even manages to seduce the grieving widow—his own wife.

I share this film here because, in many ways, *Vijay and I* visually and narratively exemplifies my approach to brown. The ways in which Wilhelm's Jewish identity is ethnicized as *barely* White and folded into his friendship with Rad—a man who literally browns other brown faces for his own gain—solidifies his identity as outside conventional modes of Whiteness, and normalcy, and reproduces his brown face as both literally and metaphorically (a deviant) brown. As the film proceeds, the subaltern subjectivity that Wilhelm performs becomes increasingly racist, as he seeks advice in the *Kama Sutra* for new lovemaking techniques so his wife won't recognize him in bed, and as he utters "German" words with an "Indian" accent when she asks him to excite her with "Indian dirty talk." The use of multiple cross-dressings and interethnic performance—Latinos as Indians, Indians as hybrid subjects, Jews as Indians—connects the characters through a particular performance of brown that converges around a sense of shared alterity. This arrangement in the film speaks to the ways in which brown is contexualized throughout this book.

Brown is, as exemplified by the film, a moving target that is applied (literally and metaphorically) to bodies to mark otherness in seemingly benign but exceedingly insidious fashion. Here the target moves between *actual* brown bodies and within bodies that are also "browned" through a process of deviant behaviors. As such, *Vijay and I* is a fitting segue for shaping a response to the question, what is brown?

In the following sections, I outline the approaches I take to rethinking brown outside, within, and through its somatic and metaphorical manifestations following September 11, 2001. I do so, perhaps naively, in the same spirit that Richard Rodriguez wrote of brown in 2002. Whereas Rodriguez approached his brown as a rewriting of its history in celebration, I attempt to map its malleability as a tool of hegemony. At times this mapping is tangential, at other times it is more concrete and laid out against the bodies of color that make up contemporary global movements. Its ebb and flow speaks to the complications of articulating identification against and with/in identity.

While the processes of racializing and categorizing people based on somatic identities and perceived differences are deeply historical in the United States, it is perhaps not until 9/11 that identification—of specifically targeted communities and peoples as threats to national security— has so *effortlessly* become incorporated into everyday life. The rapid institutionalization and immediate acceptance of the social and political practices of identification as the way it *must be* and *should be* in the aftermath of 9/11 speak to the broad machinations that go into constructing, producing, and maintaining racialized social order—essentially, the practices produced through the "historical specificity" that Hall speaks of in the epigraph to this chapter. Starting with the larger theoretical, political, and social processes, followed by documentations of brown experience, immediately after 9/11, including my own, brown here is an identification of deviance that moves from body to body in a culture that is consumed by the language of security and securitization.

Brown versus Brown

When Wilhelm asks Rad, in *Vijay and I,* whether the process of browning already browned Latinos to be waiters costs less money than hiring actual Indians for the job, Rad admits that there is no financial advantage but that there is value in protecting what he owns, explaining that hiring "real Indians" will result in them stealing his recipes and opening their own restaurants. Rad's desire to protect his "assets" by browning differently browned bodies encapsulates the ways in which the historically constructed (brown) e/raced bodies, such as Latino/a and Chicano/a identities, become subsumed within the metaphorical deployment of brown as part of the culture of identification that arose after September 11, 2001. This convergence of historical brown with "terrorist" brown produces a process of identification that simultaneously rejects and relies on past racisms. Converging multiple vectors of identities, both old and new, under discourses of security and securitization effectively animated a form of securitized nationalism that hinged on two interrelated concepts: (1) to secure the homeland from threats and (2) to identify and separate those considered a threat from those who belonged within the secured perimeters of the nation-state. The process by which this happened was largely through governmental (see chapter 2) and rhetorical practices of the Republican administration in power at that time and through the internalization of those administrative acts by the general populace. For example, in the immediate aftermath, President George W. Bush (2001c) declared,

> A great people has been moved to defend a great nation. Terrorist attacks can shake the foundations of our biggest buildings, but they cannot touch the foundation of America. These acts shatter steel, but they cannot dent the steel of American resolve. America was targeted for attack because we're the brightest beacon for freedom and opportunity in the world. And no one will keep that light from shining. Today, our nation saw evil—the very worst of human nature—and we responded with the best of America.

Language like this, along with images of mourning citizens, effectively mobilized the latent sense of nationalism that had long simmered below the mythologized melting pot of contemporary U.S. society. Undergirding this discourse of securitized nationalism was an implicit *profile* of those who fit within the secured nation-state.

Addressing the country in a joint session of Congress on September 20, President Bush effectively and implicitly outlined the profiles of both citizen and denizen, claiming that "terrorists practice a fringe form of Islamic extremism that has been rejected by Muslim scholars and the vast majority of Muslim clerics; a fringe movement that perverts the peaceful teachings of Islam." He went on to explain that the "terrorists' directive commands them to kill Christians and Jews, to kill all Americans and make no distinctions among military and civilians, including women and children" (*Washington Post* 2001).

By constructing a dichotomy between the blood lust of al-Qaeda and unmarked (and therefore, by contrast, peace-loving) Christians and Jews, Bush managed to define Islam and Christianity within a muted paradigm of clashing civilizations, even while he paid lip service to American multiculturalism by defining the attackers as Islamic extremists and not as "regular" Muslims. This rhetoric was then harnessed to promoting an American Way of Life—set against the primitivism of the Middle East—that was defined by a White, patriarchal heteronormativity, harnessed to military prowess that spoke to American exceptionalism (Puar 2007).[1] When Bush asked Americans to live our lives and hug our children, "even in the face of a continuing threat," and told citizens to "uphold the values of America and remember why so many have come here," America emerged in the discourse as a country where Christian families prayed together to protect and uphold the nation-state and its values against a powerful and unseen threat. It is during those early days of implicitly defining the core citizen as primarily White and Christian that we begin to see the first articulations of a *metaphorical* brown. This metaphorical brown represents the first of two approaches to brown that I take throughout this chapter and the chapters that follow.

In this first instance, brown becomes a metaphor or a moving and mutable signifier that can be applied to any body that is considered outside the norms of social conventions demarcated by what I call discourses of securitized nationalism following 9/11—a securitized nationalism produced by discourses such as the aforementioned speeches of George W. Bush and the subsequent translation of those early ideologies into law.[2]

Under this emerging regime, all those who did not fall within the ideological bounds of White, Christian heteronormativity were produced as suspect subjects and therefore became metaphorically brown—neither the privileged and protected *White* nor the perennially marginalized and dismissed *Black*. These metaphorical brown (deviant) bodies—from immigrants to mixed-race people to same-sex couples—are approached as *outliers* who actively work against core American beliefs.[3] Through both political and popular maneuverings, preexisting tensions between the conservative political and religious beliefs of the Republican administration, on one hand, and various rights organizations, including immigrant and gay rights movements, on the other, were obscured by a call and a mandate to rally around a constructed national ethos as a response to the attacks.

Under these post-9/11 conditions, where fear and insecurity were the defining characteristics, those who challenged that unified nationalism were considered deviant distractions. It is these supposed deviants who fall under the category of "new" brown. Here the new brown is not separate from the historical somatically defined deployments of the color but instead is harnessed and extended to any behaviors, places, spaces, and performances that challenge the hegemonic Whiteness of U.S. neonationalism. Because these deviant outliers challenge the notion of a particular and recently repopularized version of American nationalism, it was seen—and continues to be seen—as necessary to rearticulate those deviants as *a threat*. But, even while articulating the threat and asking citizens to participate in policing that threat, it is also important to construct that threat as containable and controllable, because such containment is imperative to reinforcing this particular nationalist discourse.

In other words, those who are perceived as threats are marked as threats, but not as so dangerously threatening that they can't be controlled. Because the threats are never clearly explained, and are seemingly randomly produced, brown as a category can be applied to any group and not necessarily (though it often is) to a group that is also somatically brown.

This leads me to my second approach to brown.

Because brown as a color is seen as boring, dull, the color of dirt, unimportant (Zappa's "brown shoes don't make it"), these qualities are also metaphorized onto the bodies and characters of those who are constructed as brown.

In this instance, the social value of brown as a signifier for deviant subjects is based on the social construction of brown as the "dullest and least memorable of colors." Made up by mixing the three basic primary colors of blue, red, and yellow, it lacks any visual or aesthetic merit and merely signifies boredom and abjection. This association of brown with boredom and abjection works to reimagine brown, on one hand, as devoid of character and, on the other, as insidious and parasitic in its very existence. The lack of character comes, of course, from our association of brown with all things uninteresting and unseemly: mud, dirt, feces, and so on. These are the excesses and excrements of our existence and, though serving important functions, are best not displayed or discussed. They are what Erving Goffman (1990) would call "backstage" activities.

So, we have the common, accepted understanding of brown as something that is of no import. Ironically, it's this very lack of presence that allows brown bodies, both metaphorical and somatic, to be constructed as insidiously parasitic within contemporary U.S. culture. In a culture where glamour and visibility are marks of success, brown, both as a sensible quality and as a racialized category, can only be seen as something that does not strive to attain. By being unglamorous and not aspiring to be more visible, it is always suspect. Why would someone *want* to be invisible and struggle in the land of opportunity, if not to work against that land and all it stands for?

By ignoring systemic structural practices that have marginalized colored bodies, and instead framing the discourse in terms of sloth, ignorance, and the reluctance to assimilate, the marginalization of brown is
constructed as a self-inflicted condition that needs to be supervised and
managed. This is accomplished by harnessing the two overlapping meanings of brown (the metaphorical and the somatically brown bodies) and
(re)presenting the amalgamation as a pathology that needs political,
legal, and/or popular intervention.

This sense of brown relies heavily on the convergence of the somatic,
metaphorical, and discursive vis-à-vis the popular and political. It brings
together multiple sociopolitical issues/identities/performances that separate it from the somatic history that it has been tied to. Instead, it is positioned *simultaneously* by cultural and political producers to rationalize
cultural, political, and economic changes and neonationalisms, both in
the United States and abroad. In this sense, brown becomes a new coher-
ence of racialized discourse, deployed broadly by cultural and political
producers.

For example, consider the fractured representation between the original movie *Outsourced* (dir. John Jeffcoat, 2006) and its sitcom counterpart that is the focus of discussion in chapter 3. I argue in that chapter
that the comedic representation of the outsourced space serves to con-
tain and neuter the growing fear of India's economic and political capa-
bilities. Indeed, after 9/11, an identificatory chain was produced to include South Asians under the fluid and amorphous rubric of "terrorist"
that floats in the United States. It follows along these lines: a militant
Muslim becomes an Arab; all Arabs are brown and wear turbans; all
brown, turban-wearing people are Arab terrorists; all Sikhs are brown
and wear turbans; so all Sikhs are terrorists. Similarly, Bollywood kitsch
is authentic India; India is the universal South Asia; South Asia is available for purchase on film and in fashion; and through this, brown becomes a fashion statement and cultural commodity.

As these two narratives of identity collide, collude, and circulate,
both the political state (the representative governing bodies within politics) and the cultural state (the representative creators of cultural production) have successfully managed, through strategic deployments of
identification, to police and maintain brown as particular broader *metaphorical* identity, connected mostly to colored, deviant bodies, which

then comfortably fits within popular discourses and narratives of racialized minorities.[4]

But there is a caveat to this seemingly stable marginalization: Hall (1992b), Derrida (1978), Butler (1990), and Laclau (1994), among others, have argued that marked identities (such as woman and Black) are built on exclusion and are juxtaposed against unmarked norms (such as man and White). This exclusion acts as a method of policing borders. In other words, for there to be a stable center, there must be a periphery against which it is measured. However, although this has been historically and categorically true, the widespread visibility and ongoing deployment of brown in popular culture as a cultural commodity and in political discourse as an immigration issue and terrorist threat challenge a simple center–periphery model. Furthermore, constructing it as a center–periphery model, as has been common governmental practice, hides the more powerful and insidious nature of this particular constructed identification.

Brown does not find its genesis in the marginal, the peripheral, the way most previous racialized identities have. Instead, by broadly classifying brown, and circulating it in strategic ways across the center, the peripheralization of brown seems necessary and, indeed, justifiable. In the next section, I explain this practice of the broad categorization of brown by inverting Gayatri Spivak's notion of *strategic essentialism* to *subjugating essentialism*.

From Strategic Essentialism to Subjugating Essentialism

The various examples in this chapter highlight how the political and popular deploy the convergence of a marked body with the notion of deviance, to strategically essentialize the ostensibly unidentifiable. Such an anomalous convergence circumvents any actual critical interrogation or specific identification of a deviant body. Instead, it creates a strategically essentialized deviant who is marked by random colors, behaviors, and characteristics that are generated under changing security conditions.

When Gayatri Chakravorty Spivak (1988) introduced the concept of strategic essentialism as a form of political interrogation and intervention, she argued that its value rested on its ability to acknowledge and recognize essentialism as dangerous in its uncritical application, while understanding it as powerful when critically and judiciously applied. More simply, its political efficacy lay in a critique of essentialism rather than the blind application of it. So, when a group essentializes its own identity for a larger political voice, what is that essentialism saying about the structures they are fighting to gain that voice?

Following 9/11, strategic essentialism became somewhat of a liability, as South Asian immigrants rushed to separate their brown identities along religious lines that separated the brown Muslim—the harbinger of terrorism—from the brown Christian, the devout patriot (Kurien 2003). As the possibilities of a strategically essentialist coalition to combat post-9/11 racism against South Asians were severely challenged, a form of essentialism that I am calling *subjugating essentialism* was taken up by cultural and political producers to create an anomalous and amorphous category of deviant brownness. With this the essentializing forces were/are not the political tools of the subaltern but rather the tools of the hegemon.

This essentialized brown is not separate from Latin American, Chicano/a, or Hispanic brown per se but rather is manipulated and extended to include other kinds of brown, whatever those browns may be. It is an essentialism that creates and maintains a subaltern that is subjugated in a strategic subordination. For example, the idea of a terrorist as a "Middle Eastern"–looking woman or man evokes a corresponding visual—one that has brown skin, dark hair, a generalized turban or head covering—that has been perfected over the last decade and a half.

From a security and political perspective, this crude caricature of brown serves two purposes: on one hand, it identifies a threat that can be collectively controlled because it allows the political- and/or citizen-vigilante to respond to *everyone* as a threat. It also sanctions whatever actions these self-appointed guardians of White American nationalism might take, such as removing a family of "Muslim-looking" passengers from an airline because other passengers are uncomfortable (Chandrasekhar 2003). On the other hand, such an expansive group of brown subjects allows for the shoring and demarcation of privileged race identities, specifically Whiteness. As brown becomes a subjugated essentialism that is applied to a wide and unwieldy group, those outside of it are reified and granted license to act on that essentialism by identifying— and producing the identification of and for—the deviant body.

This form of identification is not new. Indeed, the historical colonial project, as practiced by Britain and France, for example, was based on identifying and demarcating geographies through similar identificatory practices for economic and political gain. This was later extended by the American empire, when it converged strategic political interests with educational policy and funded area studies programs throughout the country. The original mandate of area studies in the U.S. academy was the study of race and identity—including U.S. ethnic studies—in the service of the political and economic interests of those in power. Therefore my impetus to frame/ground brown as identification (beyond a geographically specific community) is fueled by a desire to dislodge brown from what Dave et al. (2000, 79) have called "community studies," where race and ethnicity are studied through the academic models and practices that have roots in U.S. foreign policy–led ethnic studies programs. For me, such a dislocation proves useful because it encourages a continuous engagement with the how and why of racial and ethnic categorization and its systemic practices in the United States. In doing so, it is important to keep two realities salient. First is that we must acknowledge the colonial hand in creating and maintaining racial and ethnic identities for economic and global power. As Anibal Quijano (2007, 169) writes,

> the colonial structure of power produced the social discriminations which later were codified as "racial," "ethnic," "anthropological" or "national," according to the times, agents and populations involved. These intersubjective constructions, produced by colonial domination by the Europeans, were even assumed to be categories (of "scientific" and "objective" pretension) with a historical significance. That is, as natural phenomena, not referring to the history of power. This power structure was, and still is, the framework within which operate the other social relations of classes and estates.

This leads to the second reality: the racial categories created by colonial practices have become increasingly complicated in contemporary times and cannot be easily (if it ever was easy) applied to identities. As Prema Kurien (2003, 27) notes, "race is an important principle of classification in the U.S. that does not always fit neatly within the official ethnic categories of American society." These two realities produce the conditions that allow for brown to be circulated as an identificatory strategy, as detailed in the following pages.

Circulating Brown as an Identificatory Strategy

The broad circulation of brown culturally and its peripheralization politically and governmentally are interconnected and reciprocal. They feed off each other. This symbiotic relationship supports the cultural manifestations (as a symbol of abstract multiculturalism) at the same time as it justifies the political interventions. This is possible only because the anomalous, ahistorical nature of brown, as it is circulated in the United States, is approached as an identification (assigned to anyone perceived as a threat rather than historically grounded) that needs to be policed and controlled.

This form of thinking has become especially obvious following September 11. For example, while films, such as *Bend It Like Beckham,* that reproduce notions of American exceptionalism—in this case through an emphasis on the wonders of freedom for women's soccer in the United States—became extremely popular in the United States in the six days following September 11, 641 acts of violence against South Asian and Arab Americans were documented (*American Backlash* 2001). While American audiences cheered a British-Indian girl as she defied her parents to come to America to play soccer, living out her American Dream,[5] other Americans, over a period of months, weeks, and years, were busy demanding that random assortments of people, identified as brown threats, "go back to their own country."

Despite these calls for brown to "leave," on January 27, 2006, *Passions,* a soap opera on the U.S. television network NBC, aired a much hyped and promoted dream sequence. Mimicking a dance sequence common to Bollywood films, the seven-minute clip was meant as an introductory vision of the impending nuptials, *in India,* of the hero and heroine. For our purposes here, I am less interested in an analysis of the sequence itself. Instead, what is more telling is the circulation of this particular identification of brown in the notoriously Anglophone and ethnocentric genre of daytime soap operas. In this instance, brown, as a *cultural industry* (visualized and articulated as Bollywood), resonates with an American audience as a non-American, deliciously kitsch symbol of Other. Made to seem simultaneously exotic and benign, the brown *Passions* sequence acts as the perfect foil to an issue of *Newsweek* devoted to India, published six weeks later on March 6. The issue—from its cover featuring Indian-born model and television personality Padma Lakshmi to Pulitzer Prize–winning American novelist Jhumpa Lahiri discussing her Indian heritage (as non-American) to a call center worker pictured in front of the Taj Mahal—in its content and in its very existence, symbolizes the simultaneous fetishizing, fear, and taming of brown.

Keeping with this sudden popularity of brown in consumer culture, in 2007, both Canada and the United States debuted sitcoms that deal with the arrival of brown bodies to Midwestern locales in both geographies. In Canada, *Little Mosque on the Prairie,* created by Zarqa Nawaz, provides a somewhat stereotypical but relatively positive view of the Muslim community. In *Aliens in America,* created by David Guarascio and Moses Port for CBS-owned cable station the CW, the Tolchucks, a White family from Medora, Wisconsin, deal with the arrival of Raja Musharaff, a sixteen-year-old Pakistani exchange student, to their home. The ensuing misunderstandings and cultural differences (including Raja's arrest for buying parts to build bombs when he was buying materials to build a rocket for a school project) reproduce the formulaic, Huntingtonian "clash of civilizations" (1996) discourse that pervades U.S. political culture. *Aliens in America* reminds its viewers constantly that brown is alien. Brown is confusing and possibly (probably) threatening.

This cultural circulation of brown is juxtaposed against the ongoing debate in American politics over immigration policy. For example, the Secure Borders, Economic Opportunity, and Immigration Reform Act of 2007 (S. 1348), proposed to grant more than nine million "illegal" immigrants work visas and permanent residency cards at the same time as it sought to increase the security—and build a permanent barrier—on the border between the United States and Mexico. Thus the cultural process of identification of a particular notion of brown, through the banality of Bollywood dance sequences, is also representative of the perceived political threat of brown through immigration. Although this book focuses on South Asia and South Asians, it is important to recognize that this process of taming brown (for fear of invasion) is beyond a somatically identifiable, racial identity. The *notion* of brown is deployed as something outside the Black/White dichotomy to mark threats. Thus, offering 9/11 as their rationale, the cultural and political hegemons continue to exploit and reproduce a deeply historical fear of "otherness."

This fear is built on the discursively constructed "growing threat" of immigration, which has resulted in legal interventions over a number of years, including the 1994 "save our state" amendment, or Proposition 187, of California.[6] Under this proposition, all "illegal aliens" were to be denied public health care, public education, and any other public services. While Proposition 187 failed in 1994, owing to protests by civil rights and immigrant advocacy groups, the current immigration bill (S. 744) under debate builds on this same notion of America-for-Americans. Although the current bill grants work visas and provides services to existing illegal immigrants, it does so under a neoliberal model of benevolence that allows for corporations to keep their existing (illegal) workforce, while making it more difficult (and more dangerous) for newer immigrants to enter the country. After all, "populations governed by neoliberal technologies are dependent on others who are excluded from neoliberal considerations" (Ong 2006, 4).

To fully grasp the implications of this and its connection to brown, one must recognize that the largest numbers of illegal immigrants who are in the service sector are from Latin and South America and South Asia. In addition, as noted earlier, Arab identities are often conflated with South Asian identities and are also circulated as "threats." Within the current sociopolitics that are articulated through the lens of 9/11, the logics of historical diasporas that result in varied and multiple somatics that defy any kind of essentialist identity are forgotten, as brown is deployed freely as an identificatory strategy that can easily be transported from one marginal body to another. It becomes simultaneously the call center worker in India, the Bollywood dancer on TV, the Arab terrorist in the news, and the protestor on the street. In this sense, identification has become a more powerful tool for constructing arbitrary identities that serve strategic political and cultural purposes of discipline.

This notion that anyone could be labeled, at any given time, with an identity that is increasingly wielded as a justification for strategic cultural and political practices that work against her is significant. This strategy is not a publicly historicized discourse or condition, born in relation to another specific identity, such as our understanding of Black and White. Instead, it is a mode of identification that can move from body to body, based on seemingly unconnected cultural and political relations. But the reality is that these relations are not random. They are carefully mapped strategies to maintain a social order that preceded the present. They work together to provide a seamless, cohesive ideology that seeks to sustain a status quo that naturalizes deviant representations as "Truth," and therefore universal, and justifies the strategic and marginalizing political interventions on behalf of controlling the perceived deviant.[7] They work, in Foucault's words, as "a form of political literature that addresses what the order of a society should be, what a city should be, given the requirements of the maintenance of order; given that one should avoid epidemics, avoid revolts, permit a decent and moral family life" (as quoted in Rabinow 1991, 239). It is in the spirit of excavating the relationship between the growing anxiety of unruly immigrants and the "maintenance of order" vis-à-vis popular representations that this book is written.

Arrivals and Departures

In the introduction to his book *Passport Photos,* Amitava Kumar (2000) describes the immigrant experience as one of "shame": the visitor who walks through an airport immigration line carrying a history that is reduced to a tiny booklet that grants him permission to enter the country is always, according to Kumar, aware of how minuscule his existence can be, of the difference between the privilege of belonging and the disadvantage of always being a visitor. This notion of "visitor" and the subsequent shaming of that status as a form of effectively securing the borders of the nation-state were strategies used actively following the terrorist attacks in 2001.

The separation between citizen and denizen was a demarcation made based on the convergence of socially constructed realties: (1) the privileging of Whiteness with citizenship and (2) connecting this notion of Whiteness to structure that connects geographic location with somatics (Burman 2010). Following that September, a plethora of stories documenting the practice of shaming surveillance in the name of security that subtly color-coded citizenship were rife. The stories included my own. I was on the second plane to land in the United States after the four-day-long suspension of flights following the September 11 terrorist attacks in New York City and Washington, D.C. As my baggage was searched at Los Angeles International Airport on the last leg of my thirty-six-hour flight from Sri Lanka to Oregon, I realized quickly that the color of skin had taken on new meaning. As the only visibly brown body on the flight, I was "randomly" pulled out of line as "officials" searched my baggage. When— because my hands were trembling and I was nervous—the locks wouldn't quite turn, the two airport officials, never speaking directly to me, except to bark out impatient orders, decided that using a crowbar to pry open the suitcase was not only necessary but also the most efficient way to deal with the situation. It took quite a lot of pleading on my part to point out that once that was done, my suitcase wouldn't close and the contents would never make it to Oregon. Eventually, the keys did work, the contents were examined only to reveal the clothes and books of a doctoral student returning from fieldwork—the security guards seemed disappointed—and I was finally allowed to board the plane. I remember being deeply embarrassed by the sight of my bag spread on a conveyor belt for all to see. It was not that there was anything unusual in my belongings. But to see a capsule of my life—clothes, books, food, and some artifacts from Sri Lanka—on open display was a reminder of my vulnerability as a second-class noncitizen. And the display was deliberate. It performed "security" at the same time as it was a reassurance to those passing—those subjects whose lives were not on display—that their selves were secured by the raid on mine. When I finally returned to my apartment, I stayed up that night writing "I Will Call My Children Mestiza"—the poem that opens this book—because it was the only form of speaking back to the public shaming.

A week or so later, I started teaching a course on media and culture that had a lengthy section on the Walt Disney Company. The class and I had lively discussions, critiquing Disney's ideological, economic, and social practices. With the exception of two international students, the rest of the class had grown up with Mickey Mouse, and each had an opinion about it. As part of the discussion, I asked the students to consider the ramifications of an uncritical belief in the "magic" of Disney. A few days later, a student accused me of being "anti-American" and of not understanding "our way of life." He said that as someone from a military family, he understood that he could, if he so chose, report me to authorities under the newly enacted USA PATRIOT Act. Instead, he said he was merely thinking of reporting me to administration for teaching "un-American" values at a time when we needed to be most patriotic. While the threat of being reported to the DHS or university administration blew over, two things from that incident stood out: first, I had raised these same issues in other classes and discussion groups numerous time, prior to 9/11, and at no point in any of these previous contexts had my interlocutors translated a critical analysis of Disney into a terror threat; second, and perhaps more important, was the student's internalization of the powers that the USA PATRIOT Act had granted him as a White (thus unmarked) *American citizen.*

This latter point especially speaks to the notion of the citizen-vigilante that was embraced by many (and sanctioned politically in the calls for "alertness" by governmental entities), in which the practice of linking a brown body to a critique of an American corporation as an act of terror—along an imagined continuum of un-American practices—was not unique to me nor to that particular moment in time. Such vigilantism has become routine in post-9/11 culture and continues to be widely documented. But many of these narratives are shared publicly, not by formal news outlets or by any political entity, but through blogs and websites where such conversations are more acceptable and less dangerous. Take the following example: on the tenth anniversary of September 11, Shoshana Hebshi was on a flight from Denver to Detroit. Sitting in a three-seat row, Hebshi's fellow travelers were two Indian men whom she did not know. Although the flight was uneventful, upon landing at Detroit, the plane was redirected to a separate part of the airport where it was swarmed by armed officers, and Hebshi, a half-Arab and half-Jewish American, and her two neighbors were handcuffed, detained, and questioned by the Transportation Security Administration (TSA) and the DHS on "suspicious behavior." According to Hebshi (2011),

> one of the cops [grabbed] my arm a little harder than I would have liked. He slapped metal cuffs on my wrists and pushed me off the plane. The three of us, two Indian men living in the Detroit metro area, and me, a half-Arab, half-Jewish housewife living in suburban Ohio, were being detained. . . . They put me in the back of the car.

It's a plastic seat, for all you out there who have never been tossed into the back of a police car. It's hard, it's hot, and it's humiliating. The Indian man who had sat next to me on the plane was already in the backseat. I turned to him, shocked, and asked him if he knew what was going on. I asked him if he knew the other man that had been in our row, and he said he had just met him. I said, it's because of what we look like. They're doing this because of what we look like. And I couldn't believe that I was being arrested and taken away.

Although Hebshi and the other two passengers were eventually released with an apology and told that "it's 9/11 and people are seeing ghosts. They are seeing things that aren't there," it is also worth noting that an FBI agent told Hebshi that there had been fifty other incidents across the country on that day. (Mis)identifying brown bodies has become a routine practice, where the vigilantism is acted upon and rewarded with a deepening sense of security and investment in the nation-state.

Such actions, which violate traditional and hard-won civil liberties, and—more egregiously—leave deep psychological and emotional scarring, are often dismissed as a sign of the times and as benign: it's merely people "seeing ghosts." Many of these misidentifications emerge out of a convergence of ideas around brown somatics along the continuum identified at the beginning of this chapter, where brown somatics becomes tautologically tethered to terrorism. To a security-obsessed American nation, the answer to the question "why are brown people terrorists?" is simply "because brown people *are* terrorists." Because of this prejudice, those identified as brown must be constantly identified, surveilled, and controlled.

Many of the processes that are connected to this form of surveillance follow very rudimentary understandings of culture and cultural practices, in which a vague cohesion of dates, habits of dress, languages, and traditions are sufficient to generate a profile that can cover a wide range of individuals. For example, during the weeks of Ramadan, security is high and cases of "mistaken identity" are widely and informally documented.

An example is the case of Aditya Mukerjee, a New York–based technology expert who was traveling to Los Angeles from JFK to an annual family gathering during the last week of Ramadan in August 2013. At the airport, Mukerjee was pulled out of the security line for setting off an alarm for explosives. He was detained for several hours and questioned repeatedly by various law enforcement and airline officials during that time. When Mukerjee requested food and water—Mukerjee had been hoping to get breakfast at the airport after going through security—these were denied, the officials telling him that he would be released "soon." Though the questioning ranged from his employment to the family gathering—which included an annual visit to several Hindu temples— and his religious beliefs, perhaps the most exemplary moment of brown deviance and its systemic institutionalization comes from the genuine ignorance of an FBI agent who asked Mukerjee how many times a day he prayed. When Mukerjee's face registered surprise, the agent admitted that though he didn't mean to be offensive, he didn't "know anything about Hinduism. For example, I know that people are fasting for Ramadan right now, but I don't have any idea what *Hindus actually do on a daily basis*" (Mukerjee 2013, emphasis added). Here a security agent of the FBI is unaware of the differences between Islam and Hinduism, though he identifies Mukerjee as a product of this mashed-up identification. Eventually, Mukerjee was released and the triggered alarm was attributed to the bedbug spray that he had used in his new apartment the previous day. Here the subjugated essential that is produced by brown—where a Hindu becomes a Muslim, and a Muslim becomes radicalized during Ramadan—is a way not only to mark individuals but also to *justify acting on those suspicions.*

Certainly anxieties about foreigners, who are seen to threaten a constructed, bucolic American Way of Life, are nothing new. The United States has a long and well-documented history of such xenophobia, in which these anxieties are largely manifested in curious relationships between politics and popular culture (see, e.g., Marchetti 1993; Takaki 1998; Lee 1999; Ono and Pham 2009; Valdivia 2000; Molina-Guzmán 2010). In keeping with this long history, contemporary anxieties about foreigners are pathologized by political discourse and medicated by popular culture. As Evelyn Alsultany (2012, 2) notes, such mediated representations produce "a new kind of racism, one that projects antiracism and multiculturalism on the surface but simultaneously produces the logics and affects necessary to legitimize racist policies and practices."

Alsultany names this process *simplified complex representation*, whereby a negative representation (terrorist) with a positive one (Middle Eastern informant) has become a standard practice for representing Muslims and Islam after 9/11. Such simplified complex representations, because they seem to be "balanced and fair,"[8] nullify the inherent racism in reductive depictions of good Muslims and bad Muslims. She notes that much of this is an acute fracture between representation and reality, writing, "At the same time that sympathetic portrayals of Arab and Muslim Americans proliferated on US commercial television in the weeks, months, and years after 9/11, hate crimes, workplace discrimination, bias incidents, and airline discrimination targeting Arab and Muslim Americans increased exponentially" (161). Complicating this even further is the fact that these caricatures of the Middle East are almost always juxtaposed against a militarized White America that is consistently just and true (exemplified in part by popular fictional characters such as Jack Bauer in *24* [2001–10] and Leroy Jethro Gibbs in *NCIS* [2003–]), where democratic patriotism justifies the unorthodox and, at times, illegal means that are employed by law keepers to maintain order. It is this desire to maintain order that gives rise to what Junaid Rana (2011, 51) calls a "global racial system that incorporates 'dangerous Muslims' as a racial category," where the complicated terrain of constructing this dangerous Muslim becomes both a project of the state and the project of patriotism (50–60).

9/11 as a Signifier

Because of political and popular renderings of brown Muslims and Islam as a "new threat"—tied to a common acceptance of 9/11 as "unprecedented" in U.S. history and as the first attack on U.S. soil since Pearl Harbor—I have chosen to focus on 9/11 as a *signifier* of how contemporary notions of brown are practiced in American culture. But, at the same time, I am aware that such a reindexing of race, war, and history under the rubric of 9/11 carries its own baggage—especially the ways in which 9/11 was used to solidify long-standing desires to bound ethnic and racial identities. Sunaina Maira (2009, 30) notes that

some of this writing that emerged in the United States after 9/11 is motivated by benign interest to compensate for previous ignorance, even if in the context of fear or a sense of cultural and religious distance from Muslims and Arabs. At the same time, the hypervisibility of Muslim Americans after 9/11 is tied to the states' desire to map Muslims, and especially Middle Eastern and Pakistani communities, within the U.S. in order to monitor them and convince the American public that it is guarding against the threat of terrorism.

Here Maira's point—that "9/11 studies" unwittingly provides fodder for both the education about and the production of a particular form of Muslim that is then directly tied to the 9/11 attacks—is well taken.

In addition, marking the day as an event, or as a "breaking point" that signifies some sort of pre/postreality, allows us to ignore the history of global, transnational politics that leads to such events (Derrida 2003). It also keeps up the illusion that the United States is without culpability in larger global crises at the same time as the United States claims the mantle of the "world's greatest democracy" and bestows the title of "leader of the free world" on its head of state. Acknowledging this broader context, it is more useful to recognize 9/11 as a signifier that allowed global geopolitics and growing anxieties about outsourcing, job loss, the rise of Third World spaces—especially India and Pakistan—in the global economic marketplace, and a resurgence of conservative politics in the form of the Republican administration to give rise to U.S. neonationalisms. In addition, to locate 9/11 and the subsequent responses to it within the context of transnational global politics is to recognize and acknowledge the connection between contemporary fears of brown (as sudden) and the end of the Cold War, which coincided with the rise of Japan's industrial and economic power in the 1980s and 1990s. U.S. preoccupation with Japan during that time period was reflected in popular culture, and anxieties around economic and cultural peril were supported by a wave of fiction and nonfiction that flooded the market, warning the American public of a Japanese "takeover."[9]

In the midst of this anti-Japanese frenzy, the slow rise of South Asian economies, India's in particular, went largely unnoticed, but the parallels between anti-Japanese sentiment in recent history and the antibrown sentiments of contemporary culture should not be overlooked. Along with the sociopolitical practice of connecting popular culture and political discourse around alarmist notions of takeovers by foreigners, the reality is that the United States takes little interest in activities that do not directly impact its own political and economic agendas.

Let me elaborate: although the *New York Times,* in 1976, declared that "India's Economy Is Heading from Rags to Riches" mainly because of "a flood of money that is being sent home by Indians who live abroad, largely in the Middle East, Britain and the United States," India's seemingly meteoric rise as a global power was not visible to the American public until the late 1990s, until rumblings of job outsourcing and manufacturing became more audible (Borders 1976). Even then—at this particular juncture in the 1990s—it was South Asians *in* South Asia, and not the South Asian diaspora, that was the problem. In fact, as Vijay Prashad (2000, 6) has noted, for many years, especially during and after the civil rights movement, South Asian diaspora was the solution, not the problem. Except for racist acts that went largely unnoticed—such as the Dotbusters[10] in New Jersey in the 1980s—South Asians in the United States at this time were dismissed as a meek model minority whose presence was deemed "relatively recent"; yet another reinvention that transitions effortlessly to the present times and to ideologies of security, war, and economic battle that allow South Asians to be viewed as part of the *new* deviant browns destroying an American Way of Life. In many ways, this imagined newness of South Asian immigrants thrives because of their lack of visibility within canonical and education texts that are widely circulated about U.S. immigration and history.

Absent Bodies: South Asian Immigrants and the Politics of Visibility

Trying to locate South Asian brown is somewhat challenging, for several intersecting reasons. First, brown has long been the domain of Latino/a and Chicano/a identities in the United States. The roots of Chicano studies in the civil rights movement, and the subsequent institutionalization of Chicano/a studies in the 1970s, coupled with the rise of queer feminist Chicana studies in the 1980s, as well as historical and ongoing immigration and migration discourses that are largely tethered to Latin America typically root (and route) brown in ethnic studies.

In addition to this, South Asian brown Americans, until the 1990s, were both largely politically invisible and firmly absent from Asian American studies—a space that would have most readily fit the category of

South Asian American brown. Such an absence of the latter in Asian American studies, notes Dave et al. (2000, 6), arises for several converging reasons. Most notable among those listed by the authors is (1) the fact that the numbers of South Asians who entered the United States in the 1900s were relatively few compared to the numbers of East Asian immigrants who arrived in the United States during that period; and, citing Yen Le Espiritu's 1994 study on panethnic coalition building, (2) the fact that South Asians don't somatically blend with other commonly identified Asian groups separates South Asian Americans from other Asian groups. Such invisibility, both in an academic, historical, social and political sense translate to a sense of dislocation and isolation that has larger social consequences. This has become increasingly true in the last decade, when birthright and somatic familiarity have become ways to separate citizens from aliens. And it is in this nexus of citizenship and immigration, contexualized by historical migrations and arrivals, that brown is produced as a form of identification.

As I have mentioned before, it is simultaneously an identification that acknowledges brown as historically tethered to Latino/as and Chicano/as as well as South Asian Americans at the same time as it extends it *beyond* those somatics to connect it to a form of identity production based on contemporary social and political constructs. In other words, the history is valid, of course, and has enormous impact on how brown is understood and interrogated today. In many ways, that early history of in/visibility, especially for South Asian Americans, feeds the production of a brown identification. Because South Asian brown seems to be devoid of any historical legitimacy that ties it to an ethnic group in the United States (like East Asian Americans), it can be produced, with inaccuracy and with impunity, within many contexts. And certainly the South Asian immigrant, irrespective of her long history in America, or her contributions, both old and new, to the American economy and culture, has always remained a cultural outsider in the United States. This is especially true because of the immigration patterns and modes of arrival of these particular brown bodies to the Americas. Marked by two very different and distinct phases—the early 1800s and the 1960s   the South Asian diaspora to the United States has changed not only in terms of ethnic makeup but also in terms of the role the diaspora plays within the racialized landscape of the United

States. Life for the early immigrants (consisting solely of Punjabi men)—among the first Asians to the United States in the early 1800s—who settled in California was similar to the more carefully documented lives of the East Asian immigrants. As with the Chinese, Koreans, and, later, Japanese immigrants, Punjabi immigrants were met with outright hostility and racism, both socially and legally. And although they were from landowning families and merchant classes, they were viewed as illiterate and backward. Karen Leonard (1997, 24) quotes the 1920 report of the California State Board of Control, which warned that "the Hindu is the most undesirable immigrant in the state. His lack of personal cleanliness, his low morals, and his blind adherence to theories and teachings, so entirely repugnant to American principles make him unfit for association with American people."

While early histories of Asian immigration document the piggyback effect of Asian workers moving to the United States, this amalgamated history ignores the various roles that South Asians played in the agricultural development and economic growth of California. According to Leonard, the Punjabis "helped initiate rice cultivation in northern California, grew grapes and other crops in central California, and moved to the southern Imperial Valley to establish cotton growing." But, caught in the midst of legal and social upheaval in the early part of twentieth-century America—including the Emergency Quota Act of 1921 and the Immigration Act of 1924—it wasn't until the 1960s that the South Asian diaspora, again, predominantly Indian, began to flourish. When President Lyndon Johnson, in 1965, signed the Immigration and Nationality Act, removing the national origins system and replacing it with a regionally based quota system, the *type* of immigrant had changed drastically from the earlier laborer and working-class immigrants to a more educated, middle- and upper-middle-class population. Reflecting changing economic conditions both in the United States and in South Asia, a large number of professionals from South Asian countries, including India, started immigrating to North America. Especially in the 1980s—corresponding to the rise in technology, free trade, and what was later to be commonly known as the brain drain—large numbers of South Asians filled American metropolises. But this long history of South Asian migration to the United States is hardly known outside academic circles.

Certainly there are growing numbers of archives and libraries that carry considerable historical documentation of South Asian immigration.

But commonsense history more easily recalls East Asian American and European migrations and immigration. In fact, in 2007, when I gave a lecture on South Asian migration to a group of graduating seniors at a four-year college on the East Coast, the students were shocked that "Indians had been around for that long." A student told me, "I assumed they were in Britain for a long time, because I saw *Bend It Like Beckham,* but I didn't know Indians came to the U.S. in the 1900s!" As we continued to talk about history and (in)visibility, it was abundantly clear that for many of the students, Indians, whether American or not, were recent arrivals whose trials and tribulations were more easily accessed via media texts than through secondary education.

And there is strategic value in ignoring the history of migration and reinventing a population as relative newcomers. Disconnecting South Asian immigration from popular canonized history (such as the history taught in middle and high school) allows the (re)creation of a minority that exemplifies the American Dream as it is being *lived* rather than as weighted down by slavery, railroad work, or illegal migration that forces the United States to acknowledge its own culpability in these enterprises. South Asians are presented as the best and the brightest whose contributions to society are in keeping with both a new model minority and neoliberal transnational networks of exchange, both economic and cultural (Prashad 2000, 7). This desire to present a new model minority, à la Louisiana governor Bobby Jindal and South Carolina governor (Namrata) Nikki Haley, who represent conservative political and economic policies that are built on the mythologies of the American Dream, has become a U.S. staple. In fact, Jindal was once called the "great beige hope of the Republican Party" (Scott 2009). And Haley (who has artfully changed any sign of brownness into Whiteness through her name) solidified her American credentials in June 2011 by signing off on anti-immigration legislation modeled after Arizona's SB 1070 law. Following the signing of the bill, Republican senator Larry Grooms justified this right to racial profiling by claiming that "they cling together in illegal communities and bring with them drugs, prostitution, violent crimes, gang activity." The echoes from the past resounding into the present, and rearticulated by the likes of Donald Trump more recently, are hard to overlook.

Falling within this neo-xenophobia, post-1960s South Asian Americans have vacillated in a space devoid of history, created for them by America's complex and contested relationship with the racialized other. This ahistorical existence is especially problematic within the post-9/11 U.S. sociopolitical, economic, and cultural context for two reasons: (1) it always questions the *authenticity* of Americans who are of South Asian descent and (2) by mass-producing a generic South Asian immigrant experience within popular culture and archiving it as a commodity, it removes the need for a discussion of this particular brown as a disruption of the Black/White racial binary of the United States.[11]

Identity versus Identification

I have argued up to this point that brown is an unbound and constantly updated category of subjugating essentialism that is maintained by political and social means. Here I want to explain how identity and identification converge and diverge within this context. This work builds on the significant contributions to the study of race in cultural studies to understand the shift from identity, as the nomenclature of race, to identification, as something grounded in xenophobic notions of security and threat, following September 11, 2001. Since 9/11, the ethos and pathos of nationalism and nationhood have changed in the United States, where brown has become a *malleable identification* that neonationalist discourses use as a ranking logic of belonging that re-creates a hierarchy of nationalist belonging. Arriving at this through Derrida's notion of *différance,* perhaps the most cogent description of this process comes from Stuart Hall. Hall (1990, 225) argues that identity is inherently tied to identification, where identification becomes a process through which identity is negotiated and renegotiated. He writes,

> Cultural identities come from somewhere, have histories. But, like everything which is historical, they undergo constant transformation. Far from being eternally fixed in some essentialised past, they are subject to the continuous "play" of history, culture and power. Far from being grounded in a mere "recovery" of the past, which is waiting to be found, and which, when found, will secure our sense

of ourselves into eternity, identities are the names we give to the different ways we are positioned by, and position ourselves within, the narratives of the past.

Extending this, here we can certainly add *the present* as an identity interlocutor. But, unlike in the past, when discourses of racism were bounded, at least to a large extent, by the nation-state, current discourses of race are positioned against and within more global notions of Otherness. The events of 9/11 created a culture and society focused on a constant threat of terror, where the perpetrator of such terror is ever present but unidentifiable, except when introduced against what he is *not*. Within this contemporary narrative of what is not, both our popular and political nodes have become centers of simultaneous surveillance and discipline. Much of this surveillance and discipline happens through a two-pronged approach to citizenship as identity: (1) the notion of illegality and (2) once legal, a *ranking* of citizenship. For example, the recent anti-immigration laws in states that have some of the largest numbers of Mexican and Latin American immigrants, such as Arizona and South Carolina, indicate the rise of the neonationalist xenophobias. The opposition to such laws is seen as un-American and unpatriotic, and in turn, the introduction and support of such laws are seen as a form of patriotism and "true" Americanism. This is even clearer when we consider that, in South Carolina, a governor whose Sikh parents emigrated from India to the small working-class town of Bamberg, South Carolina, introduced the anti-illegal immigration law. Nikki Haley, born Nimrata Randhawa, has spoken publicly about the challenges her family faced as immigrants in South Carolina, but this hasn't stopped her from trying to make life even more difficult for those following a similar path to a "better life." Haley's rabid anti-immigration stance highlights the complexities of contemporary nationalism and the struggles of "imperfect" citizenry (under the sociohistorical conditions of belonging) to find their place within a (new) system that subtly demands a perfect citizen, even as it denies or rejects the existence of such perfection. More simply, while the *rhetoric* of multiculturalism keeps the myth of the American melting pot alive, social and political *practices* do not; in fact, they demand a rejection of such.

This ranking of citizenship, which creates a hierarchy of belonging, results in a struggle to define, be, and be part of a neoliberal reinscribing of race that is grounded in an anomalous triangulation of birth–national–citizen. Then, in its simplest form, identity can be understood as a noun—a meme for creating a sense of self—whereas identification, following Steve Martinot's (2010) approach to racialization, is a transitive verb. Essentially, the level of individual agency that one assumes in identity has been reinscribed with additional powers when it becomes identification. With the latter comes the ability to identify self and other as insider and outsider, essentially creating regimes of identification: discourses that create categories of identities that converge under the rubric of security and terror. This becomes a way to naturalize the construct of alterity and parity. For example, consider the very naming of the DHS. A governmental arm named "Homeland Security," in charge of securing the national border through various processes of identification and verification, functions as a reminder that some belong and some do not.

To further clarify, I borrow from Craig Robertson (2006, 189), who writes, "What becomes accepted as objective practices of verification in 'fact' produce the very criteria they utilize—verification produces the verifiable object it requires." Through such a process, categories of identification are created so as to maintain order. As Paul Gilroy (2004, 39) writes, "'race' refers primarily to an impersonal, discursive arrangement, the brutal result of the raciological ordering of the world, not its cause." It is in this way that brown, in its current malleable form, becomes deployed in contemporary culture. Identification strategies form a system of consensus surrounding identity that naturalizes the system of racialized hierarchies that we come to accept as "normal." Thus the identification produces the categorical criteria of popular tropes of identity. For example, the same ideological notions of disruptive, savagist unacceptability that were publicly articulated against Blacks during the twentieth century are the same tropes used against various peoples, ranging from citizenship to sexual orientation, in present-day culture. Therefore this notion of identification—almost ephemeral in its fluidity and less somatically tied to a particular group—makes identities conceptual rather than fact. In the following chapter, I further elaborate on this particular permutation of brown.

2
Un-American
Surviving through Patriotic Performances

We are in a crisis of belonging, a population crisis, of who, what, when, and where. More and more people feel as though they *do not* belong. More and more people are *seeking* to belong, and more and more people are not *counted* as belonging.

—TOBY MILLER, *CULTURAL CITIZENSHIP: COSMOPOLITANISM, CONSUMERISM, AND TELEVISION IN A NEOLIBERAL AGE*

It's July 2009 in Boston, Massachusetts, and I'm waiting for the traffic light to turn green. A car pulls up alongside mine and moves just a little ahead. In his rear window I see a sticker of the American flag, while another sticker proclaims that "these colors may bleed but they never run." Several other bumper stickers claim pride in being American. The traffic moves slowly, and I'm now alongside the car of the patriot. A small statue of god Vishnu sits on his dashboard, and prayer beads hang from the rearview mirror. He looks over at me, momentarily animated by seeing another brown face in the traffic, but looks away and races forward when the light turns green. The last thing I see is the American flag that never bleeds but is apparently not immune to fading.

I thought about that strange juxtaposition of Vishnu with the American flag for a long time. In many ways, it became a visual aid for my thinking of home, after 9/11, and its relationship to the fluidity and malleability of brown that I articulate in the preceding chapter. For me, it underscores the function of brown as shorthand for many transgressions, but in this instance specifically, for the fear of being seen, literally, as a traitor or, even worse, un-American. It exemplifies a response to the most concrete xenophobia we have seen in recent times: a rabid, visual articulation of *amantes patriae* in the form of bumper stickers and American flags, where "those who 'looked Muslim' had to signal their allegiance to 'America' and being 'American' by the same logic of visibility that marked them as racially unAmerican, in order to avoid becoming victims of racist violence" (Grewal 2003, 548). The racist violence—and it's accompanying necropolitical practices, where birth and death (or acute physical violence) were based on a perceived un-Americanness—constructed a false binary between "terrorist" and "patriot," where the violence against brown bodies was reinscribed as misguided patriotism rather than being understood as acts of real violence. And the actual blame was shifted from the perpetrator of that violence to some abstract "terrorist" as the person(s) responsible for inciting the violence on behalf of the nation-state. Here the twin discourses of terrorist and patriot introduced a new race-scape through a false binary, where *brown* animated a particular division between the two categories. Such a false binary begs the question, what is the relationship between these two performances of terrorist and patriot? And how do these manifest in everyday life and political culture, which in turn give meaning to abstract notions of belonging? Furthermore, following Wendy Brown,[1] in a time when the twin discourses of security and terror are in full effect, how does location work to construct subjectivity? Although the answers to these questions are interrogated through concrete examples in later chapters, here I delve into them as the skeletal foundation that guides the protean existence of brown.

I expand on the most basic response to these questions: that for brown to retain its malleability (terrorist, Middle Eastern, Vishnu, Hindu), it has to be measured against a less abstract, and more grounded, concept (American). This grounded concept, in and of itself, can also be rather fluid and abstract,[2] but it has to resonate as a unified cultural center in the collective imaginary of the populace. For example, in the case of the driver of that car in Boston, the fear of being seen as a fundamental Islamist, despite being an Indian (American) Hindu, results in a desire to showcase a loyalty to America through the display of American patriotic paraphernalia. This display pledges allegiance to an America that is constructed as a single, unified home/land. In fact, these twin concepts of home and land, the focus of this chapter, became a valuable commodity, a form of ideological real estate following September 11. From citizen vigilantes identifying and harassing those who should "go back home" to the tsunami of American flags that proclaimed people's place in the unified nationalism, concretized by the creation and institutionalization of the DHS, the contest over home was the not-so-silent battle cry in the aftermath. The need to prove belonging to the United States of America, as a response to the conflation and generalization of their own identities with and through terror, became of primary importance to many who were perceived as brown threats. For example, as a response to the most virulent forms of violence directed at them, because of the conflation of their turbans with both these "other" transgressive identities, the Sikh community was forced to quickly and actively start an educational campaign to prove that they were not terrorists, and not Middle Eastern.[3] Unlike Espiritu's (1992) panethnic communities, who consolidated identities for power,[4] Sikhs were forced to speak out *against* other diasporic, immigrant, and browned bodies because of the nonexistent connection made between their turbans and radical Islam. This labor of proving difference continues long after 9/11. As recently as December 2013—at the behest of the Sikh American Legal Defense and Education Fund (SALDEF), which felt such a study was necessary after the Oak Creek massacre in 2012—the Stanford Peace Innovation Lab conducted a "multithreaded" study of American perceptions of Sikhs in America. The resulting publication, *Turban Myths: The Opportunities and Challenges for Reframing Sikh American Identity in Post-9/11 America,* was produced in an effort to understand and respond to continuing anti-Sikh sentiments in the country. Although the study is important in that it formally documents certain facts that had until its publication been anecdotal—facts such as 49 percent of Americans believe that Sikh is a sect of Islam and 70 percent cannot identify a Sikh man in a picture as a Sikh—here I want to underscore more the very *need* for such a study, especially longer than a decade after September 11. The convergence of Sikhism with radical Islam speaks to the ways in which brown is produced and circulated as a form of policing boundaries between identities that harm and identities that do not harm, and the ways in which the rhetoric of "they" and "us" was used to demarcate a spatial difference between those who were wronged (mostly White Americans) and the savage perpetrators (brown bodies from uncivilized spaces) of those crimes. Even the most childlike response to the events—"why do they hate us?"—was, in its immaturity, a naive patriotism that marked un-self-conscious belonging: the unifying "us" who were hated.

The rampant use of the American flag to showcase that particular brand of parochial nationalism was not unique to conservatives, whose rabid patriotic roots have long been documented. Instead, it became a source of seeming comfort, a symbol of location that connected the displayer of the flag, as "the most universally recognizable symbol of American government," to the space it represented. I say "seeming comfort" here because, in many ways, it was more than just comfort and shared empathy (Hopkins 1991). For communities of color that could be (and were) mistaken for terrorists, it was a symbol of *security* through a declaration of "fast patriotism" (Kelly 2003)[5]—the right kind of mark (patriotism) to compensate for the wrong kind of marking (brown).

When George W. Bush famously declared, shortly after the attacks on 9/11, "that you are either with us, or with the terrorists," there was a frenzied response by those who could be "you" to make sure that they were "us." As Sikh and other South Asian businesses and persons were attacked as representatives of terrorism, their collective efforts centered around survival through patriotic performances that included the display of American flags and stickers declaring their love for and support of troops and country. The semiotics of such a display was straightforward and easy to read, and because of that ease, many communities of color capitalized on the flag as a form of shorthand for citizenship. Store owners plastered their walls with American flags; some even went so far as to verify through billboards that they were Sikhs and not Muslims, in case their turbans caused confusion; and every brown home proudly displayed the flag.

In an almost embarrassing display of solicitation, they formed respectful rings around gatherers at various rallies and memorials, enthusiastically waving flags. Perhaps one of the most iconic images of that response, in the immediate aftermath of 9/11, was a young Sikh child waving an American flag as she was perched on an adult's shoulders. This image was circulated widely and included in educational posters produced by organizations such as SikhNet when it started becoming clear that terrorism had become equated with brown, brown with turbans, and that there was only one visible (non-Muslim) community who fit this "profile" generated in the aftermath.

But despite these efforts to educate the public, stories like the one on September 17, 2001, in the *New York Times* have become somewhat of a norm: the newspaper notes that on September 15, a gunman in Arizona went on a shooting rampage against "Muslim" business owners in Mesa, Arizona. Frank Roque's shooting spree, resulting in the violent death of Balbir Singh Sodhi, a Chevron gas station owner, would go on to become one of the most horrific acts of neonationalism following 9/11. Roque

A downloadable poster produced by SikhNet (http://www .sikhnet.com/) immediately following 9/11. It was meant to be displayed as a "safety measure" against being mistaken for a terrorist or Muslim.

then went on to shoot at a Mobil gas station clerk who was of Lebanese descent, before firing several shots into the home of another family, this time of Afghan descent. Neither the Afghan family nor the Mobil station clerk was injured, but Balbir Singh Sodhi went down in history as the first innocent Sikh to die after 9/11 because of how he looked.

From shooting sprees like Roque's to bumper stickers like my fellow motorist's in Boston to rallies and protests by various organizations, the post-9/11 social culture became one that demanded action on the part of its citizenry to *visibly prove* its love, loyalty, and fidelity to the country. This culture of proof, whether violent or not, was then harnessed to a neoliberal ethos that demanded a commitment to the core American value of capitalism, where the most patriotic action was seen as consumption and consumer pleasure. As Lynn Spigel (2004, 237) notes,

> by the weekend of September 15, television news anchors began to tell us that it was their national duty to return to the "normal" everyday schedule of television entertainment, a return meant to coincide with Washington's call for a return to normalcy (and, hopefully, normal levels of consumerism). Of course, for the television industry, resuming the normal TV schedule also meant a return to commercial breaks and, therefore, TV's very sustenance. . . . So, even while the media industries initially positioned entertainment and commercials as being "in bad taste," just one week after the attacks the television networks discursively realigned commercial entertainment with the patriotic goals of the nation. In short— and most paradoxically—entertainment and commercialism were rearticulated as television's "public service."

In the following section, I show how this paradox of entertainment–public service was used and extended to discursively demarcate an American identity that solidified the borders of the country, where a suspect brown was constructed as the enemy of these consumerist pleasures and juxtaposed against those who belonged to and were of the nation-state.

Buy, Buy, Baby

In the same way that Paul Gilroy's (2004) description of how Albilonia (Old Britain) in *After Empire: Multiculture or Postcolonial Melancholia* is unable to process and mourn the end of its empire and enacts its imperialism through anti-immigration policies, so does the United States articulate its growing anxieties about the end of the *American* empire. Almost bewildered that the end came upon them before they had a chance to fully enjoy the fruits of imperialism, U.S. policy makers bolster and maintain the notion of a Tocquevillian exceptionalism by incessantly reminding themselves and the citizenry of the privileges and practices of belonging. This particular form of patriotism manifest in a citizen consumer, in the aftermath of the attacks, was based on maintaining and performing consumer culture as a sign of free choice.

In fact, almost immediately following the attacks, President Bush encouraged citizens to show their patriotism by asking for the "continued participation and confidence in the American economy" and, shortly after, encouraging citizens to "get on board. Do your business around the country. Fly and enjoy America's great destination spots. Get down to Disney World in Florida. Take your families and enjoy life, the way we want it to be enjoyed"—the implicit encouragement, then, is that patriotic citizenship is performed vis-à-vis hyperconsumerism and entrepreneurship. This call to fly and to visit Disney World becomes the *labor* of citizenship (even in the midst of an emerging recession) and an American way of life—which goes a long way in explaining the reaction of the student who saw me as a threat when I critiqued Disney (see the introduction). As Inderpal Grewal (2003, 556) notes, as "the connection between civil society and corporate and state institutions has led to an American form of democracy in which consumer culture makes possible all kinds of identities, including national identities, it follows that shopping would become a civic duty. . . . To be American was thus to go shopping as usual."

This sort of yingyang of work and leisure—where one works endlessly to be able to spend money on leisure—becomes a way to enact sovereign rights. Furthermore, it essentially positions consumption as a war effort, where the normalcy of American life—essentially consumerism—becomes support for the troops as well as support for the War on Terror that was to follow shortly after September 2001 in the Middle East. Here an absurd enactment of necropolitics—"contemporary forms of subjugation of life to the power of death (necropolitics) profoundly reconfigure the relations among resistance, sacrifice, and terror" (Mbembe 2003, 39)—ensues, where the military intervention into another nation-state, the loss of lives there, and the economic burdens of war become inextricably linked to a consumer spectacle in the United States.

Furthermore, this patriotic citizenship of consumerism and capitalist leisure is presented as truly and uniquely American, subtly allowing the boundaries of the nation-state to be solidified through the codification of these practices. Within the borders of *this* nation—as opposed to other nations, where such luxuries and opportunities don't exist—life is split between the accumulation of capital and the spending of this accumulated wealth. Such a middle-class, suburban identity, because of the history of slavery, the long and hard struggle for civil rights, and contemporary struggles around immigration, is also implicitly White, separating the United States from darker spaces from which the violence erupted and where the barbaric other lives. This demarcation crystalized the inherent contradiction of a borderless, utopian transnational existence that proponents of globalization have long celebrated. With the attacks, the United States revitalized and solidified its borders at the same time as it created Orientalist images of countries in the Global South.

To expand on the latter point, I want to return to the notion of subjugated essentialism that I introduced in the introduction. There I explained that subjugating essentialism works by having those in power create an essentialist identity of otherness that works strategically for those in power—as opposed to Spivak's notion of *strategic* essentialism, which was advocated as a tool to emancipate those who are powerless. In the aftermath of 9/11, such a subjugating essentialism was largely mandated through the notion of tolerance, especially by then president George W. Bush and his administration, who repeatedly asked the American public to tolerate Muslims as *not terrorists.* For example, in a speech on November 24, Bush encouraged Americans to recognize the differences between Islam as it is practiced by those who are peaceful and Islam as it is practiced by those who are not, stating, "Americans understand we fight not a religion; ours is not a campaign against the Muslim faith. Ours is a campaign against evil" (Bush 2001b). Demarcating the boundaries of the country via implicitly identifying Americans as "we" (who are not Muslim), while also asking for tolerance of those who were/ may be perceived as outsiders vis-à-vis Islam, hid the rhetorical power of defining otherness within this proclamation of peace and justice.

Following Michel Foucault, it is important to recognize the subtle and psychological violence that is inherent in discourses, such as these, that work to produce a passive alterity, thereby normalizing the codified practices of social demarcations. In Bush's proclamation here, the defining alterity is evoked through the iteration and reiteration of articulating difference ("*Americans* understand that we fight not a religion") and respecting difference ("ours is not a campaign against Muslim faith") by emphasizing that difference not as an equal but as so singularly alien that it must be protected by the tolerance of Americans. In this instance, Muslims at home need to be tolerated *and protected* as outsiders, not as citizens who are protected under the laws of the nation-state. In essence, "at the same time that the state represents itself as securing social equality and rhetorically enjoins the citizenry from prejudice and persecution, the state engages in extra legal and persecutorial actions toward the very group that it calls upon the citizenry to be tolerant toward" (Brown 2006, 84). Case in point: the creation of the DHS as a means of protecting the citizenry also produced a variety of strategies and laws that expelled bodies that had theretofore been left alone by the state. With the institutionalization of the DHS, the ideological and political functions of home and belonging became firmly tethered to a form of security and citizenship where, following Giorgio Agamben (1998), the legal system produces and maintains a nation-state that organizes its citizenry as either deviant (brown) or nondeviant (White) from birth to death.

Homeland Security and Intolerant Patriotism

In response to the attacks of September 11, on October 8, 2001, Executive Order 13228—the establishment of an Office of Homeland Security (OHS) and the Homeland Security Council—went into effect. Led by former Pennsylvania governor Tom Ridge, the OHS was intended to provide support to more independent government entities like the Immigration and Naturalization Service (INS) in tracking, and coordinating responses to, possible acts of terrorism in the United States. In 2002, President George W. Bush declared a motion to extend the powers of the OHS by creating it as a more independent, and more powerful, *Department* of Homeland Security. While noting that the creation of such a department was "the most significant transformation of the U.S. government in more than a half-century," the Bush administration nonetheless deemed that such a transformation was necessary because it was the most efficient way to protect the "American homeland." In "transforming and realigning the current confusing patchwork of government activities into a single department," the first order of business was to fold the border operations into one of four areas of DHS (Bush 2002a). Under this configuration, the daily operations of the U.S. Coast Guard, the U.S. Customs Service, INS, the Animal and Plant Health Inspection Service of the U.S. Department of Agriculture, and the TSA (also a post-9/11 creation) came under the purview of the DHS. Justifying the need for such a centralized system of power in a (supposedly) functioning democracy, the Bush administration laid out the following scenario as an example of what could happen were the DHS not a functioning entity:

EXAMPLE: REMOVING BARRIERS TO EFFICIENT
BORDER SECURITY

Currently, when a ship enters a U.S. port, Customs, INS, the Coast Guard, the U.S. Department of Agriculture, and others have over-lapping jurisdictions over pieces of the arriving ship. Customs has jurisdiction over the goods aboard the ship. INS has jurisdiction over the people on the ship. The Coast Guard has jurisdiction over the ship while it is at sea. Even the Department of Agriculture has jurisdiction over certain cargoes. Although the Coast Guard does have the authority to act as an agent for these other organizations and assert jurisdiction over the entire vessel, in practice the system has not worked as well as it could to prevent the illegal entry of potential terrorists and instruments of terror. Consider this scenario: if the Coast Guard stops a ship at sea for inspection and finds there are illegal immigrants on the ship, the Coast Guard relies on the INS to enforce U.S. immigration law and prevent their entry. If the Coast Guard finds potentially dangerous cargo, it relies on Customs to seize the dangerous cargo. Unfortunately, these organizations may not always share information with each other as rapidly as necessary. So, instead of arresting potential terrorists and seizing dangerous cargo at sea, our current structure can allow these terrorists to enter our ports and potentially sneak into our society. The system might also allow the dangerous cargo to actually enter our ports and threaten American lives. Under the President's proposal, the ship, the potentially dangerous people, and the dangerous cargo would be seized at sea by one Department that has no question about either its mission or its authority to prevent them from reaching our shores. (Bush 2002a)

This Rambo-esque description of the DHS is one of the many examples listed in the document released by the government in 2002. This made-up scenario of the imminent threat that needs to be corralled effectively and seamlessly conflates terrorists and immigrants, making official almost three hundred years of racism in the United States and laying bare contemporary xenophobia that emerged long before 9/11 but was made concrete by the events of that day. At the same time that the official rhetoric called for tolerance and declared that "ours is a country based upon tolerance and we welcome people of all faiths in America," it did so by subtly, or perhaps deliberately, marrying two antithetical elements within one entity: home and terror (Bush 2002b). Through the official and repetitive use of "homeland," "our land," and "American people," the DHS now gets to define who is of the home and who is not. The American homeland is deployed as a politically powerful term, where the emotional weight of the home is securely harnessed to the boundary of the nation-state. The shoring up and stabilizing of home through a governmental structure is meant to make those who are not of the home more unstable and insecure. Though 9/11 allowed (and continues to allow) political and social powers to consolidate and broadly enact racist legislature in the name of security and securitization, it should be noted that such practices have a long history in the United States, especially against Latin American and East Asian communities who were, because of their form of arrival into the country as indentured laborers, seen as the quintessential foreigners. The move to expel these bodies from U.S. soil has a long and violent history. For example, following the Mexican–American War (1846–48) that annexed much of the current Southwest from Mexico, lynching and discrimination of Mexicans living in that region were commonplace. During the Great Depression of the late 1920s and 1930s, repatriation efforts were made to get Mexicans away from the annexed areas back to Mexico and have ensured ongoing racial and ethnic conflicts in the region. This early practice of acquisition and expulsion has carried over to recent times, when the Mexican and more generally Hispanic labor force work as a gray economy within the United States but continue to be denied rights of citizenship and legal status, while confronting harassment and xenophobic violence, even as that particular brown population grows and surpasses in number Whites in the United States. Although there have never been conventionally defined terrorist attacks along the south-western border of the United States, the border continues to be a treacherous space to cross. Paralleling treaties to secure the southern borders of the United States in those early years, Asian immigration to the country was also carefully policed, with several laws consecutively enacted to force repatriation or exclusion. These laws resulted in a piggyback effect of various Asian communities moving into the United States—such as the Japanese succeeding the Chinese as the prominent labor force following the Chinese Exclusion Act of 1882 and Korean and Asian Indian immigrants taking over from the Japanese following the 1907 Gentlemen's Agreement between Japan and the United States—during different periods. But despite these brief moments of welcome, over the last two hundred years, legislating bodies have worked tirelessly to demarcate the geographic and cultural borders against those who are seen as interlopers in the (small yet powerful) White-centric culture that is the United States, ensuring that any non-White presence remains largely on the margins.

Such practices are most recently legally codified in the states of Arizona and South Carolina. In Arizona, Senate Bill 1070—the Support Our Law Enforcement and Safe Neighborhoods Act, most commonly known as SB 1070—was introduced and put into effect as the strictest anti-immigration bill in the United States. Using federal regulations put into effect after 9/11 to combat terrorism and terrorist activities, SB 1070 was presented as the implementation of federal laws on state and local levels. The intent "is to make attrition through enforcement the public policy of all state and local government agencies in Arizona. The provisions of this act are intended to work together to discourage and deter the unlawful entry and presence of aliens and economic activity by persons unlawfully present in the United States." The conflation of illegality, citizenship, rights, and economics embedded in this opening preamble is indicative of the ongoing separation between the realities of being and becoming American in the age of neoliberal imperialism and the hackneyed metaphor of America's multicultural melting pot that has rarely, in the last 150 years, welcomed non-White aliens. But it should also be of no surprise that Arizona would introduce such a law. The Mexico–Arizona border has had a long history of xenophobic hypervigilantism protecting it, where crime and illegal aliens have long been linked. For example, in 2005, then president George W. Bush, speaking of the DHS, declared in Tucson, Arizona, that

> since the Department of Homeland Security was created, agents have apprehended nearly 27,000 illegal immigrant fugitives. Thanks to our determined personnel, society is safer. . . . Illegal immigration puts pressure on our schools and hospitals . . . it strains the resources needed for law enforcement and emergency services. And the vicious human. . . . Smugglers and gangs that bring illegal immigrants across the border also bring crime to our neighborhoods and danger to the highways.

This language of scarcity and violence that Bush relies on to justify the oftentimes unethical and illegal practices of detention and deportation is deeply historical. Such language was used to construct slaves as inhuman, violent, and childlike in both legal and institutional contexts as well as in mediated representations such as newspaper cartoons, cards, ornaments, and music within popular culture (Lehman 2007; Smolko 2012). In addition, as early as the nineteenth and early twentieth centuries, newspapers ran cartoons that showed "Asiatic hordes" as parasites "stealing" wealth from hardworking White Americans. In many of these images, Chinese and Japanese immigrants were depicted simultaneously as having Fu Manchu–like cunning and brilliance and as bucktoothed simpletons who needed to be deported. During World War II, iconic American artist and writer Dr. Seuss produced a lengthy series of anti-Japanese cartoons and images that reproduced these early sentiments of East Asians as bucktoothed villains. Over the years, maintaining the illusion of American multiculturalism, such overtly racist humor has become less public and visible. Instead, couched in democratic values and a free society, they reflect what Simon Weaver (2011) calls contemporary forms of *embodied racism*. Weaver defines embodied racism as humor that focuses on parts of the body, on phenotype or on corporeality. It is a racism with an *order-building and hierarchical propensity,* and is an invention of modernity alongside the development of race and biological racism. Embodied racism contains many of the themes and stereotypes of biological racism but lacks the systemic totality that biological racism exhibited in earlier periods of modernity. It appears as a contemporary racism that does not display the dominance of early biological racism, and it exists alongside, and intermingles with, other forms such as cultural racism. (414, emphasis added)

Essentially, Weaver argues that this form of humor ignores the historical structures (and racist biological distinctions) that have generated the images and instead harnesses itself to characteristics of otherness that include "the systemic totality of older, often academic, forms of biological racism" (419). It is this kind of embodied racism that, in 2009, allowed (now retired) Los Alamitos, California, mayor Dean Grose to circulate, via e-mail, a cartoon that read, "No Easter egg hunt this year." The accompanying image showed rows of watermelons superimposed in front of the White House, indicating that watermelons had replaced the annual Easter egg hunt under the Obama presidency. Following a public outcry and calls for resignation, Grose did eventually step down, but not before strongly denying any wrongdoing, claiming that there was no racist intent and that he had had *no knowledge* of the historical and racist connotations between watermelons and Blackness as shorthand for the "happy darkie" (who wanted nothing but a sweet treat to keep him working) stereotype. Essentially those who canonized a relationship between the fruit and Black intellectual ability, in a defense of slavery, are forgotten or erased from memory, as the watermelon becomes a form of shorthand for a racist definition of Black identity. Now these images circulate as humor, separated of their racist past, and are deployed onto a succession of colored bodies du jour that occupy the time of (White) patriots whose paranoia results in a sense of White solidarity and a valorization of disenfranchising violence (Martinot 2010). And in states like Arizona, this paranoid patriotism is harnessed to the militarization of the U.S. border, justifying the formalization of oftentimes violent institutional racism (Kaplan 2004). Following this paranoid logic of marking difference and separating, even those who are born in the United States are effectively, quintessentially brown and therefore not "of the home."

Thus the institutionalization of the DHS, tethered to discourses of immigration, securitization, and citizenship, was harnessed to tolerance, within a multicultural framework, rather than acceptance. This distinction is a significant one, as Wendy Brown (2006) has noted. In her work, Brown maps the trajectory that tolerance has taken from being a form of benign and well-behaved racism to the highest form of democracy and democratic practice. In her critique of this neoliberal trajectory of racist performance masquerading as democratic principles, Brown notes that the state is able to use the rhetoric of tolerance to enact its own undemocratic principles in the name of security. As such, the dependence and reiteration of tolerance against brown (read deviant) bodies implicitly assume intolerant performances. What I mean by this is that by asking citizens to tolerate brown bodies, the state essentially indicates and reinforces the otherness of those bodies as outsiders, at the same time expecting intolerant behavior from its citizenry as a form of patriotism. Essentially, the discourses of tolerance tell us that to be intolerant is as patriotic as tolerance. This is done most effectively by effortlessly connecting intolerant patriotism to the home at the same time that the immigrant/brown body is constructed as outsider. Though such demarcations are subtle, they reinforce the nation-state as a space that is split between inclusion and expulsion on a mythic belief of multicultural acceptance.

On September 8, 2006, the *Los Angeles Times* ran a story with the headline "Officials Plead for Tolerance as 9/11 Anniversary Nears." The article reported that religious leaders, both Muslim and Christian, and law enforcement officials were asking that the fifth anniversary of the attacks go unmarked by *further* violence. The newspaper also reported that the attacks of 9/11 had "ushered in a new era of cooperation between local Muslim leaders and law enforcement officials. . . . With their help, Los Angeles County sheriff Lee Baca formed the Muslim American Homeland Security Congress, which meets regularly to discuss terrorism issues and educate officers about the Muslim community" (Quinones 2008). The article also quotes Hussam Ayloush, director of the local chapter of the Council on American-Islamic Relations, as saying, "Muslims in

America are the first line of defense against terrorism conducted falsely in the name of Islam." This article—in its headline and subsequent discussion—is exemplary of the normativity of intolerant patriotism and its strategic use to construct the home/land. The headlining plea for tolerance is redolent with a normalizing of violent expectations, wherein the plea for tolerance carries an implicit belief that intolerant violence is the *expectation,* given the circumstances.

Also unspoken of, but clearly identified, are the recipients of this violence: unpatriotic Muslims, or, in the case of "mistaken identity," Sikh/Hindu (read brown) people. By such implicit identification of brownness and terror, the corollaries, or audience, produced by such are the White patriots who defend the homeland against foreign invasion. And their violent zealous defense is normalized as an expectation. Essentially, "pleading for tolerance" makes intolerance the norm. Within such a normalization of violence as a form of patriotism, the quotation from Ayloush, who speaks of Muslims and Islam in the same breath as terrorism, becomes even more problematic. His position on the Council on American-Islamic Relations (at least at the time the article was published; Ayloush would later become a board member of the Muslim American Homeland Security Congress, also quoted in the article) provides a level of insider status that gives additional weight to the *expectation* that the country seems to have of othered brown bodies: educating mainstream America about Islam and other forms of brown, to ensure their—the others'—own safety. Essentially, arguing that Muslims in America are the first line of defense—and referencing it in terms of warfare—and putting the burden of *creating* tolerance on the victims of the crimes (brown bodies) rather than on the perpetrators (intolerant patriots) implies a level of wrongdoing on the part of the victim. Such a burden of security and assimilative tolerance on bodies marked as other is not without precedence.

As bell hooks (1994) has noted, in the 1960s in the United States, during school desegregation, the labor of integration and assimilation was the burden of the Black community, not the White—even though segregation was a White creation. From being bussed to White schools to being forced to assimilate in the midst of ongoing and undocumented violence within these schools, hooks argues that the labor of educating White racists and eradicating racism vis-à-vis integration became the physical and affective labor of the African American community. The internalization of this physical and affective labor by brown bodies after 9/11 also results in studies like *Turban Myths* and in the organization of International Turban Day events in the United States (and internationally) since September 11. *Turban Myths*, for example, gives recommendations for "educating" the public about Sikh turbans, including outreach and community-building activities, noting that "the future of Sikhs in America depends on the vibrancy of its community" (Stanford Peace Innovation Lab and Sikh American Legal Defense and Education Fund 2013, 31).

In both these examples—hooks's from the 1960s and the article in the *Los Angeles Times*—White affective and physical labor is to "protect" the homeland from outsiders. Such a burden results in ongoing "other" labor, where members from the Sikh community, and other more "easily" identifiable brown communities, continue to educate the American public.

Home Is Where I'm Invisible

In *Home: A Short History of an Idea*, Witold Rybczynski (1987, 217) writes that "domestic wellbeing is a fundamental human need that is deeply rooted in us, and must be satisfied. If this need is not met in the present, it is not unnatural to look for comfort in tradition." In this section, I want to expand on what Rybczynski makes implicit: that there is a connection between belonging and nostalgia. In essence, that nostalgia (what he calls tradition) is a response to a lack of belonging (home). In keeping with this, in the third definition of *home* that I outline in this chapter, I look at how the diaspora itself responds to the social realities that are created by the two other versions of home outlined previously: homeland security and the intolerant patriot. Essentially, if homeland security is based on securing the homeland, who feels secured by it? And what responses are generated by the "unsecured" immigrant/alien/citizen to intolerant patriotism, as outlined earlier, which reinforces the sense of insecurity from the previous question? As a response these questions, I posit that the twin discourses of security vis-à-vis the patriot and the government produce a diasporic and immigrant brown subject and subject position that is always suspect, and in turn, the realization of their own suspect status reinforces the sense of alienation experienced by brown bodies. Here the "affective recircuitry"[6] is directed both inward, as a way of policing one-self, as well as at each other (Burman 2010). The impact of this is twofold: (1) because the language of security and safety that has permeated every-day culture allows a certain carte blanche to act in ways that are physi-cally and mentally abusive toward the suspect bodies (e.g., the actions of the intolerant patriot and the attempts to humanize him as kind until something triggered the violence), it animates racism as patriotism, and (2) it reinforces and amplifies the sense of alienation that immigrant/diasporic/othered subjects experience, at the same time as it encourages the othered body to actively take part in its own marginalization and othering.

Miss America Terrorist

On September 15, 2013, Nina Davuluri was crowned Miss America 2014. The child of Indian immigrants, Davuluri is the quintessential poster child for the American Dream. Her parents, mother, Sheela, an informa-tion technology specialist, and father, Chaudhury, an obstetric gynecolo-gist, moved to the United States in 1981 from India shortly after their marriage, and Davuluri was born eight years later. Raised in New York, Kansas, and Denmark, by the time she was crowned Miss America, Davuluri had graduated with a bachelor of science degree in behavior and cognitive science from the University of Michigan, where she was on the Dean's List, had won the Michigan Merit Award, and was part of the National Honor Society. According to various biographical information, once her tenure as Miss America concludes, Davuluri plans to enter medical school to become a physician. Davuluri was not the only Asian American, or even Indian American, at the 2014 pageant. First runner-up Crystal Lee is the offspring of a Chinese American father and Taiwanese mother (Jeong 2013), and Miss District of Columbia Bindhu Pamarthi's parents are also, like the Davuluris, originally from Andhra Pradesh (Chitnis 2013).

But it is the backlash against Davuluri's win—and not the title—that made headlines. Despite a platform titled "Celebrating Cultural Diver-sity through Cultural Competence" and "wooing the judges" with a Bolly-wood dance routine, Davuluri's win was seen as a loss for America and American patriotism by the majority of viewers, who were watching the live telecast on ABC from their homes. Outraged by her win, intolerant patriots used Twitter to express their disbelief that an *Arab* had won the title of Miss America. Statements like the following—posted on Matt Binder's (2013) Tumblr blog *Public Shaming*—were tweeted throughout and following the live telecast:

> Miss America is terrorist. Whatever. It's fine.
> #Miss America ummm wtf?!! Have we forgotten 9/11?
> Miss America right now or miss Al Qaeda?

Some were even more violent, and abusive: "a fucking god damn terrorist 9–11 bitch won MISS AMERICA WTF!! Got to be Merican to win miss Merica #LoveitorLeave it," one person noted (Binder 2013). Another wrote, "Her original plane to America landed in the World Trade Center. She lost her father" (Binder 2013). Following the statement with an emoji of a gun to a turbaned face, another asked, "Arab Miss America, really?" (Binder 2013). And, acting on the imagined continuum of Islam, brown, and South Asia mapped in the introduction to this book, several other commentators—including ones who said, "Is it ironic that Miss New York is Muslim . . . ?" and "So a Muslim is representing New York and wanting to be miss AMERICA? That's not ironic at all"—coded Davuluri's brown body as a threat to both a national consciousness and national security (Binder 2013). By making assumptions about religious affinities and affiliations based on skin color (brown) and then coding those religious beliefs (Islam/Muslim) as quintessentially un-American (the denial that Muslim New Yorkers exist), viewers' commentaries, shared through a very public forum like Twitter, created a matrix of racism rationalized by and through patriotism. Essentially, the vitriol directed at Davuluri was not because she wasn't White *but because she was brown.* The latter part of this distinction is important to note, because it speaks to the reindexing of race that preceded 9/11.

After all, Davuluri was not the first Miss America of color—in fact, exactly thirty years earlier to the date, Vanessa Williams became the first Black Miss America, and since then, seven African American women have won the title; in 2001, Angela Perez Baraquio became the first Asian American to win the title, and she was celebrated for representing the diversity of the United States through her Filipino-Hawaiian heritage. Although some of these contestants have had their share of controversy,[7] none of them had been accused of un-American activities or of being a terrorist, as Davuluri was. Underscoring this is the fact that, in addition to Davuluri, there were two other Asian Americans who made it to the final round—none of them, as the pageant was broadcast, received the kind of patriotically motivated virulence that Davuluri did. What also created both anger and anxiety around this particular pageant was that there was a contestant that many of these Twitter-venting viewers thought was more representative of the country: Miss Kansas, Theresa Vail. Lead-

This image of Nina Davuluri following her crowning as Miss America was the most circulated picture of the event. It epitomized "Indo-chic" and exotic and, through that exoticism, symbolized America's multicultural ethos. At the same time, it marked her as an outsider. Photograph by Lucas Jackson for Reuters.

In contrast to Davuluri's exoticism, this meme of Miss Kansas Theresa Vail, as true patriotic American, was widely circulated on Twitter. Screenshot from the *Huffington Post*.

ing up to the pageant, the popular press covered Vail extensively, declaring that "the Miss America Pageant won't know what hit it when it lays eyes on Miss Kansas, Sgt. Theresa Vail" (Grout 2013). This was in large part due to the fact that Vail refused to cover up her tattoos (the Army Dental Corps insignia and the Serenity Prayer) during the swimsuit competition and also because she is "an expert M16 marksman, a bow hunter, a skydiver, a boxer and a mechanic. . . . She can skin a deer, she has a great squirrel stew recipe (it features sauerkraut) and, one day, she hopes to hunt bear with her bow and arrow" (Grout 2013). This latter description of Vail, which emphasized her skills as a marksman, especially resonated with many of the post-9/11 patriots, who called her a "real American Woman" (Grout 2013), with *Fox News and Commentary* host Todd Starnes (2013) tweeting at the end of the pageant that "the liberal Miss America judges won't say this—but Miss Kansas lost because she actually represented American values."

The collective votes of the at-home viewers—via telephone, Twitter, and Facebook during the pageant—garnered Vail the title of "America's

Choice" at the pageant. In light of this title, her loss was seen as a rejection of American "choice" and representation, with tweets expressing outrage at Davuluri's "illegal" status—"The Arab wins??!!!"—and juxtaposing this against what was seen as quintessentially American about Vail: "Miss Kansas is in the army and is a country girl!!! C'mon" (Hafiz 2013).

This last statement exemplifies the convergence of the intolerant patriot and (homeland) security as central discourses of an American identity. Anything outside this convergence, which is increasingly amplified as representing the homeland—as Davuluri's brown body does—is seen as suspect.

On August 18, a month before the Miss America pageant and its ensuing controversies, New York City mayor Michael Bloomberg (2013) noted in a *Washington Post* op-ed that "New York is the safest big city in the nation, and our crime reductions have been steeper than any other big city's. For instance, if New York City had the murder rate of Washington, D.C., 761 more New Yorkers would have been killed last year. If our murder rate had mirrored the District's over the course of my time as mayor, 21,651 more people would have been killed."

Bloomberg was using these statistics to defend New York's controversial stop-and-frisk policy, which had been declared unconstitutional by various civil liberties organizations and had been the subject of several news stories in the *Post.* The stop-and-frisk policy has been a longstanding practice in the New York City Police Department but has gained special prominence since the attacks on the city in 2001. Under New York's Criminal Procedure Law Section 140.50, stop and frisk authorizes police officers to stop a person whom the officer believes has either committed or is about to commit a crime and demand her name, her address, and an explanation for her "suspect" behavior. In addition, the officer is authorized to search the suspect for weapons and other instruments that may be harmful to the public.

While Section 140.50 makes no reference to what constitutes suspect behavior or processes for identifying such behavior, the New York Civil Liberties Union (n.d.) notes that statistical evidence provided by the New York City Police Department shows that nine out of ten people stopped have been completely innocent and that African Americans and Latinos disproportionately make up the numbers of suspects who are stopped and frisked. In the midst of class action lawsuits against stop and frisk, and extensive news coverage of the policy, actor Kal Penn—best known for his title role as Kumar in the Harold and Kumar film franchise—shared with his Twitter followers the "Great op/ed by @MikeBloomberg on the merits of 'stop-question-frisk,'" attaching a link to Bloomberg's comments. When people asked whether he was being sarcastic, Penn responded no and that it was "a good policy." As the Twitter conversations grew, he noted that it was "sad to see such activist judges ruling against public safety." As the conversation went back and forth between Penn and his Twitter interlocutors, Penn continued to defend stop and frisk, arguing—in response to one follower who said Penn might have more sympathy if he were stopped and frisked—that he had indeed been a victim of violent crime and using the poorly thought out and popular racist argument that African Americans and Latinos are the perpetrators of most crimes as justification for the disproportionate stopping and frisking of these two groups (Gandhi 2013). As outrage over Penn's remarks gathered momentum, Rinku Sen, president of the Applied Research Center and publisher of *ColorLines,* along with Deepa Iyer, executive director of South Asian Americans Leading Together (SAALT), released a joint statement declaring their opposition to stop and frisk and to Penn's support of it. In it, they noted that

> stop and frisk sounds so benign yet it covers up the violent humiliation experienced by hundreds of thousands of young black and brown men annually. Beneath the numbers is the human impact of this sort of policing. It involves being thrown to the ground face down. It involves cops dumping your belongings on the street while they taunt you with predictions that you'll never amount to anything. It involves having this happen to you a dozen times before you're 16 years old, and continuing into your adulthood. This sort of police enforcement not only hurts the individual, but also entire communities whose members are treated as "others" and automatically deemed unwelcome suspects in their own neighborhoods. . . . Especially since September 11, South Asians are routinely targeted as would-be terrorists in many settings. . . . South Asians have endured harassment at airports and at the border, interrogations and detentions by immigration authorities in the name of national security. (Sen and Iyer 2013)

At the same time as this statement was released, Sen and Iyer also reached out to Penn and asked that he reconsider his stance on stop and frisk. In response to their joint statement, coupled with growing public outrage, Penn eventually retracted his support for the policy, stating, "I have and still do oppose racial profiling in any form. I want to thank SAALT and the Applied Research Center for reaching out and starting to educate and dialogue with me about these issues" (Sen and Iyer 2013).

Penn's initial support for such routinized surveillance and systemic disciplining of othered bodies seemed even more ironic considering that one of the largest-grossing installments of the Harold and Kumar franchise that made him a household name, *Harold and Kumar Escape from Guantanamo Bay* (dir. Jon Hurwitz and Hayden Schlossberg, 2008), is a seemingly tongue-in-cheek criticism of post-9/11 racial profiling. When Kumar is mistaken for a terrorist by an elderly passenger who morphs the bearded and stoned Kumar into a turban-wearing terrorist in her mind, she also mistakenly—in her heightened sense of vigilantism—hears Kumar use the word "bomb" instead of "bong," as he refers to a smoke-less bong he has brought on board. In addition, Penn has also repeatedly spoken about his experiences of racial profiling at airports, decrying the realities of "flying while brown."

His inability, or, perhaps more correctly, his unwillingness, to make connections between those experiences and state policies that violate civil liberties for additional marginalized populations speaks to the internalization of oppression experienced by othered bodies. In many ways, Penn's support of the stop-and-frisk policy emerges out of the same affective space that compelled South Asian Americans, especially Sikh Americans, to perform *amantes patriae* by draping themselves in flags and proclaiming "we are American" as well as the strategies with which they sought to distance themselves ethnically and religiously from Muslim American communities after 9/11. A sudden rise in patriotic vigilantism requires one to embrace the public disciplining of other marginalized subjects as a way to overcome one's own experiences as a marginal subject. It is also this same affective space—the desire to belong at the same time one recognizes that one doesn't—and the actions that are taken to reconcile that dissonance that result in a nostalgic longing and pastoral elevation of the motherland for many diasporic subjects.

Nostalgic Homes

It's summer 1999, and I'm traveling from Ohio to Oregon with a friend. The car ride is long and tedious because we're pulling a small trailer holding six boxes of books, a dresser, two suitcases, and a plant—my life's belongings in the United States up to that point. We are exhausted and hungry, and somewhere in Iowa we choose the first exit with a motel sign on it and decide to stop for the night. The town is small, and as we pull into the motel parking lot, a tumbleweed crosses the road like a ghost in the streetlight. I am simultaneously charmed and a little nervous. It seems lonely, cut off from reality. More importantly, my companion is White and I am brown. My six years in the United States thus far have taught me that such combinations are not always welcome, even before 9/11. My fears are put to rest when I walk into the lobby of the A-frame motel. A middle-aged woman dressed in *salwar kameez* greets me with a huge smile. Once we work out the necessary paperwork for us to stay the night (she asks me repeatedly whether we need two rooms instead of one), we move on to more substantial discussions—like establishing through name and ethnicity that I am from Sri Lanka, my parents are traveling and moving to other parts of the world, and that I am on my way to start my doctoral program—information that is clearly of more importance to her than the paperwork that is required for our stay. As the conversation veers to family and where I'm from, she invites us to dinner at the motel manager's apartment that she occupies with her husband and daughter. "After all," she tells me matter-of-factly, "you are one of us and it's late." She steers us to the back of the building, where her husband is seated reading a newspaper and one of her daughters (the other is in college, "like you," she nods at me), a teenager of fifteen or so, is watching MTV while doing her homework at the kitchen table. As she's getting the meal ready, Mrs. Patel[8] continuously asks questions about my life, school, family, and future plans, hardly waiting for answers but pausing occasionally to throw a suspicious and disapproving glance at my male friend—who is sitting silently watching us, unable to comprehend how we are suddenly eating a warm meal of rice and curry in the back of a motel in a small town in the middle of Iowa.

As she chatters away, Mrs. P suddenly turns to me determinedly and tells me that I need to stay another night to "watch the film at the Y." The film at the Y, she explains, is a cultural event organized by the Indian families in the neighborhood where they screen Bollywood films at the local YMCA so that their children, second- and third-generation Americans, "would know what India was like." In many ways, Mrs. P's need to re-create Home, with a capital *H*, within her U.S. home speaks to what Witold Rybczynski (1987, 217) makes implicit when he notes the connection between belonging and nostalgia, previously mentioned.

Mrs. P tells me emphatically that these film meetings are important because they are also a way to socialize and ensure that the children have the opportunity to meet future partners who are "more like us because, you know, otherwise these children think they are American and forget where they come from." At that moment, she seems oblivious to the fact that her daughter hardly looks or acts "more like us," *in the way her mother defines "us."* For Mrs. P, "us" is defined by a sense of ethnic identity and belonging that delineates the space of Home from this home: history and nostalgia, from the reality of living and working in the United States as immigrants, working in one of the most stereotyped industries for South Asians—as motel owners. While stereotypes of motel owner and corner store Indians are part of popular culture (Apu in *The Simpsons*, for example), they are also increasingly used as racist epithets. I remember seeing "American owned and operated" signs displayed prominently outside several motels to indicate that ownership was White, not brown, shortly after September 2001. More recently, commenting on Davuluri's win, a Twitter user going by the name of OneProudHonkie asked, "how can you be Miss AMERICA and look like you should be a gas station clerk or motel owner? this country though."

I met Mrs. P a couple of years before the World Trade Center and Pentagon attacks, and though we exchanged a couple of e-mails after my brief visit, we eventually lost touch. But that evening, and its conversations, has stayed with me for more than a decade and a half. After the events of September 11, I've revisited that evening in my mind over and over again, trying to connect what was unspoken about diasporic identity and the crises of otherness, and the subsequent escalation of antibrown racism in the United States. I wondered how their sense of home and belonging may have changed because of those events in September. I recalled how, over dinner, Mrs. P told me that they'd arrived in the United States in the late 1970s and, over the last two and a half decades, had been back "home" eight or ten times. She explained that these trips might increase in frequency as their daughters became older because "it is good for them to know where we come from and our values and ideas." It didn't seem to occur to her, or if it did, she refused to acknowledge the fact, that her daughters were American, by birth and—based on my interaction with her younger daughter—by disposition as well. Mrs. P's desire to teach them "where we come from" and "our values and ideas" seemed to be important to her mainly because she saw her *own self*—as a first-generation other—as different. Her desire to give her children roots seemed to come from her own sense of alienation. Mrs. P is not unusual in her longing for security through a nostalgic construction of her place of origin as the quintessential home. Immigrants, whose somatic and ethnic identities aren't easily assimilated into the mythology of the melting pot, tend to look back at what was left behind, namely, a sense of inclusion and its corresponding sense of security that that sense of home evokes. While these origin geographies stay frozen in memory as a higher moral, cultural, and social authority for many immigrants, the reality is that the countries themselves continue to evolve, responding to and changing with global economic shifts. But this reality becomes irrelevant, as the ethnic performances and cultural artifacts become nostalgic extensions of the mythologized homeland—much like the films from Bollywood shown at the local YMCA—where "Hindi movie theaters act as anchors in the daily lives of the migrants. When new immigrants arrive, they turn to these centers for information and help with their transition" (Prashad 2000, 114).

Over the years, and especially since 2001, I've thought about that teenage daughter and how she feels about growing up in the middle of Iowa and taking day trips to Chicago (also described by her mother) to see various Hindi actors who would visit the city and give performances to the Indian community of that area, in the midst of hyperpatriotic vigilantism. She was also on my mind, years later, when I did fieldwork on U.S.-based Third World social movements and talked to American teenagers whose activism in India came out of a sense of alienation and otherness that they were only able to articulate after leaving their parents' homes. A few years ago, at the annual general meeting of one of the organizations I was studying, I spoke to several members who were Indian American. Born to Indian parents in the United States, these men and women were actively involved in an organization that sought to protect India from and provide alternatives to the systematic social, cultural, and environmental havoc caused by large transnational corporations. Their general conversations were peppered with words like "back home" and "going home." When I explicitly asked them their reasons for involvement in the association and other cultural and social events, overwhelmingly the answer was that it gave a sense of connection to "home." One of the young men, Mohan,[9] a college student from California, spent several hours talking to me over the course of four days as the annual general meeting of the organization continued. My first conversation with him was marked by his tentativeness about going to India. I asked him whether this was something he planned on doing because the organization provided support for volunteers who wanted to help with any of the grassroots projects that were already in place in India. He stared at his hands for a while and then responded,

> I feel really torn between wanting to go to India but feeling afraid and then guilty because I'm afraid to go there. I have never been there, you know, and I was thinking that maybe by getting involved and doing something with [*he names the organization*] I would be able to resolve this conflict. I'm planning to go back [*laugh*], OK, not "go back" because I've never been there, but go there next summer and do some work or something [*he trails off and looks vague*]. (Silva 2003, field notes)

His evocation of "going back" at the same time he tells me that he is afraid of going to India is illuminating, and not unusual for second- and third-generation offspring. The desire to "go back" can be attributed to the fact that he is perceived as "different" to his peers who have a more concrete sense of (somatic) American identity, even though he appears to be completely American in a performative sense. In fact, to me, Mohan looked like the majority of American teenagers I've met in the country thus far—and a lot like Mrs. P's daughter. He was wearing blue jeans and a Gap T-shirt. All the while that he talked to me, he twirled a baseball cap in his hand and flipped back long strands of hair from his eyes as he stared down thoughtfully at his cross-trainers. But it was clear that despite the accoutrements of American teen culture, Mohan still felt a profound sense of dislocation from America at large, one that forced him to consider as home a geography that he somewhat feared and that he had never visited. This feeling of alienation is not unusual, especially in a country where brown bodies have become marked as "threatening" or "alien" following the attacks of September 11, 2001. Considered "un-American" because of the perceived somatic similarity to a random Middle Eastern identity, South Asians have increasingly come under attack, both physically and ideologically, since 9/11. While the events of that day remain an interstices—an unnamed, unfathomable space rather than a single event—for all within and outside the United States, the repercussions of those acts have been especially difficult on immigrants and their offspring. Also, incidents such as this highlight mainstream beliefs that South Asians rose out of a vacuum—a migration inaccurately perceived as so recent that "they" don't belong here. It is perhaps this perception that fuels the feelings of alienation that many of the conversations seemed to share. Mohan's crisis of belonging was apparent as the conversation continued:

> "Do you know what you want to do?" I ask him as he tells me that he is very confused about his identity and sense of self.
>
> "[*He laughs*] No, to be honest not really. I got involved in the organization because I wanted to find out who I was. I mean, I have all of these things that I do with my family that are Indian and I have no idea what they mean or anything. All I know is that they are Indian and because of that, important. (Silva 2003, field notes)

There is almost a question mark at the end of that statement. He looked at me as if for reassurance that these things are indeed "important." I didn't want to respond to his subtle plea because I had no response to give him, so we continued on. "Do you take part in a lot of events and activities?" I asked him.

> Well, my parents do and when I'm at home I go for things because it's at least a way to learn a little bit about India. (Silva 2003, field notes)

I asked him why these things were important simply because they were Indian. He looked surprised at my questions and responded with, "Well,

I'm Indian, right?" And after a moment, as the silence continued, "at least, Indian American." Mohan's elevation of the ethnic self over the American self is very similar to Mrs. P, who still saw herself and her American daughters as Indian.

The cultural practices become what Hamid Naficy (1998, 4) sees as an "attractive method for becoming discursively emplaced." And for many of the second generation, like Mohan, these events and organizations are ways to connect with people who have the same sense of dislocation that he feels—a space of emplacement to combat the displacement. An interview with him also included a fellow member of the organization, Saro, who seemed to have a more assertive approach to how she wanted to go about reclaiming her identity as an ethnic Indian:

> "I really wanted to find out more about who I was and felt that this would be a good opportunity."
>
> "Why?" I ask her.
>
> "Well, a lot of them are like me—ABCD[10] [*laughs and looks at me knowingly*]—American and Indian. So I felt they would understand my confusion better and help me understand myself."
>
> "Did you?" I ask her [*Mohan interrupts before Saro can answer*].
>
> "Yeah, she's really good. She's already decided that she's going to India and doing work there. And she's already learning the language too. I don't speak it at all" [*Mohan looks despondent*].
>
> Saro responds, "It took me a while to figure things out though. I mean I had no idea either, but being with this group really helped because they've done the same things that you have done and gone through the same stuff so it's easy to figure things out."

Several themes emerge in this conversation. One is Saro's confusion about her own identity and the desire to resolve that confusion in a way that clearly claims an identity and a history that she shares with a common group. Interestingly, Saro's search for identity results in a return to the less familiar rather than an assertion of her identity as an American. As part of that process, she has carefully constructed herself as an Indian through language, community involvement, and a single-mindedness that makes Mohan envy her. Mohan's own crisis of belonging and his tentativeness in articulating that crisis manifest in his admiration for his friend as "really good" and his anxiety that he doesn't speak "the language." I point out that there are many different languages spoken in India and ask whether there is one that he thinks he should learn. He tells me that it will probably be what his parents speak. I ask him what that is, and he "thinks" it is Punjabi. When I ask him why they both put so much emphasis on language, especially to go back to a country of multiple languages, and one where English is readily spoken, they both have identical responses: it is about community, a sense of belonging that marks them as "Indian" rather than as foreigners.

This sense of community and camaraderie is central to South Asian diasporic identity but is also negotiated very differently based on generation. For example, Mohan, Saro, and the daughter of the motel owner seem to simultaneously embrace and fetishize, and then discard and forget, ethnic performances, depending on the social and political circumstances. The motel owner, and other older immigrants I have spoken with, are less fluid in their movement between the ethnic–Western dyad. But whatever the depth of the relationship and the ability to negotiate their ethnic selves, the films and the social and cultural events serve two very significant purposes: first, they allow for a common understanding of cultural values and practices that the older diasporic community hopes will not be forgotten, and second, they become—for the younger generation—venues for connecting with people who have split identities like they do. Ironically, based on my observations, perhaps it is to these second and third generations that the cultural *consumption* is most important, even though they are among the first to discard it depending on circumstances. Interacting with people "more like them" provides a sense of belonging in a society where racial divisions are mostly marked by Black or White—and where their own marking carries little currency in debates of race. And whether this is articulated emphatically, like for Mohan and Saro, or whether it is, like the following conversation, more subtle and nuanced, the *ethnic* performance carries a sense of belonging that is necessary for emotional well-being.

My friend Ravi was born a couple of years after his parents moved to the United States in the late 1960s and was raised in the suburbs of Chicago, Illinois. A child of educated and affluent parents, Ravi has little of the tentativeness of Mohan, or the assertiveness of Saro, when it comes to questions about his identity. He is confused by my interest in his identity, jokingly accuses me of "overthinking race," and sees nothing to indicate or understand his upbringing as "different" from his non-Asian peers in the suburbs. But nevertheless, we continue our conversation about growing up American to immigrant parents. Ravi starts laughing when I ask him about being a brown American. He reminds me, again, that he thinks that this conversation is "silly" and wouldn't really help my research because he isn't very "different" from the average, Midwestern American, especially because he didn't have a particularly "Indian" upbringing. He warns me that this conversation/interview would derail my research. I tell him that I'm interested in all experiences and forge on. Despite this un-Indian upbringing, I ask him whether there was anything that was connected to his ethnic background. At first, Ravi denies that there was anything significant that marked him as "Indian." I ask him whether he knew other Indian American families. He tells me that he knew them from the "temple": "We went to temple every week and we had a social network and there were about ten of us [Indian Americans] who hung out together at school—we kind of banded together, you know so that we had each other if something happened in school."

He pauses as he comes to the end of the statement and realizes what he has just said: "if something happened in school." Ravi's interpellation of race-based violence as a real possibility, and the precautions taken against this as completely natural, speaks to the issues of security and insecurity that I have raised throughout this chapter. By naturalizing the protection against violence, and seeing it as something inevitable, he has also internalized his second-class status as a citizen at the same time he performs belonging, publicly. After making the statement, Ravi looks away for a full twenty seconds or so, realizing that all this doesn't sound like "nothing," and then says almost defiantly, "Well, I mean I guess it sounds like a lot, but I know many kids who had much stronger Indian influences here than mine." He pauses and thinks about it more, and then changes the subject, telling me that he thinks "the women especially get really caught up in the cultural aspects, the guys less so." He laughingly tells me that he played soccer outside the temple with the other boys while his parents, their friends, and the daughters of the families attended the ceremonies. We start talking about visiting India, and how that experience has changed over time. Ravi tells me he first visited India right "after high school and I hated it. It was completely different than what I had expected. I mean, I don't remember a whole lot of it except that I kept thinking that this is nothing like I thought it would be. Honestly, it was so . . . polluted. And after we got back, my American friends here kept asking whether I had done this, or done that, like these key Indian events that have been broadcast all over the world that we are expected to do when we're there, and it hadn't even occurred to me to do those things." When I ask him if this first impression has changed over the years, he says yes, and that food especially has become, in his own words, "sort of my own connection to the community." Though reluctant to partake in any large-scale performance of South Asian identity connected to the diasporic community, and even more reluctant to admit to any feeling of alienation or difference, Ravi still finds a sense of identity and belonging through the preparation of food, calling it "comfort food." It is ultimately the consumption of home and belonging, even as he denies any significant connection to the community.

Ravi, especially, highlights the complexity of this nostalgic identity. Like many of his generation, he has a deep desire to belong, to be American—a White, middle-class American—through performance and consumption. But ultimately, and unconsciously, he re-creates, as Saro and Mohan and many other non-White immigrants do, a deep and abiding relationship to a distant space that is nostalgically marked as "home."

If the events of 9/11 reinstated the home/land as a "birthright"—and this coeval existence as the mark of belonging—for those whose births were outside the home/land (and therefore were lesser, "naturalized" citizens), home became an elusive, seductive, and prized possession. Such anxieties about color, race, birth, and, ultimately, death (as many of the brown diaspora learned about after 9/11) had theretofore been constructed—within the myth of the melting pot—as historical or isolated and shared silently among the brown bodies who refused to overstep their place. The silence surrounding the deeply historical anti–South Asian violence in the United States (outside academic writing, where this is somewhat more documented) can be summarized around two intersecting points: (1) the construction of Asian and Asian American and (2) the history of that panethnic group largely tied to East Asian diasporic movements and solidified by the disciplinary boundaries and focus of academic study. Essentially, the carefully policed borders of ethnic studies within the United States long ensured that the category and study of Asian Americans mirrored the general community borders of separation between East Asians and South Asians. Because the former consisted of larger numbers, and a much more detailed and formally documented history, and the latter gained more prominence in the 1960s, the arrival of South Asian brown as "new" and without proper routes/roots has long ensured a sense of dislocation for South Asian Americans. Such a dislocation has only intensified after the events of 9/11, when cases of "mistaken identity" resulted in vandalism of properties, arrests, harassment, and even death. Within this broader context, where one's invisible body is now a suspect body, the nostalgic longings for a mythical home seem to have become a coping mechanism for the sense of alienation and distance that the anti-immigrant outcries bring out.

3
Expulsion and What Is Not
Defining Worthiness of
American Citizenship

One of the essential characteristics of modern biopolitics (which will
continue to increase in our century) is its constant need to redefine
the threshold in life that distinguishes and separates what is inside
from what is outside.

—GIORGIO AGAMBEN, *HOMO SACER:
SOVEREIGN POWER AND BARE LIFE*

If we wanted to describe the complex politics of identity in contemporary American urban society, we could contrast four such vectors:
first, a population largely demobilized, with little or no ability to
move out of predefined and enclosed spaces; second, a population
with highly constrained but extensive lives of mobility; third, a highly
mobile population which is nevertheless excluded from certain key
places; and finally, a population living in a voluntarily imposed, increasingly fortress like space, but which, from within that space, as
a result of a variety of technologies, is granted an extraordinary
degree of mobility.

—LAWRENCE GROSSBERG, *IDENTITY AND
CULTURAL STUDIES: IS THAT ALL THERE IS?*

Previously I defined *home* within the parameters of legal residence,
(model) citizenship, and patriotism, approaching these identities as the
cornerstones of a post-9/11 society that is bound by a hypervigilantism
couched in discourses of security and securitization. Within this hypervigilantism, the need to identify and control brown becomes a primary

function, and one that utilizes (and relies on) both political and popular culture. Since the home/land imparts, through its very discourse and existence, as I've illustrated previously, a tangible value that is coded in a particular appearance (that is not brown), that value is only manageable and maintained through what it is judged against. Through this abstract ideo-mathematical equation—which I define as an algorithmic process by which identities are added and subtracted that seem to logically feed race biases—*what is not* is what becomes brown. It is the "what is not"— and the practices by which it is constructed and maintained—that I focus on here. Essentially, I look at the ways in which the noncitizen, the non-patriot/foreigner, and his space become constructed as counter to the patriotic and perfect citizenry of home/land. I do so by juxtaposing representation and reality to provide context for the merging of truth and fiction-as-truth.

I approach such a merger as a form "lenient disciplining" (Foucault 1979) that produces and maintains a socially acceptable form of hierarchy around identity. In *Discipline and Punish,* Michel Foucault (1979, 25) writes that, "in our societies, the systems of punishment are to be situated in a certain 'political economy' of the body: even if they do not make use of violent and bloody punishment, even if they use 'lenient' methods involving confinement and correction, it is always the body that is at issue—the body and its forces, their utility and docility, their distribution and their submission." In this repositioning of the body as the object of codified violence, rather than the act itself, Foucault provides an important segue into understanding how and why certain representations of contemporary immigrant experiences in popular culture act as a form of ideological disciplining that mirrors and extends the political disciplining of everyday life and law. In keeping with this, I turn to both news events and mediated popular representations to illuminate how contradictions between immigrant/visitor realities and mediated popular representations collide to reinforce the notions of American exceptionalism and American expulsion.

Here expulsion comes from being unexceptional or without the correct "credentials" or "legitimacy" to be "worthy" of U.S. citizenship or without the right to belong *to* the country—as opposed to *of* the country, which is already tied to a form of unchallenged legitimacy. Following Foucault's notion of lenient methods, I turn to specific examples of the codified body (as brown deviant) that is emblematic of the anti- or unexceptional subjugated essential, that is produced and bracketed through both the events of 9/11 and the long history of racism in the United States. Each instance that I expound on here carries with it the contradictions of what it means to belong in America. The contradictions themselves work together to make the possibility of belonging, as explained and defined in the previous chapter, a convoluted process that seems impossible to navigate for the brown body, whose somatic features and imagined identities lead to a plethora of identifications that negate the right to belong.

Reality and Representation

On September 15, 2001, Balbir Singh Sodhi had just stepped outside his gas station to inspect the work landscapers had completed for him when Frank Roque—mistaking Sodhi as Middle Eastern because of his turban— shot and killed him. When he was eventually arrested and led away, after a shooting spree that saw him attack other "Middle Easterners" (see the introduction), Roque shouted, "I am a patriot" and "I stand for America all the way." Caught up in the patriotic fervor, foregrounded by a racist history that gripped the country, Balbir Singh Sodhi's murder of mistaken identity became the first documented assassination of a civilian following September 11, 2001. Such an act of violent racism is tragic in and of itself, but what makes Sodhi's assassination even more profound is that he had moved to the United States to get away from the very persecution that killed him—that of identity and religion. Sodhi left India in the late 1980s to escape the anti-Sikh movement that gripped India during that time and arrived in the United States because of a belief that he would be free of persecution in the Promised Land. Initially moving to California, and working as a taxi driver, Sodhi and his brother decided to move to Arizona for a more quiet life in safer communities outside metropolitan areas. In 2000, the two brothers bought a gas station and house in Mesa, Arizona—a town they thought was safer than the Los Angeles and San Francisco Bay Area neighborhoods in which they had previously lived and worked. Balbir Singh Sodhi was looking at flowers that had been planted in front of the gas station when Roque pulled up and fired a gun at him. While Sodhi's murder was met with outrage by the neighborhood community that he was part of, it mostly instilled a sense of fear in the Sikh and South Asian community at large. It was the first tangible sign of violent antibrown patriotism.

Following his murder—the first of many violent crimes committed in the name of the United States and of patriotism following September 11—Sodhi's name was committed to memory on the Arizona 9/11 Memorial as an important reminder of the ways in which the United States responded to the attacks and so that Sodhi's name could bear witness to those who had unduly suffered because of the misguided actions of the 9/11 terrorists. The commemorative monument, located in Phoenix's Wesley Bolin Memorial Plaza—commissioned under executive order 2003-02 by then (Republican) governor Jane Hull and completed under (Democratic) governor Janet Napolitano—is meant to be a "permanent Memorial in honor and memory of those who lost their lives in one of this nation's most horrific tragedies and to those who kept their spirits alive through unity and sacrifice, and to serve as a meaningful place for families to go to reflect upon these events for generations to come" (Hull 2003).

But since its completion and unveiling in 2006, the monument has become a contested symbol of 9/11, of domestic and international politics, and of the ongoing immigration laws of that state. The memorial—consisting of a steel canopy laser cut with various responses to the attacks that appear and fade with the movement of the sun—is intended to (according to the bipartisan commission that designed the project) immortalize the diverse responses, both national and international, to the acts of terror and to provide a broader context to understanding 9/11. As such, among the statements that acknowledge the firefighting heroes of New York City and immortalize the time of the attacks, are also the statements "09 15 01 Balbir Singh Sodhi," "Foreign-born Americans afraid," and "Must bomb back."

Such statements reflect the reality of a violent patriotic citizenship that erupted following the attacks. As the FBI noted of hate crimes in 2002,

> the preformed negative opinion, or bias, was directed toward ethnicity/national origin. Consistent with past data, by bias type, law enforcement reported that most incidents in 2001 were motivated by bias against race. However, crime incidents motivated by bias

against ethnicity/national origin were the second most frequently reported bias in 2001, more than doubling the number of incidents, offenses, victims, and known offenders from 2000 data. Additionally, the anti-other ethnicity/national origin category quadrupled in incidents, offenses, victims, and known offenders.

Although such statistical evidence by law enforcement agencies, as well as the real fears and lived experiences of non-White peoples in the country, was presented to a larger public in various ways, it was the statements that referred to this "broader context," and that were documented on the Arizona monument, that raised the ire of conservative lawmakers. Despite the aggressive attacks against communities of color across the country, and the specific location of Arizona as the first antibrown murder following 9/11, Greg Patterson, a well-known conservative blogger and former Republican state lawmaker, who is "credited" with rallying co-conservatives around the issue, declared that the monument "is a criticism of the United States! . . . I'm not saying these things can't be spoken. . . . But this is the *official* 9/11 memorial at the Arizona state Capitol grounds, and this is not how I want my family to remember 9/11, and I don't think it's how many Arizonans want to remember 9/11" (Gutel 2006, emphasis added). The use of "official" to justify the erasure of Sodhi's murder speaks to the FBI's statistical evidence that national origin (in addition to citizenship) was what was suspect within 9/11 discourses and practices of othering. In the controversy surrounding the monument, securing the nation from the "what is not" is done through a renarrativizing of the "official language" of the monument. The story also became popular fodder for anti-Napolitano conservatives, who opposed the governor's seemingly left and anti-American politics, and was a central talking point of the Republican challenger to Napolitano's seat, Lee Munsil, during that election cycle. Two weeks after the monument was opened to the public, Munsil held a press conference at the site, challenging Napolitano's patriotism and declaring that

a memorial put in place supposedly to remember the losses of 9-11—an evil attack on our nation that killed thousands of innocent Americans—instead reminds us of American failings and American mistakes, real and imagined, before and after 9-11. . . . This Governor

does not get it. She does not understand the nature of our oppo-
nent or the gravity of the war we are in. Her support for this memorial, along with her failure to secure the borders of our state five
years after 9–11, is evidence that she cannot be trusted to take seri-
ously the threats to the security of the people of our state and of
our nation. (Munsil 2006)

Successfully circumventing any discussion about "American failings and
American mistakes, real and imagined," and what that statement means
in terms of context for 9/11 as well as other historical events around race,
the monument essentially became tied to immigration reform and border security (from brown bodies that were either unconnected or connected only by geographic proximity to the perpetrators of the attacks).
In his speech, to rousing applause and cries of support, Munsil seamlessly connected the attacks of 9/11 to Arizona's immigration laws. By
essentially declaring the governor's lack of support for the war in the
Middle East as an extension of her inability to implement immigration
laws in the state of Arizona, Munsil wove a narrative that connected
brown bodies of radical Islamic terror to immigration and immigration
reform. Undergirded by Arizona's geographic placement as a border
state, the popular sentiment seemed to be that the monument needed to
represent a vision of the United States as imagined by conservative, anti-
immigration politicos rather than taking a broader and more diverse approach to understanding 9/11 outside of its place/date. As part of this
desire to isolate 9/11 as an unprovoked and ahistorical attack on the
American way of life, anything that contradicted or questioned that uni-
polar vision was declared inaccurate.

It was to address these "inaccuracies" that, on January 19, 2011, at the
fiftieth legislature of the House of Representatives in the state of Arizona,
Republican representative John Kavanagh introduced House Bill 2230:
An Act for Providing Modification of the September 11, 2001, Commemorative Monument in Arizona. Kavanagh, in his presentation and
defense of the bill, argued that some of the statements on the monument
were "anti-American" and without merit. Although newspapers and eye-
witness accounts reported that Roque had specifically targeted "Middle
Eastern–looking" people to shoot down in a misguided attempt to protect the United States, Kavanagh argued that he was "unconvinced" that

there was a direct link between Sodhi's murder and the events of 9/11, saying, "He was the victim of a madman. He was not a 9/11 victim. . . . I don't mean to (dismiss) what happened to this individual. I don't mean to trivialize it" (Walsh 2011a). Kavanagh argued that a *separate* plaque could be made for Sodhi and that his primary concern was with the "other" statements that seemed "political." Despite the claim that Sodhi was not a "primary" concern or target, the erasure of his name continued to be one of the statements of contention.

It is against the backdrop of these kinds of sentiments and heated debates that Kavanagh formally introduced HB 2230 to the Arizona legislature, requesting that the administration remove

> the existing panels containing the following phrases from the monument that is dedicated to the commemoration of the events and effects of the attack on the United States on September 11, 2001:
>
> 1. "Fear of foreigners"
> 2. "09 15 01 Balbir Singh Sodhi, a Sikh, murdered in Mesa"
> 3. "Foreign-born Americans afraid"
> 4. "Feeling of invincibility lost"
> 5. "Must bomb back"
> 6. "You don't win battles of terrorism with more battles"
> 7. "Violent acts leading US to war 05 07 1915, 12 07 1941, 08 04 1964 & 09 11 2001"
> 8. "06 03 02 Congress questions why CIA & FBI didn't prevent attacks"
> 9. "FBI agent issues July 2001 warning in 'Phoenix Memo'"
> 10. "03 13 02 New Afghan leader elected"
> 11. "Middle East violence motivates attacks in US"
>
> The department of administration shall sell the panels containing the phrases listed in subsection A of this section to a scrap metal dealer or other person in the business of recycling scrap metal.

In response to the bill, and to the possibility that Sodhi's name would be removed and transferred to a "business of recycling scrap metal," Sodhi's immediate family as well as the broader Sikh community rallied to convince Governor Jan Brewer to veto the bill. SALDEF organized an online petition asserting that "Mr. Kavanagh believes the tragic hate crime was unconnected to 9/11. SALDEF is outraged at the disrespect the Arizona state legislature has shown Mr. Sodhi's memory, family, and the Sikh

American community." The petition concluded that the bill "disrespects the memory of the first fatal hate crime victim in the wake of 9/11." In response, thousands signed the petition, writing in that "he [Sodhi] is not related to terrorism America is a great country but sometimes it can be filled with a country of idiots! He's Sikh not even Islamic!" and that "this definitely sounds racist. What else, other than racism, would motivate a person so much to REMOVE a plaque in the memory of someone who died? And then to sell it as scrap metal speaks volumes about the lack of class, etiquette, respect, and concern for human rights in general." As thoughtful public critique, such as the examples cited here, generated attention to SALDEF's petition, Representative Kavanagh finally met with members of Sodhi's family. Following the meeting, Kavanagh admitted that he "misunderstood the case" and that he "apologized for dredging up the sorrow once again" and "for any misunderstanding" (Walsh 2011b). As a result of that meeting, he proposed a "correction" to the monument, even if Brewer was to sign off on the bill, that replaced "Fear of foreigners" under Sodhi's name with "First backlash hate-crime victim." On April 29, 2011, in the presence of Sodhi's family, Governor Brewer stamped "no" on the bill, expressing concern "about the unintended consequences that would have resulted from this bill . . . the removal of Balbir Singh Sodhi's name from the 9/11 Memorial would have been a serious mistake with hurtful ramifications for the Sodhi family and the entire Sikh community in Arizona" (Brewer 2011).

Although the bill did not pass, and Kavanagh has moved on to bills securing other facilities,[1] the six-year controversy around this monument highlights the realities of subjugated essentialism as a disciplining practice. Because Sodhi seemed a terrorist to Roque, he was killed. Because he wasn't a Muslim, he wasn't a victim of 9/11 to Kavanagh. The inability, in both instances highlighted here, to make a direct link between terrorism and brown bodies results in an imagined identity that exists outside of reality. And such imagined identities stand in for ongoing disciplining practices by legislature, the misguided patriot, and popular culture.

It is against a backdrop such as this—where the imagined brown body is (re)presented as multiple versions of the "real"—that I approach the relationship between reality and representation. Here I mainly focus on comedic representations for two reasons: (1) because of the popularity of the genre in U.S. culture and (2) because humor is seen as a radical contrast to the reality of 9/11 and its postpolitics and culture, even as they serve the same disciplining purposes. In addition, as Richard Dyer (1984) notes, humor and horror provide one of the most effective ways of articulating and constructing marginalization. Both genres validate the hegemonic structures of "normalcy" by setting the stereotyped (humorized or horror) characters against a (White, straight, middle-class, etc.) norm—a norm that the audience, regardless of its own identity—is expected to identify with.

Here Dyer articulates the popular culture version of Foucault's lenient disciplining. While this positioning is subtle—and we are expected to laugh or be horrified and embarrassed at the (supposedly) inconsequential acts of cultural misunderstanding—the misunderstandings themselves are showcased to reinforce difference. Located within these differences, the success of the unwieldy, unworldly, and inelegant immigrant speaks to the exceptionalism of American society and validates the Tocquevillian assertion that "the position of the Americans is . . . quite exceptional, and it may be believed that no democratic people will ever be placed in a similar one" (de Tocqueville 1945, 334). The uncomplicated and humorous representations of a particular brown immigrant that have now become a staple of U.S. popular culture—like the Harold and Kumar franchise, the short-lived sitcom *Aliens in America,* and even *Outsourced*—largely trivialize the process of securing citizenship; render the trauma invalid, or even overexaggerated; and act as a form of lenient disciplining through misrepresentation.

On October 1, 2007, *Aliens in America* premiered to very positive reviews, with the *New York Times* calling it "fresh, funny and charming in a tart, sardonic way, one of the best sendups of adolescent angst" and the *Los Angeles Times* declaring it a "hopeful sign that we may finally be emerging pop-culturally into the post-post-9/11 age . . . in which we are ready to find a little humor in the Clash of Civilizations." This latter observation by the *Los Angeles Times* encapsulates the reasons that this show is an excellent exemplar of brown, despite its short life on the television screen.

The notion that there is "humor in the clash of civilizations" solidifies the existence of clashing civilizations, and the premise that such clashes are humorous detracts from the very real traumas experienced by being othered within U.S. society. In addition, little to no attention is paid to the amalgamation of inaccurate details that went into making the main character of the show, Raja Musharaff, representative of brown spaces, and that amalgamated culture that "clashes" with the norm. It produces a Pakistani Muslim (with a Sanskrit name mostly used by Sikhs and Hindus rather than Muslims) as both the representative of Islam and the mistaken perpetrator of jihad, which makes up many of the narrative arcs throughout the series. Here the protean existence of brown that I refer to in the introduction comes into play: because Raja, the protagonist, is suspected by many of the folks in Medora, Wisconsin, including his own host family at various instances, because of his "Muslim" (read brown) appearance, the show reinforces the absurdity of the misunderstandings at the same time as it neutralizes them as a form of well-meaning and humorous misguided patriotic ignorance.

Raja Musharaff's arrival as a sixteen-year-old Pakistani exchange student to the home of the Tolchucks of Medora is meant to impact their lives positively, mainly because Raja was meant to be European White and to provide a cultural elevation and high school "cool" to the awkward teenage son, Justin. The pilot episode opens with a voice-over from Justin Tolchuck, who explains his trauma of being a teenage boy in high school. As the camera moves down a school hallway where students move away from the audience's viewpoint in disgust, Justin narrates,

> Let's say a space alien landed in my own town. If he was sixteen years old, he would go to my high school. And let's face it, his life would probably suck. Everyone would make fun of his giant head and his big bug eyes. He'd be an outcast, a loner. Definitely a virgin. There'd be nothing he could do about it, except wait for his spaceship to take him home. I didn't have a spaceship. And each year of high school was worse than the last.

So, the alien in America at this particular moment is a sensitive high school teenager who feels out of place but whose alien position is quickly displaced by the exchange student who arrives in their midst: a *real* alien—with a big head and bug eyes—as defined by U.S. border control and security. In the moment that Raja arrives, in all his awkward social solicitation, Justin's sense of alienation is quickly put into perspective (as a common condition shared by many *American* teenagers who navigate the liminal space between childhood and adulthood), and through that perspective, Raja-as-Other is produced (because he occupies the liminal space of Otherness). Instead of the White European savior the Tolchucks are expecting,[2] Raja arrives, doffing and bobbing his head, skinny, unsophisticated, and, most importantly, brown. Dismayed by the "Muslim" appearance of Raja in his *salwar kameez* and topi cap, the pilot episode (as well as the entire series) deals with the Tolchucks' naive racism—which is meant to be funny and inconsequentially educational in its absurdity—as they come to terms with whom they are hosting. At the airport, as the senior Tolchucks and Justin stare at Raja, Mr. Tolchuck is prodded by his wife to say to Raja, "Son, there may be some confusion. The boy we *ordered* was supposed to come in from London" (emphasis added). While the audience is meant to laugh at the absurdity of the "order," in reality, that is exactly what the Tolchucks have done. As Raja explains that he did fly from London because it was his transit stop from Pakistan, the Tolchucks stare at him in disbelief. Raja continues bobbing his head and thanks them for welcoming him: "You are such good people to open your home to me. I praise and thank Allah for bringing you into my life." And then, loudly, with hands raised to the sky: "Thank you, Allah, for the Tolchucks." This embarrassing display of naive gratitude—which a English-speaking exchange student from South Asia is unlikely to do—visibly dismays the Tolchucks and foregrounds their racist interpretations of Raja's actions as the episode continues. Here "proper" behavior and multicultural acceptance become the onus of the Tolchucks, whose behavior we recognize as "extreme" and gauche, because they don't represent the melting pot mentality of the United States and their behavior comes across as well-meaning ignorance rather than racism.

While we focus on the cosmopolitan limitations of the Tolchucks—especially as Middle America—the image of Raja remains a *realistic* interpretation of Pakistan and, by extension, of brown, Islam, and terror. Here brown becomes an unworldly boy in traditional clothing, praising Allah loudly at airports, risking his own life and the lives of others around him. The gratuitous use of prayers to Allah, which heralds the arrival of Raja to Middle America, reinforces the xenophobic fears of those around him—as seen by the nervous looks from the Tolchucks and others. Raja's naïveté in praising *his* God in an American airport reinforces the stereotype of brown bodies as manically pious and as bodies who are reckless, perhaps even arrogant, about what that piety means and ties that piety to those who will and did commit violence on American soil. In that moment of grateful worship, when everyone turns to look at him in dismay, the misstep of making himself unnecessarily visible is Raja's—and not some inherent racism in the United States.

Because the attacks of 9/11 travel along a seamless chain that is tied to airports, prayers, and Muslims, the obligation to "behave" is on the brown body. Such an obligation animates the relationship between those who are protected by the state (the powerful) and those who aren't (the powerless). Such protection, after 9/11, was not based on birthright or the legal privileges of such but through the codified fears that your physical self produced for the more properly embodied (White) citizen. And therein lies the obligation: because the brown body produced a securitized anxiety, the responsibility of *not* increasing that anxiety is the labor of the brown body. Such responsibilities, and their ideological disciplining, are tightly woven into the fabric of everyday life, even outside mediated representations, where the consequences of disregarding that obligation are reported regularly.

In 2009, for example, Atif Irfan, a tax attorney, and his extended family were flying to Orlando, Florida, from Washington, D.C. After boarding the flight, and while the plane was still at the gate, Irfan and his family were suddenly asked to disembark because of a "suspicious conversation" reported by a fellow passenger. The "suspicious conversation" was a comment made by Irfan's wife about which location of the plane—wing, engine, back, or front—was safest to sit in. As they have repeatedly stated, no part of the conversation contained the word "bomb," "explosion," or "terror." After being questioned and cleared by the FBI at the airport, the Irfans were still refused their seats. In fact, the airline, AirTran, refused to rebook them on a later flight, or any flight, until the "matter was cleared," even though the FBI *had* cleared the matter and the same FBI agents lobbied on behalf of the passengers to get them back on the flight. Also removed from the flight, along with the Irfans, was family friend Abdul Aziz, a Library of Congress attorney who just happened to be on the same flight and who had been seen talking to the Irfans and was, therefore, suspicious by association.

Such incidents are not isolated. More recently, on May 7, 2011, Imams Masudur Rahman and Mohamed Zahloul were boarding a Delta subsidiary flight from Charlotte, North Carolina, to attend, ironically, a conference on Islamophobia. After the men had undergone two security screenings and had boarded the flight, the plane taxied back to the gate because the pilots felt that the two men may make "other" passengers uncomfortable. Two other attendees of the same conference were also detained at other airports. Here the ideo-mathematical equation I refer to at the start of the chapter arrives at a calculation that makes it obvious that the "other passengers" were largely nonbrown, or at least not visibly brown.

A few days later, on May 13, an American citizen of Pakistani origin was removed from a Southwest Airlines plane after she ended a phone call by saying "I've got to go," as the plane was taxiing, and a passing flight attendant heard the sign-off as "it's a go." The hypervigilantism of misheard calls to action is of course laughed off in popular culture, where under similar circumstances Harold and Kumar are able to eventually escape from the most notorious detention center in recent history. But it's not just a mishearing of words or language but the very performances of an unidentifiable brown that moves from body to body that occupy those who see themselves as the guardians of the nation-state. On the same day, on landing after a flight from Mexico City to Los Angeles, an Alaska Airlines flight was met by a slough of FBI agents and other security personnel after a flight attendant was alarmed by the orthodox Jewish prayer observance of tefillin. A spokesperson for the airline stated, "The three passengers were praying aloud in Hebrew and were wearing what appeared to be leather straps on their foreheads and arms. . . . This appeared to be a security threat, and the pilots locked down the flight deck and followed standard security procedures" (Gorman 2011). The appearance of prayer—as brown—and the translation of that as a "security threat," which is punitive, speak to the ways in which "certain territories and people *require* and beseech domination, as well as forms of knowledge affiliated with domination" (Said 1993, 9). Under this new language of securitization and citizenship (belonging), the domination that Said refers to comes from the various punishments (interrogations, missed flights, public scrutiny) that reconstruct the White/Christian/middle-class ethos as the new normal. Then, juxtaposing this new normal against popular mediated representations, what the Tolchucks (and, by extension, the rest of America—Protestant, White Middle America) are supposed to learn is tolerance in its most benign and useless form, where "tolerance discourse . . . designates certain beliefs and practices as civilized and others as barbaric, both at home and abroad; it operates from the conceit of neutrality that is actually thick with bourgeois Protestant norms" (Brown 2006, 7). Here Raja is not presented as a caricature of brown but as a wholly naturalized representative that needs to be understood and *tolerated*, but never accepted, for whom he is. The tolerance is encouraged by asking Middle America to see the other as an object of a barbaric space who is simultaneously odd *and* useful: Raja is impressed by the Tolchucks' middle-class home and cleans, vacuums, and helps with chores, much to the delight of Gary, the dad, who encourages the servitude but doesn't demand the same of his teenage son. As Raja scrubs plates at the sink, with a dish towel over his right shoulder, Gary comes by, drops off more dishes, and pats him delightedly on the shoulder. The image of Raja's servitude, which resonates with colonial overtures of a generous sahib who is delighted with his servant, is foregrounded by Justin's voice telling the audience that his dad has never before seen a teenager clean dishes. Although these conversations and exchanges are meant to highlight the misunderstandings about and resulting racism against people of color in the United States, the absurdity of the situation and the reduction of the complex relationships to differences between "the Orient and the Occident" make the systemic deployment of the racism inconsequential. For example, when Franny poses the ultimate post-9/11 query "what about the terrorist question?" to Gary and he responds with incredulity, Franny informs him that "they pose as students; Bill O'Reilly said so" and chastises him for not watching more news. When Gary defends his response by saying, "It's Medora, Wisconsin," Franny's counter of "So, Medora is not important to blow up? Where is your civic pride?" is, in the most generous of readings, meant to highlight Franny's naïveté and provide some critique of Bill O'Reilly's credibility as an authority on the "terrorist question." But the focus on Medora as a possible location for attack—rather than the accuracy of O'Reilly's claim that "they" pose as students—deflects from any real critique of American ig-norance, either popular (Franny) or political (O'Reilly). While Medora's lack of value as a city worth blowing up remains contested, what is not up for debate is whether "they" pose as students and attack the United States. Such careless and subtle reinforcements of the inherent differ-ences between "them" and "us" are even more intensified when Raja goes to school the next day (sans Justin, who fears that he will be "crucified" if he is seen with Raja). We are introduced to his experiences by Justin as the voice-over narrator (as the camera pans left and right and the audi-ence sees students staring): "OK. You know that nightmare when you are standing in front of your class naked? Well, it was what Raja was going through. Only it was worse because he was wearing a *salwar kameez*." Here, like a bad take on an advertisement by People for the Ethical Treatment of Animals, it is apparently better to be naked than to be seen in clothing that marks and solidifies your otherness. As if to re-inforce the stereotype, we hear a teenager shout out, "Apu, where is my slushy?" Within the genre of the comedy, a critical reading of the natural-izing tendencies to conflate Indian Apu with Pakistani Raja is impossible; instead, the shout reiterates the notion of the amalgamated identities of the laboring brown body as a corner store owner, made popular by a car-toon character.

Although we don't know Raja and Pakistan very well outside their possible connection to terrorism, we *do* know Apu from *The Simpsons*: Apu Nahasapeemapetilon, PhD, is the owner of Kwik-E-Mart, the fic-tional corner store in the wildly popular cartoon. Apu's "arrival," via popular media, has a long and storied history,[3] where racism from the past becomes amalgamated as present reality, so much so that, in 2007, chain store 7-Eleven transformed twelve of its stores into Kwik-E-Marts to promote the release of the movie *The Simpsons*, even selling in them products made popular by the cartoon series. The campaign was enor-mously successful from a financial perspective, and *Advertising Age* raved about the marketing strategy, writing,

> Yes, thanks to the miracle of cross-promotion, you have blundered into a parallel cartoon universe. For a brief moment, you are a Simpson. And it is soooooooo great. Grab a box of KrustyO's cereal, or a six-pack of Buzz Cola or an ice-cold Squishee. And then, for a

taste of life imitating art imitating life, head for checkout, where
there is no under-employed Indian immigrant named Apu on duty,
but there is an Ethiopian immigrant named Getachew. ("They're
asking me to say 'I Apu,'" he offers.) (Garfield 2007)

The review—and the Ethiopian immigrant who is asked to pretend to
be a brown man—along with the economic success of the campaign itself, speaks to several intersecting issues about brown and race(ism) in
the United States that can be harnessed to the surge in representations
like Raja.

Although popular culture may not be the space of "true" representation, it is indeed "a theater of popular desires, a theater of popular
fantasies. It is where we discover and play with the identifications of
ourselves, where we are imagined, where we are represented, not only to
the audiences out there who do not get the message, but to ourselves for
the first time" (Hall 1992b, 32). So within such a context of being imagined and represented, especially to *ourselves,* the Apus and Rajas become a form of internal colonization in that to be outside these representations is to not live up to American expectations of brown immigrant
status. The internalizations of such expectations of marginality result in
the support for legal and social disciplining of one's own self and other,
othered subjects, like in the aforementioned cases of Penn, Jindal, and
Haley. Whereas the caricatures offer a form of how-to for brown bodies,
this conflation of a caricatured cartoon character with a "real" person
reinforces the marginality of brownness, thereby simultaneously articulating *and* neutralizing its perceived threat to American society at large.

In an attempt to further "educate" the audience on the irrationality of
stereotyping, we are witness to an uncomfortable exchange in Raja's new
classroom, as the teacher attempts to integrate him into the class by introducing him as a "special guest"—"a real live Pakistani who practices
Muslimism. This means that we have the opportunity to learn about his
culture and him from us. So let's start a dialogue [*looks at Raja*]. Raja,
you are so different from us. How does that feel?" As Raja looks at her in
confusion, the teacher turns to the class to ask "how everyone else feels
about Raja and his differences."

STEPHANIE, *student, raises her hand*: Well, I guess I feel angry because his people blew up the building in New York.

TEACHER: Oh! That's good. [*smiles approvingly at Stephanie*]

RAJA: But that's not true.

TEACHER: Raja, in America you have to wait 'til you are called on [*turns to the class*]. Now, who else is angry at Raja? [*the entire class raises their hands*]

While the absurdity of the claims of "Muslimisms" and rage against Raja as a Pakistani are exaggerated for comedic relief, the fact that the scene has no resolution, and that Raja never has the opportunity to respond, leaves the viewer with the notion that random terror *is* possible and that the anger against brown bodies as a whole is an ignorant *but natural* response by people who love their country. More simply, the exchange highlights the racism but neutralizes its impact on actual people by saying that such a response is patriotic. Also, introducing Raja as a "real live Pakistani," much like the practices of the world's fairs described later, reconstructs him as an anthropological study and solidifies his alien status that justifies the violence, vis-à-vis collective, ideological anger against him. Here the humor masks the trauma that someone in Raja's position would go through and trivializes the anxieties—of being misunderstood and labeled as outsiders—experienced by many South Asians and South Asian Americans following 9/11.

A similar narrative unfolds in *Harold and Kumar Escape from Guantanamo Bay*. In keeping with the stoner-buddy genre, Kumar (Patel) brings a smokeless bong on board a flight to Amsterdam, much to the chagrin of Harold (Lee). When a fellow passenger imagines that she sees a bearded and turbaned Kumar say "bomb" (instead of "bong"), Harold and Kumar are sent to prison at Guantánamo Bay, Cuba. Their escape, coupled with romantic heroism and modern minority stereotyping, made the second installment of the Harold and Kumar franchise wildly successful. While the majority of the film was a cultural exemplar of lenient disciplining—be responsible, stick to your place, anyone can be successful, and so on—some moments of the film shone with insightful racial commentary. For example, the film starts by poking fun at the battle for the number one spot of uber-marginalized, *between* minority groups. The verbal battle for ethnic superiority—who is more colored—highlights what Elaine Kim (1993) notes is the "Raise the Red Lantern" condition: the hegemons create a system that pits those below them against each other, thereby ensuring that they are left alone. Under this system, while "the notion of the formally equivalent citizen in representative democracy suggests that all individuals of different constituencies have equal access to and are represented within the political sphere," it also hides "the degree to which strata and inequalities continue to exist . . . facilitating the capitalist system in which one dominant class group prospers" (Lowe 1996, 144). Such socially and legislatively systemic inequalities result in a struggle for place and space among people of color, where powerfulness versus powerlessness is routinely performed in everyday contexts (like Ethiopian immigrant Getachew being asked to claim that he is Apu, another marginalized but culturally powerful brown character). This is exemplified in an exchange between Kumar and a TSA agent who pulls Kumar aside for a "random" search while Kumar is entering the airport terminal. Kumar and the African American TSA agent enter into a heated discussion about the "randomness" of Kumar's selection, with Kumar accusing the agent of racism and the agent responding, "Racist? Dude, I'm Black." Kumar responds, "Please, dude, you're barely even brown . . . compared to me, you look like Matthew Perry." This brief conversation regarding who is more "colored" highlights one of the racialized shifts in contemporary U.S. society that allow brown to move more freely as a de facto identity outside "conventional" nodes of color and identity. What I mean by this is that, with the events of 9/11, the issues surrounding unresolved tensions between Blacks and Whites in the United States have largely become invisible, where such invisibility creates its own racialized tensions and notions of "authentic" colored identities between the groups themselves, as both Elaine Kim (1993) and Lisa Lowe (1996) have shown us in the past.

More recently, in *How Does It Feel to Be a Problem?*, a young Palestinian American tells author Bayoumi (2008), "We are the new Blacks"—this declaration summarizes the general sense of crisis that brown bodies have felt after 9/11: that they have become the contemporary versions of fear and loathing within the current political economy of the body. But while hypervisibility brings corresponding disciplining practices that are both subtle and obvious, *visible displacement* also creates tensions, where racial tensions between minority groups increase as each struggles for visible minority status and the rights that such visibility brings. But, in keeping with the genre of comedy, especially stoner-buddy comedies, such moments of insightful critique are few and far between. Instead, the film relies on more comforting narratives about the United States, including the joys of immigration and the ease with which entry is granted. Such representations neutralize any anxiety about the more real experiences that belie the American mythos of accepting the tired and huddling masses that yearn to breathe free and rewrite the history of the violent racist and anti-immigrant policies and practices that have long gripped the country.[4]

When *Harold and Kumar Escape from Guantanamo Bay* does reference locations—which act as moments—that are significant to the discussions around race and racism in the United States, those references make sense *only* to those who have experienced the trauma or share that history in some form. For example, it would take some effort to recognize the significance of locating Kumar's family in New Jersey: a location of one of the most anti-Indian movements in recent history. In 1986, many Indians in Jersey City were victims of random acts of violence at the hands of a group of gang members who called themselves Dotbusters—referring to the *bindhi* worn by Indian women. When a local newspaper highlighted the growing number of incidents, Jersey City Dotbusters responded with the following:

> I'm writing about your article during July about the abuse of Indian People. Well I'm here to state the other side. I hate them, if you had to live near them you would also. We are an organization called dot busters. We have been around for 2 years. We will go to any extreme to get Indians to move out of Jersey City. If I'm walking down the street and I see a Hindu and the setting is right, I will hit him or her. We plan some of our most extreme attacks such as breaking windows, breaking car windows, and crashing family parties. We use the phone books and look up the name Patel. Have you seen how many of them there are? Do you even live in Jersey City? Do you walk down Central avenue and experience what its [*sic*] like to be near them: we have and we just don't want it anymore. You said that they will have to start protecting themselves because the police cannot always be there. They will never do anything. They are a

week [*sic*] race Physically and mentally. We are going to continue our way. We will never be stopped. (Chitnis 2014)

Among the most brutal of these acts was the beating of thirty-year-old Navroze Mody in June 1987. Mody, who was returning home after meeting a friend at a local restaurant, died four days later from his injuries. But, in a country where history—even recent history—and especially racialized history, is carefully ignored in a wave of amnesia, these realities hardly make it to popular culture.

Mapping the racism between the Dotbusters of the 1980s and immigrant experiences of the fictional Patels from New Jersey that culminate in their son being sent to Guantánamo Bay because of a case of "mistaken identity" is not an easy task, or one we are necessarily invited to do by the creators of the franchise. Instead, the narratives of immigrant triumph and the humorous challenges of the actual journey become the more prominent reality: one where Harold and Kumar conveniently come across a makeshift boat that is carrying Cubans to America, and the two escapees are invited to join the boat of merry travelers. We see them discussing the value of TiVo with a genial Cuban—"I'm telling you, Jorge . . . the first thing you have to do when you get to America . . . buy a device called TiVo, OK? Freedom means nothing if you're a slave to regular programming. . . . I promise you that"—while the boat, made from a scrap truck, bobs gently on calm seas against a spectacular sunset. Once on shore, the Cubans grab suitcases and skip merrily (literally) onto the land of opportunity, as Harold and Kumar wave at the "nice people."

This mediated image of nontraumatic entry into the United States belies the realties whereby the U.S. Coast Guard along the Florida shore carefully enforces the "wet feet, dry feet" policy—caught while in water, returned to Cuba; caught on land, allowed to apply for residency—an inhumane law that results in numerous deaths each year as people desperately try to swim ashore while avoiding detection by the patrolling boats. In July 1999, for example, six rafters who tried to swim ashore were blocked and pepper sprayed by the Coast Guard. The dramatic events were broadcast on live TV, and as two of the rafters made it to shore and four were left behind at sea for repatriation, protests erupted across Miami. As the events were played out on local and international media, it became clear that the Coast Guard had acted against policy and that in fact, "at one point, the coastguards used water hoses, and one refugee in the water was hit with pepper spray" (BBC 1999). Owing to a public outcry, the four men left at sea were brought onshore and were given over to authorities for "possible" naturalization. The images of this dramatic event, where the rafters actually fight to survive and, in many instances, are not successful, contrast sharply with the bucolic romanticism of the images of arrival in *Harold and Kumar Escape from Guantanamo Bay.*

Once the boat arrives safely, with no Coast Guard intervention, in Miami, Harold and Kumar head over to meet their college friend Raza. Again, irony abounds—and this is perhaps the intention (and therein lies the problem)—as the two escapees, both othered Americans, seek the help of an "Arab" to get "back home." While "they are a post-collegiate multicultural odd couple in a world where ignorance and prejudice do battle with hypersensitivity and political correctness," as noted in the glowing review of the film in the *New York Times,* and the irony may be intentional, the expectation that an audience viewing the film is critically engaged with the metanarrative of that irony is perhaps too much. Throughout the film, White ignorance—in the form of the elderly woman on the plane who sees a bearded Arab every time she sees Kumar; the deputy secretary of the DHS who believes that Harold and Kumar represent an alliance between North Korea and al-Qaeda; in Alabama, the friendly hunter, his wife-sister, and their inbred son; and, finally, the Klan, who mistake Harold and Kumar for Mexicans—stands in for White racism. But these representations, in keeping with their comedic forms, are so extreme that, much like the racism in *Aliens in America,* or even in NBC's *Outsourced,* they are seen as benign and, unlike the representations of color, are not *universally real,* especially because the film does include reasonable, rational, and thoughtful White men, such as Beecher, who try to convince Fox that his behavior against Harold and Kumar is unreasonable and unfounded and *un-American.* Basically, we are expected to recognize the "extreme" stereotypes of Whiteness as their worst, and therefore most humorous, among *many* identities of White.

This subtle separation of a multidimensional Whiteness from the colored bodies is undergirded by the essentialized performances of both ethnicity and outsider. Even in the midst of chaos, Harold maintains his aura of model minority. From the moment the film begins, Harold is

Cuban Refugee Rescue in Shark infested Sea

This image is part of a series of images captured by gladiator43 for CNN iReport (http://ireport.cnn.com/docs/DOC-773399). According to the accompanying story, gladiator43 was sitting on the balcony of a cruise ship when he saw a small speck on the ocean that turned out to be the refugee boat. All twenty-three passengers were rescued, but many are not always that lucky.

In contrast to the desperation and challenges faced by refugees trying to get to the U.S. border in makeshift boats through shark-infested waters, Harold and Kumar enjoy a peaceful and bucolic ride back home.

represented as slightly neurotic, uptight, and, perhaps most significantly, asexual—this despite that he is flying to Amsterdam to follow a woman. Harold's ingratiation and submissive adoration of Colton Graham, the uber-successful fiancé of Kumar's ex-girlfriend—reinforce the historicized representation of East Asian men quietly taking over America by faithfully, and somewhat insidiously, mimicking Whiteness. In contrast to Harold, Kumar is uncouth, wild, often dumb, and impulsive. From the opening scene—when he uses the toilet to defecate while Harold is taking a shower—Kumar exemplifies the image of the alien and uncouth brown body and reinforces the notion that "the Hindu is the most undesirable immigrant in the state. His lack of personal cleanliness . . . so entirely repugnant to American principles make him unfit for association with American people" (Leonard 1997, 24). But this undesirable brown quality is tinged with a fear that represents larger geopolitical economic machinations: much like Raja, who is presented as having a natural aptitude for the sciences, Kumar too is seen as a science prodigy—in a flashback we know that his dad started teaching him advanced calculus in the sixth grade and also that he has a medical school interview—reinforcing the stereotype of the scientifically advanced but socially stunted brown body. The practice of neutralizing the intelligence because it cannot be harnessed to productivity is a common practice, one that allows the mediated success of the brown image to thrive, despite the ongoing anti-brown sentiments that followed (and continue to be true in the aftermath of) 9/11. Although the Bush administration publicly decried acts of anti-brown violence as reactionary and racist, since 2001, the sense of anxiety against Others has been carefully managed and kept constant by legal and political means.

In 2001, for example, George W. Bush extended the NSA's power under the Foreign Intelligence Surveillance Act of 1978 (FISA) to allow warrantless wiretapping of the communications of individuals and organizations with connections to the Middle East, South Asia, and other geographic locales deemed as potential threats. This was justified by the Bush administration as a *necessary precaution*. With the passage of the FISA Amendments Act in 2008 (reauthorized in 2012), the NSA has what the American Civil Liberties Union (2015a) calls "almost unchecked power to monitor Americans' international phone calls and emails." President

Barack Obama has supported the wireless wiretapping program and its reauthorization, deploying the same rationale as George W. Bush had previously.

Similarly, during the election cycle of 2010, the state of Oklahoma put question 755[5] on the ballot, concerning banning of Sharia and international law. The ballot passed with 70 percent in favor of the ban. This codification of Islamophobia ignored the reality that international laws are not the jurisdiction of the state and that Sharia law is the domain of the mosque and is not applicable in the American legal system. Instead, what the state voted on was whether their collective xenophobia should be codified under the state legal system. And apparently, more than two-thirds of the state decided that it should be. Calling the legislation a "preemptive strike against Sharia," its sponsor, state senator Rex Duncan, declared that he "sees this in the future, somewhere in America" (Siegel 2010). And it is to ensure the future of America that other such laws have followed: Arizona law SB 1070 and South Carolina's SB 20.

These precautionary and preemptive measures that masquerade as justification for "legalized" racial profiling articulated the realities of contemporary American democracy: the state of exception as the norm (Agamben 1998). Under these conditions of constant crisis, and the ability to circumvent the constitutional rights of citizens, especially those whose citizenship is gained rather than given, the everyday practices of brown bodies are scrutinized and managed under the rule of (new) law. Within this notion of management, true *citizenship*—whether they are *actual* citizens—is a topic of much conversation. Part of this (re)construction of the quintessential American is the ability to juxtapose it against what is *not* American.

Space, Race, and Everything in Between

If the Rajas and Kumars of this world behave and act the way they do, then their behavior is underscored by the question, what kinds of spaces produce "these people"? It doesn't matter that, in Kumar's case, the space that produced him is New Jersey. What becomes subtly reinforced is that his somatic body produces an image of savagery that is correlated with contemporary geopolitical conditions by his very existence. Kumar's New Jersey roots are absorbed into Raja's routes, where the person of the country and the visitor converge around a space that is mythically created as simultaneously exotic and abject, in its difference, from the secured nation-state. Such exotic abjection is then harnessed to reinforce the othered body as outsider, where *their* behaviors are incommensurate with the values and practices of the protected space.

Geographer David Sibley (1995) calls these imaginary or created spaces that are naturalized as real *imagined geographies*—socially constructed spaces where the imperfect must not mix with the perfect, where space is demarcated according to one's socially constructed senses of self and worth. Throughout his work, Sibley eloquently articulates how arbitrary relationships of power are naturalized through spatial relationships. Sibley argues that these imaginary geographies "cast minorities, 'imperfect' people, and a list of others who are seen to pose a threat to the dominant group in society as polluting bodies or folk devils who are then located 'elsewhere'" (49). These marked bodies are moved to a space that contains them and that simultaneously becomes a space of vicarious titillation. At a time when alien bodies are a national pastime in the United States, there is a fervent desire among the governing bodies, as well as social processes, to "educate" the masses about "these people." Such armchair anthropology[6] produces a particular kind of expert citizen, one whose knowledge comes from the vicarious consumption of othered spaces. Such secondhand expertise is then harnessed to the anxieties around brown bodies—whether those arise from terrorism, outsourcing, or population density. Bracketed by these conditions, various spaces, whether they are located within (ethnic enclaves) or outside the United States (Middle East, Asia), become increasingly restructured as "control zones" to organize people into "proper" locations. As Allen Feldman (2001, 59) writes, "the social control zone is a spatial logic that exceeds its explicit administrative grid and serves to bifurcate urban space into normalized space and pathologized space." This ideological bifurcation that is foregrounded by a fear and loathing of and dependency on foreign bodies results in a curious relationship between entry and consumption: the desire to close off the borders of the nation-state is in sharp contrast to the consumption, from food to clothing to mediated representations, of all things foreign. Such vicarious consumption as a form of control has a two-pronged logic: (1) the consumption allows a certain cosmopolitan tolerance for Americans, where the consumption of other spaces entertains, while also marking their own lives as "civilized," and furthermore, (2) this notion of tolerant cosmopolitan consumption is "part of a civilizational discourse that identifies both tolerance and the tolerable with the West, marking nonliberal societies and practices as candidates for intolerable barbarism that is itself signaled by the putative intolerance ruling these societies" (Brown 2006, 6). This practice is not without history and precedence. The nature of empires, whether they are British or American, requires the movement and consumption of goods from colonized spaces to the seat of empire as a mark of successful imperialism.

The best historical corollaries to contemporary mediated representations of "other spaces" and the vicarious consumption of exotica are perhaps the world's fairs, dating back to the 1900s and still in practice. These fairs "were carnivals of the industrial age, communal activities undergirded and directed by corporate boards and interests of the state," and as a form of state-mandated edu-tainment, they were considered central to the elevation of the average citizen (Brown Goode, as quoted in Hinsley 1991, 344). Essentially, world's fairs were meant to "illustrate the steps of progress of civilization and its arts in successive centuries, and in all lands up to the present time," where they would become "an *illustrated encyclopedia of humanity*" and an effort to educate and "formulate the modern" (346).

As such, "the goods shown at world's fairs did not just cater to middle-class taste, they helped form that taste. People were educated about what to buy, but more basically, they were to be taught to want more things and quite new things. . . . This education took on society-wide and even international dimensions. The consumer society was being born" (Benedict 1983, 2). And within this context, education and modernity stayed tightly connected to the colonial enterprise, where subject and object were divided along the might of the ruling *geographies.* Subjects of the empire recognized their subjectivity by looking at the imported colored bodies on display, while the colored bodies recognized themselves as objects—without the rights of color or class to be a consumer—by being on display. As James Gilbert (1994, 21) writes of these displays and this time period, "most significant was the emergence of culture as an instrument and privilege of class and status, an expression of unity, allure and superiority of Western civilization."

Said's definition of Orientalism supports a similar articulation of knowledge construction that sharply divided the East from the West (the exotic Oriental native object from the civilized Occidental subject) and the spectacular nature of that object as a commodity for voyeuristic consumption. This voyeuristic consumption is based on a symbiotic relationship that allows for *both* the object-performer and subject-consumer to construct notions of subjectivity and self-worth based on location.

In contemporary times, the ideological premise of world's fairs—as sites of "modernity" and "privilege"—has transmuted to television and film. With shows like *The Amazing Race* (2001–) and the Bachelor and Bachelorette franchises, for example, transporting viewers to exotic locales, where contestant-participants—all American—describe their experiences with natives, the world's fair is brought to contemporary living rooms. Many of these shows, both within and outside reality television, were especially created to "educate," directly or indirectly, the public about brown spaces and lifestyles (Alsultany 2012). In their mediated form—as both dangerous and delightful—these spaces simultaneous give voice to and quell anxieties about the rise of brown and brown spaces. In doing so, these geospatial settings, much like the world's fairs, produce an understanding of subjectivity and subject position that is taken for granted and acted upon within contemporary U.S. culture. Essentially, brown spaces produce an understanding of the brown body for those within the protected nation-state/homeland.

Because subjectivity is spatially constructed, and determined by the geography one speaks for and from, "the self . . . can be reconceptualized in spatial terms as different modes or vectors of spatial existence" (Grossberg 1996, 101), where, among the many different forms that minoritized spaces take as locational sites, one is "the production of an enclave culture that molds the enclave space and vice versa" (Laguerre 1999, 97). Essentially, the production constructs the culture and the person as inextricably linked within the boundaries of the (constructed) cultural performance. Such culture and cultural performance are built on the assumption that multiple characteristics or competing trends cannot exist in the same location (de Certeau 1984, 117), and in the event that cultural homogeneity is challenged, that heterogeneity is reinvented as a monoculture, within the geography of television.

AZNTV and Monocultural Consumption

Owned by Comcast, and targeting "the fast growing, affluent and multigeneration Asian American community, as well as a broader American audience interest in the Asian experience" (AZNTV, n.d.), AZNTV was aired as a paid cable channel from 1996 to 2008. With programs ranging from *Gourmet Moments,* a Singaporean cooking show, to *Saara Akaash,* an Indian drama in the vein of mainstream soap operas, AZNTV brought together the entire cultural mélange of Asia in one mediated space. The programs jostled together to cover the spectrum of an amorphous Asia for both Asian Americans and American "tourists" alike seeking an Asian experience from the comfort of their living rooms. For a cable channel targeting a niche audience, AZNTV was enormously popular, but it was not able to withstand competition from more established channels like ImaginAsian TV. AZNTV's demise in 2008 was met with outrage by a devoted audience, who demanded its return to cable. When that demand fell on deaf ears, the channel's audience turned to online message boards to vent their frustration and regret. Several online message boards ran laments like these:

> The loss of AZN was a great shock to me, a white American. I followed many of the historic series such as Jueoug, Dae Jo Young and more. Their scenery, acting and overall historic qualities were superb and the subtitling was sharp, not done in a quick flash as most are, it gave you time to read it all.

> I have enjoyed on this channel that I cannot find anywhere else. The Korean Drama series such as Emperor of the Sea, Jewel of the Palace, and the most recent Dae Jo Young (136 ninety (90) minute episodes . . . lol) have been almost inspiring with their portrayal of characters who sacrifice all for Love, Duty, Honor, Responsibility and Integrity. Their individual struggles and how they deal with adversity were truly remarkable. Of all the things I will miss the most, these Korean Dramas rank high on my list, even if they were in sub titles. Other programs such as Luxury India with Jay Menon showed

aspects of India not really shown elsewhere. Other programs I occasionally watched were from various countries throughout Asia that showed culture and sights I did not know about, and deeper insights into things I have some knowledge of. For me, the loss of this channel is a loss and something I will have a difficult time replacing . . . if I can at all. So . . . GOODBYE AZN . . . I have really enjoyed our time together and am sad to see you go. Hopefully there can be another that will take your place in the future as I believe you have given a greater depth to my life and my knowledge and respect for culture.

And in response to Broadcasting and Cable's online report on the end of AZNTV, a viewer wrote,

Say it ain't so!!!!! I love the shows on this network, I'm a big fan of the Korean Dramas—Loved COFFEE PRINCE and THAN YOU, and curently [sic] AJUMMA—what em [sic] I going to watch now??? By the way I'm also not Asian and I'm addicted to the Dramas and movies, much better than regular tv programming by FAR!!!!!

Much of the outcry, interestingly—or perhaps even predictably—was from viewers who identified themselves as "non-Asian," similar to those cited here, but who felt that the network provided some "authentic" insight into Asian culture and geography.

Though I do not want to dwell on these fan responses, what this sample collectively illuminates is that the Asian American space and the cultural enactment within it, much like Sibley's (1995) notion of the "folk devils" in the imagined geography, are fetishized as a consumable cultural experience outside the "regular"—the sanctified and normalized space of the nation-state.

The viewer who identifies himself as a White American subtly, and perhaps unconsciously, presents himself as a connoisseur of sorts who is able to appreciate the more interesting aspects of Asiana and has made a genuine effort to get to know the exotica presented for his pleasure. Similarly, the viewer who has been introduced to new ways of thinking about "Love, Duty, Honor, Responsibility and Integrity" through Korean drama also used the channel to further his or her knowledge of unfamiliar spaces and geographies.

And it is here, at this juncture where the ideology of knowledge vis-à-vis cultural consumption—the commodification of an amalgamated Asia—neatly separates the native, the Asian American, who lives *within* that space of AZNTV and the tourists, other Americans, who *visit* it for the spectacle that is Asia. But though the space of difference is carefully demarcated, we cannot lose sight of the fact that the hegemony of White America is established through language. In case we are nervous tourists, we are reminded by AZNTV in its promotional material, that the shows are in English or subtitled in English, for minimum discomfort.

Natives are, after all, only as attractive as their ability to communicate with us, when they are not jabbering gibberish in our faces. Indeed, the observation of the "White American" that the "subtitling was sharp, not done in a quick flash as most are," tells us that this is a superior tourist destination.

Speaking to this power of language and the linguistic turn in demarcating inclusion and exclusion, Amitava Kumar (2000) muses of an exchange between the character Foster, played by Michael Douglas, and a Korean grocer in the film *Falling Down* (dir. Joel Schumacher, 1993). Foster responds to Mr. Lee's statement that he is Korean and not Chinese by stating, "Whatever. You come to my country, you take my money, you don't even have the grace to learn my language?" Of this exchange Kumar writes, "What Foster doesn't realize is that not only is it not his country alone, it is not his language anymore. (That should be obvious to the ordinary American viewer, except that it *wasn't* obvious to everyone. And it isn't.)" (18). While Kumar goes on to document the real-life translation of these moments of racism by citing the murder of Vincent Chin in Detroit, since 9/11, this kind of go-home racism against South Asian Americans has grown exponentially. This notion that non-White Americans are a special category, required to stay in special places or spaces (preferably out of the country, in their own country) or to go back home to those spaces, is not new; it is just a curious mix of the virulent with the subtle.

I bring together these vignettes not merely to document oxymoronic acts of benign racism but to question the very existence of such a channel in a broader context of understanding the intersection between race and racial re/presentation in popular culture. AZNTV, as a symbolic representation of how we understand "Asia" and the continued Orientalist enterprise, highlights the interesting paradox of Asian immigrants in the United States. It is essentially a special network for special people—an amalgamated community who are constructed simultaneously as consumable and consumer. These intertwined identities seem hardly accidental when considering the realities of new global economies: global free-market economies and transnational ventures have entered the United States into a wary relationship with rising Asian superpowers India and China. These economic relationships that result in both an increase in immigration of brown bodies to the United States and outsourcing of jobs to brown geographies (leaving behind job and economic losses domestically) animate the kinds of representations that privilege the West as a civilizing influence on barbaric spaces. To neutralize the growing anxieties around these shifts and to reinforce the continued superiority of the United States, mediated images reconstruct Orientalist imaginaries of these landscapes that neutralize any real threat and, much like the ideological project of the world's fairs, reinforce the superiority of the West. The monocultural consumers of AZNTV, who speak of honor and history, are similar to those who applaud *Aliens in America* for showing humor in the clash of civilizations.

There's *Outsourced,* and Then There's *Outsourced*

In spring 2006, both *Time* and *Newsweek* focused their respective issues on the growing economic power of India. *Time* magazine took the opportunity to put a face on "India Inc." with a close-up of a smiling Indian woman wearing traditional wedding jewelry and a headset while a sunburst surrounded her head and explained "why the world's largest democracy is the next great economic superpower—and what that means to the rest of us." *Newsweek* warned that "Asia's other super power steps up," with a picture of sari-clad Padma Lakshmi in a Namaste pose. In some sense, the magazines perfectly demonstrated the pathology and medication that I start this book with. Some stories indicated that "they were just like us," whereas other images were carefully placed to ensure that India was India—the Oriental homeland. In the *Newsweek* coverage of India's economic rise, visual imagery is used to simultaneously warn of the threat of Indian domination and neutralize such a threat by focusing on India's Third World status.

A New York City–like skyline of the new India awash in early morning sun—the symbolic dawn—is foregrounded by men prostrating near the Ganges River in age-old tradition, as India worships both river and revenue. Although this image could be read as portraying India's successful marriage of old and new, the stories that make up the rest of the issue continue to focus on the sharp divisions between old India and new India—apparently a crisis of identity that distracts from what India could actually become, thereby warning the reading public of India's rise but also alluding to the fact that the promised progress may never come to actual fruition because of the country's provincialisms.

This subtle and insistent emphasis on difference and otherness, which successfully neutralizes any claim of actual power or threat to the United States, is echoed in even more recent coverage of India by *Newsweek*. In July 2011, in a story titled "India Conquers the World," *Newsweek* contributor Joel Kotkin noted, "The international importance of India itself is rising to an extent unmatched since the onset of the European-dominated global economy in the 17th century. And with the country's economy growing at roughly 8 percent a year for the past decade—more than double the rate of the United States—India's influence can only continue to strengthen." According to Kotkin, this strength comes in large part from economic support provided by the significant numbers of diasporic Indians in the United States and the United Kingdom. Kotkin noted that "in the United States, recently published data estimate average household income at $50,000, but it's $90,000 for ethnic Indians—and a 2007 survey found that between 1995 and 2005, more companies were launched by ethnic Indians than by immigrants from Britain, China, Japan, and Taiwan combined." The actual "human interest" angle of the story is threaded through by a focus on the Lalvani family, whose "voyage from refugees to moguls embodies a worldwide phenomenon: the growing size and sway of the Indian diaspora." The cosmopolitan successes of this particular narrative of India that could cause considerable consternation for the U.S. reader—who is navigating the worst economic recession since the 1930s—are mitigated by the Gunga Din narrative that Kotkin tells of the actual India: "Back in India, conditions remain harsh despite the country's recent advances. The average life span in Mumbai is barely 56 years, a full quarter century less than in Britain and the United States,

These two covers, featuring Padma Lakshmi for *Newsweek* (2006) and an unknown model as a bride-goddess of technology for *Time* magazine (2006), were published weeks apart and speak to the urgency and interest with which brown spaces are approached both as economic threat and source of consumer pleasure. *Time* photo-illustration by Arthur Hochstein.

and poverty across the country remains at shocking levels, with four in 10 Indians living on less than $1.25 a day. Statistics like that are scarcely an incentive for members of the diaspora to return to their homeland." This narrative of the harsh conditions left behind for a better life in the United States is not an uncommon one, of course. In fact, the metaphor of the proverbial streets of gold that forms the foundation of the American Dream and its many possibilities drives a great deal of migration.

But, just as the mythology of an American meritocracy is increasingly challenged by global geopolitical economic conditions, India becomes tethered to the Middle East. In this brown space, Middle Eastern terrorism and Indian economics merge, so that brown is produced as an amalgamation along yet another continuum that spans from economics/livelihood to terrorism/life.[7] Here the relationship between economics and terrorism becomes intertwined through a shared geographic proximity and shifts in trade and tariffs between outsourced and outsourcing nations.

Certainly, since its trade liberalization in the 1980s, India has become one of *the* geographies of outsourcing. Unlike most other South Asian countries—such as Sri Lanka, Bangladesh, and Pakistan, where consumer goods manufacturing remains one of the most profitable avenues of outsourcing—India has used the growing technology market to reverse the brain drain of the 1960s and, through the privatization of the telecommunications sector, has brought the global market home, or so American news outlets like *Time, Newsweek,* and even *Wired* magazine tell us. As these news stories circulate, the economic "rising" of a Third World space brings its own anxieties and remedies, especially as outsourcing continues to cause considerable anxiety for American workers, whose jobs seem to be rapidly disappearing.

These inherent contradictions are subtly and thoughtfully interspersed within the film *Outsourced,* directed by John Jeffcoat and released in 2006. Although it relies on some standard motifs of India, it manages to convey insights into the disparities that exist within the globalized economy and the realities of a translocal existence. When Todd Anderson, a manager at a U.S.–based novelties company, finds out that his job and entire department have been outsourced and that he must travel to India to train his Indian counterpart, he initially refuses. But threatened with unemployment and no stock options, he agrees to travel to Gharapuri, India, to reduce call times from twelve to six minutes. With little motivation, and no knowledge of India, Todd travels to Mumbai to complete the mission and get back home as soon as he can. Although the plot itself is predictable, and the film concludes cleanly with all loose ends tied up in some very improbable ways, what makes this film more complex are the vignettes and relationships that are made visible throughout.

Todd's relationship with Perum, his Indian counterpart, becomes a metaphor for his own relationship with India. Perum's naive but good-natured approach to management and his general geniality showcase Todd's own arrogance and eventual transcendence. Much like for Foster in *Falling Down,* language is a central component of the negotiation of self and other for Todd. He is irritated by the pronunciation of his name as "Toad" rather than "Todd" but sees nothing wrong in his own mis-pronunciation of worker Manmeet's (Mun-meeth) name as "Man-Meat." During training, Todd points out to the workers that "the customer feels comfortable if they are talking to a native English speaker." When he is told by Asha that "we *are* native English speakers. English is the official language of our government. You got it from the British, and so did we. We just speak it differently. Sometimes our pronunciation is better. We say 'Internet,' and you say 'inner-net,'" Todd ignores the claims of this shared history of colonialism and reiterates that the employees should learn from the customer about America—essentially partaking in a trans-local education.

This education is useful to everyone involved, because we learn later through a conversation that emerges out of a chance encounter between Todd and Bob, another customer service manager from the United States, that language is central to success. As Todd explains his order from corporate, Bob sympathizes with him—"India: I'll Never Do It Again" (laughs)—and tells him that the time requirements are impossible unless Todd hires "the accent-neutrals" away from Bob. This product fetishism (Appadurai 1990)—in the form of both consumer and service provider—where the location of production becomes invisible through the uniformity of language, is even more cunningly reflected in another exchange between Asha and Todd: Asha points out that it is deceptive to tell a customer that they are in Chicago when they are located in India.

TODD: A lot of Americans are upset about outsourcing.

ASHA: But sir, most of the products they are buying are made in China.

Extending Appadurai's notion of product fetishism, what this exchange highlights is the complicated relationship between product *and* body and product *as* body within contemporary global politics. More simply, it is easier to separate the product from the body that produces it, as inconsequential to the identity of the nation-state (even though that producing body has significant impact for the domestic economy and therefore its peoples), than it is to separate the product from the physical body of a person who is seen as an interloper or an economic thief. This is especially true if the product is seen as quintessentially "American," such as the cheese heads, burger brandings, and American bald eagle head sold by the fictional Mid-American Novelties Company. Alternatively, the performance of the body—language, accent, and mannerisms—intimately marks belonging. Any perceived difference reinforces otherness and allows that body to be constructed outside the socially codified borders of the nation-state. Once the body is constructed as an outsider/interloper, it becomes the object of codified violence. As feminist scholars have noted, once a body becomes an object, the violence against it, both psychological and physical, is not only naturalized but also seen as insignificant and without consequence. So not hearing an "accent-neutral" at the other end of the phone is cause for discomfort and anger, but a product made in China, because it symbolizes something quintessentially American, goes unnoticed. This contradiction is artfully showcased in the film and invites the viewer to understand the inherent double standard of global circulation and distribution.

This is even more thoughtfully examined through a side narrative running through the film: Todd starts noticing that any food he leaves behind is surreptitiously left on the wall separating the guesthouse from the outside world by the guesthouse cook/servant. Out of curiosity, he climbs up to look over the wall and realizes that there is an entire domestic economy happening across from the cloistered and bucolic space of the garden. Around a public well, surrounded by ramshackle two-story buildings and a carefully laid out grid of claw-foot tubs—remnants of British colonization—an entire business of clothes washing and drying is under way. As Todd stares in bemusement, he makes eye contact with a man wearing a T-shirt that says "Shop Till You Drop" and who is busy pulling water out of the public well. As the film progresses, Todd takes over the practice of leaving his tray on the wall, and eventually, toward the end of the film, as he realizes that his self-imposed hostility toward India is unproductive—iterated through a symbolic cleansing in the public pond in the village center, following Holi—he accepts Shop Till You Drop's invitation to come across the wall separating them. We follow Todd as he walks through a different economy—one where the residents don't separate everyday living from work and where the narrow pathways are bordered with homes haphazardly strung together with waste plastic, cloth, and cardboard boxes in a continuous stream of communal living, eating, washing, and breathing—and ends up at a lunch prepared by his guide's family. As the honored guest, a lone egg is transferred to his plate, and the rice and gravy are topped with a naan branded with a Volkswagen logo from the heating device. The Western waste used for cooking purposes, viewed against the frivolous items sold to the American public by Mid-American Novelties, highlights the disparities of the globalized experience.

Such thoughtful critique is largely absent from the television series by the same name that premiered on NBC in spring 2011. NBC's *Outsourced* followed the same general story line as the cinematic version but foregrounded certain call center workers for comedic purposes and changed the personalities of both Todd and his assistant manager in an effort to introduce a more comedic context. In the sitcom, Todd is a genial and accommodating Westerner who is constantly harassed by his cunning and greedy assistant manager, Rajiv Gidwani. Possessing none of the charm of Perum, Rajiv is seen as a pompous buffoon who is easily foiled and outwitted by Todd with very little effort. Similarly, Manmeet's character is an Americanized playboy who simultaneously romances two unsuspecting American women, all the while asking Todd—as the epitome of American cosmopolitanism and boyish charm—for advice about American masculinity. As the series progresses, Manmeet becomes Todd's sidekick—the native foil to Todd's genial imperialism. Todd's geniality especially extends to the most disruptive and unproductive of his workers, Gupta. Gupta is a well-meaning buffoon who is always at the receiving

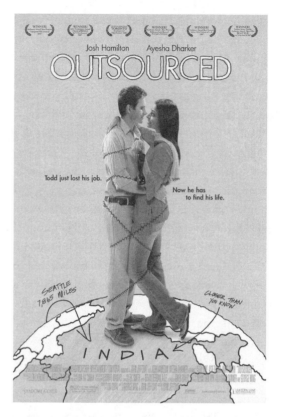

When the film version of *Outsourced* debuted in 2006, it provided a somewhat critical and nuanced view of outsourcing and its realities. In contrast, the ensemble comedy based on the film, which debuted on NBC in 2010, relied heavily on an East–West divide, and the ensuing misunderstandings, to generate its humor.

end of Rajiv's wrath but is protected by Todd. In a benign but stunningly telling turn of neoimperialism, here brown men are being saved from other brown men by White men. Gupta's friendship, toward the end of the series, with Charlie Davies—a more consistent presence of Bob than in the film version, with none of the complexity of that brief character—reinforces his childlike status and justifies the protection, so much so that Gupta eventually moves into the same guesthouse as Todd and is taken care of by the latter.

In the film version of *Outsourced*, Todd's romance and sexual relationship with Asha, one of the workers, whom he later promotes to assistant manager, are interwoven within the larger plot and become another instance of recognizing difference through culture and cultural practice, especially through important contradictions and convergences. Cinematic Todd finds out that the land of *Kama Sutra* has strong-willed, independent women like Asha, who chooses to honor the arrangements for marriage made by her parents rather than be with him, though the film ends with Todd's return to Seattle and a phone call from Asha, which leads the viewer to believe that she may have changed her mind, though there is no outright resolution of this.

In the comedic interpretation of this complex romantic relationship, Todd "applies" for Asha's hand in marriage and is rejected by her (without any of the subtle conversation between their predecessors about class and economic responsibilities, and the resulting expectations). Todd's rebound relationship—often witnessed and commented upon by Gupta, who has bored a hole in the floor between his room and Todd's—with Pippa, an Australian call center manager, is juxtaposed as a modern, progressive romance against the naive and archaic approaches to relationships that the Indian workers practice, including the wooing and subsequent marriage of Rajiv Gidwani.

Similar to the sitcom, the film also plays into the Orientalist imaginary of a savage and poor India through long shots of overcrowded streets and public urination, but there are also significant moments that interrupt the Orientalist gaze. High-rise buildings and the pristine beaches of Marine Drive are woven into the narrative of abject poverty, and the call center itself is outside the city limits of Mumbai because of the cost of real estate in the city—made even more dear, the audience learns, by the number of call centers that are being opened in the area. This separation between the node of transnational economics and the node of everyday life, the city center, highlights the complexities of a rapidly growing India and exemplifies the growth of a form of rural cosmopolitanism that is an increasing reality for countries partaking in the outsourcing economy. In this rural cosmopolitanism, the spaces become simultaneously hyper-globalized and hyperlocalized, as spaces either on the outside or out-skirts of the actual city space. As in the cinematic representation of *Out-sourced,* it is neither profitable nor realistic to assume that a city such as Mumbai, with its high real estate costs, and which serves as home to the largest film industry in the world (Bollywood), would actually house a large business process outsourcing center in the midst of the city. But such realities are ignored by the 2011 comedy, as it locates the call center in the center of Mumbai, where the city is depicted as a rural village com-munity overrun by fortune-tellers, tea kiosks, and coconut vendors who gather right outside the doors of the call center. This visual seems to fulfill the Orientalist desire for exotica that many of the previously discussed AZNTV viewers sought in their television viewing. The gaudy spectacle of color—on a daily basis, as well as through the ubiquitous holiday of Holi that now stands in for India in popular culture—and the comedic antics of the Indian workers and the people on the street reinforce the childlike status of the natives as both other and nonthreatening, within the context of a global economy. In contrast to the film, which encour-ages the viewer to see *beyond* the native as other, the television version asks us to fully embrace the native as a source of humor. Because the genre of the situation comedy requires the most mundane interpretation of complex problems and provides only the most basic of resolutions, it also effectively neutralizes any actual anxieties about the situation—in this case, the very real fallout from outsourcing and the ongoing reces-sion in the United States. For instance, the story line of the laundry worker in the film version—an important vignette that connects past imperial-isms to the present—is absent from the sitcom. In its place, we see a grossly overplayed story line where Gupta is left homeless.

When Gupta's homelessness is discovered by Todd (of course), and is resolved by his relocation to Todd's guesthouse, the realities of economic disparities that are highlighted throughout the film are largely absent, and such challenges are neatly and humorously resolved in a way that allows for the possibility of more Gupta buffoonery (vis-à-vis the shared home space). Along the same lines, cinematic Todd's ignorant decision to consume an iced treat at the Gharapuri station and his resulting health issues are part of a narrative of transcendence and education through food. As the film progresses, the consumption of native food becomes the practice rather than the disease-inducing exception. As Todd's body adjusts to the food, so does his personality, culminating in his dinner with the family in the slums behind his guesthouse—with no ill effects. In contrast, television Todd's active consumption of the food, despite a warning from Charlie, who brings his own American sandwiches to eat in the shared dining room of the call center, indicates an easy adaptability and general "conquering" of the challenges of Third World existence.

Whereas the film uses food to show adaptation and some form of insightful transcendence, the television series presents it as just another conquest—a generic Third World at its chaotic, diseased, and demented best that neutralizes the charged topic that it is covering. Thus the comedic representation nullifies the anxieties that the American population has about outsourcing and its impact on their own lives. As the audience laughs at the antics of the call center workers in NBC's *Outsourced,* they are laughing away the very real fears that a brown space has the wherewithal to threaten their way of life, to become as powerful as, or even more powerful than, their own nation-state. And through this process, the series medicates their pathologized anxieties about global economics and cultural circulation.

Laughing *at* India, rather than *with* India, allows a sense of security and comfort—a benign form of xenophobia that is presented as multicultural education. This construction of the space, as a spectacle for the pleasure of an American audience, reinforces the notion that people from these spaces are also products—exotic products that reinforce their *cultural* value as alien Other. At no point is the audience invited to acknowledge that the situation comedy is entirely performed by, for, and within the First World. Whereas the cinematic version was a crosscultural collaboration, including both North American and Indian actors, and was mainly filmed in India, the cast for the situation comedy are entirely North American or European. To break into popular media, these actors enact a form of strategic essentialism based on their somatic selves within the confines of an imaginary Mumbai set in Studio City, California. Their performance as a caricature of their roots/routes—a form of enlightened Jim Crow—solidifies the Orientalist fantasies of the armchair anthropologists. Though Kwame Appiah (2006) warns us that a shard of a mirror does not reflect back an *entire* image, in a time when shards have come to mean the entire mirror—when brown is reflected back only as terror and titillation—the creation of shows like *Outsourced,* sitting alongside *Harold and Kumar* and *Aliens in America,* says a lot about U.S. cultural politics.

4
Blackness in Brown Times
The Medicalization of Racism

> Interrelationships among exceptions, politics, and citizenship crys-
> tallize problems of contemporary living, and they also frame ethical
> debates over what it means to be human today.
>
> —AIHWA ONG, *NEOLIBERALISM AS EXCEPTION*

> To engage in a serious discussion of race in America, we must
> begin not with the problems of black people but with the flaws of
> American society—flaws rooted in historical inequalities and long-
> standing cultural stereotypes.
>
> —CORNEL WEST, *RACE MATTERS*

If brown has become the new face of somatic and ideological racism and
terror, then how does such a reindexing of race hierarchy contribute to
reproducing Blackness? In this final chapter, I take up this question and
map the pathological/medicated relationship between historical racisms
and their contemporary manifestations within the securitized state. Many
of the observations here stem from a desire to understand more fully the
impact that Barack Obama's election had on American identity politics (beyond the predictable failure of post-racism), especially in relation to brown
identification and anti-Black racism. The notion of post-race America,
though completely false and unbelievable even at the time it was first ban-
died about in 2008, still set a context for reproducing Blackness, and does
even today, through a particular lens of neoliberal racism. This neoliberal
racism, divorced from a slave history, is reproduced as a critique of the
immorality within Black communities: an immorality that is marked by

laziness, sexual promiscuity, and violence that impede African Americans from pulling themselves up by their bootstraps. In this chapter, I map the various areas that make up and reinforce this pathological notion of Black immorality, and the medicalized popular responses to it, as converging vectors that produce Blackness as hopeless—and as already helped.

(Im)moral Races

Recently, a friend and I were having a discussion about the dismantling of the Voting Rights Act of 1965 (VRA) and eroding civil liberties against historically marginalized populations. In our conversation, we were making the connection between those legally enacted racist practices and the racial profiling of brown bodies—and I was trying to explain my basic premise for this chapter: that the focus on brown bodies through terrorism and immigration has allowed anti-Black racism to seem passé and without merit. After going back and forth, my friend concluded that "the bus of racial profiling and eroding civil liberties will continue. The question is, who will get thrown under it next?" This question of who is next is a significant one that needs some interrogation, and though the question is ongoing and without a definitive answer, its answer is worth trying to map out here. Although I am neither explicitly mapping the history between Black and brown race politics and solidarities (Márquez 2013), nor providing a definitive answer to the question of victimhood as posed by the bus question, I am making a loose map of how systematic marginalization happens within ongoing racial formations and negotiations within the United States, especially after September 11, 2001. I frame this by questioning what the racialized pathologies and the corollary medications of post-9/11 anxiety mean to the Black/White racial binary that is the popularly historicized approach to race in the United States, and I extrapolate on the impact that fifteen years of brown identification have had on Black politics.

Essentially, I argue that because brown has now been deemed dangerous along the same lines that Black was historically produced, more contemporary discussions around Black identity have intensified around "morality" (West 1993), especially through a neoliberal immorality. More simply, here immorality marks the ways in which the notion of meritocracy is rejuvenated within contemporary neoliberal politics (Harvey 2005).

In this context, "individual success or failure are interpreted in terms of entrepreneurial virtues or personal failings (such as not investing significantly enough in one's own human capital through education) rather than being attributed to any systemic property (such as the class exclusions usually attributed to capitalism)" (Harvey 2005, 65). Under these conditions, the social welfare state is deemed unnecessary and excessive and its dependents, largely peoples of color, "too lazy" and lacking in a morality-based work ethic to succeed and partake in the American Dream.

This neoliberal ethos that ties an abstract moral aptitude to capitalist labor and resources also allows the disassociation of race and class and their parallel history in the United States and attributes poverty and marginalization to an *individual's* lack of motivation, an ability to work hard, to partake in *honest* and *fair* labor in a capitalist economy. In doing so, it successfully ignores systemic structures of slavery and migration (forced and otherwise) that were integral to how race and class were coproduced in the United States and the continuing impact of this systemic organization of power and resources on the everyday populace (Roediger 1991; 2005; Smith 2006). To map this rather complex terrain, I start with the present and move toward the recent past to connect the processes of creating immorality at the expense of history and truth.

Teaching Black(ish)

In his analysis of culture, Raymond Williams (1961, 64–65) introduces the term "structure of feeling," describing it as "firm and definite as a structure suggests, yet . . . operat[ing] on the most delicate and least tangible parts of our activity. . . . This structure of feeling is the culture of a period." For Williams, it is the cultural moment of a particular time, but without the optimism of a zeitgeist. More simply, it represents (perhaps in the crudest of definitions) the perceptions and values of a particular generation—not always spread evenly but nonetheless present as a form of shared meaning—and "appears in the gap between the official discourse of policy and regulations, the popular response to official discourse and its appropriation in literary and other cultural texts" (Buchanan 2010, 455). Williams's notion of structure of feeling, as defined here, provides the context for understanding the complex possibilities and failures of the popular situation comedy *Black-ish* (2014–) and its relationship to larger cultural conditions, both past and present, in a time of brown(ish) racial politics.

Thirty years after *The Cosby Show*[1] (1984–92) brought the first upper-middle-class Black family, the Huxtables, to network television, and in the midst of ongoing anti-Black violence in various parts of the United States, *Black-ish* debuted, in fall 2014, to positive reviews on the ABC network. Billed as a representation of what it means to be African American *today*, the network introduces the show's Johnsons as follows: "Andre 'Dre' Johnson (Anthony Anderson) has a great job, a beautiful wife, Rainbow (Tracee Ellis Ross), four kids and a colonial home in the 'burbs. But has success brought too much assimilation for this black family? With a little help from his dad (Laurence Fishburne), Dre sets out to establish a sense of cultural identity for his family that honors their past while embracing the future." Despite the question of identity and assimilation, the show's creator, Kenya Barris, has, throughout promotions for the show, declared that the comedy is more about culture than about race. According to Barris, "we are living in a post-racial Obama society where race and culture are talked about less than ever," and the show is a representation of what it means to be an *American* family rather than a *Black* family. This is echoed by Fishburne, who is, in addition to being the family elder, also a coproducer, who noted that "ultimately, if you live in America and you've been in America, let's say, for the last 10, 15, 20 years, you're probably a little Black-ish anyway."

Based on Barris's own life, *Black-ish* focuses on the culture clash between Dre's need to teach his "color-blind" children that the world is still a dangerous place for them, while also wanting to enjoy his economically privileged upper-middle-class (White) life. His struggle to make his children (teenagers Zoey and Andre Jr. and six-year-old twins Jack and Diane) understand their roots and the realities of contemporary culture is made more challenging by Bow (an anesthesiologist), who was raised by a Black mother and White father, both hippies. Bow and her hybrid identity, along with the requisite progressive politics that go along with her hippie upbringing, are at constant odds with Dre and his more pro-Black politics—politics that appear extreme, dated, and unreasonable, even when they speak to very real concerns and realities. His father, Earl "Pops" Johnson, who is perpetually afraid of White people and their politics, encourages Dre in his seemingly parochial racial identity. Occasionally, Dre's mother, Ruby, who is separated from (but continues to have an on-again/off-again sexual relationship with) Pops, arrives at the household, and her conservative pro-Black mothering/mating clashes with Bow's more progressive and "enlightened" (read White) ways of doing both.

Initially, the audience is introduced to Dre's identity crisis through a promotion he receives to senior vice president of the advertising company for which he works. Even as he celebrates what he sees as "living the dream," Dre learns that the promotion has a tagline: senior vice president for urban division, that is, Black demographics. Because it looks like he got promoted for being Black, and not "in spite of being Black," Dre realizes that there is an incongruity between the promotion (and its reasons) and the lives his kids are living. Although all episodes deal with Dre's seemingly maniacal need for Blackness, and his long-suffering family's response to this "unreasonable" and humorous identity crisis, perhaps the most "simplified complex representation" (Alsultany 2012) of this lesson on Black absurdity and misguided morality is one that commemorates Martin Luther King Day.

Titled "Martin Luther sKiing Day" (Barris and Shockley 2015), the episode opens with a montage of Martin Luther King Jr.'s images and a voice-over from Dre, who notes, "No matter what they threw at him, he always managed to keep his temper in line and, arguably equally important, his mustache. I mean, this thing is always on point. So every year, to properly celebrate Martin Luther King Day, the Johnsons partake in a long-standing tradition we in the community call 'Black Ski Weekend.'" The audience is expected to laugh at the thought of Black people engaging in a sport defined and marked by White privilege and to appreciate the irony that Dre does not see: that he is perhaps more *Whiteish*, based on his interests and his commitment to the annual ski weekend, and that his Black identity is an affectation rather than an actuality. This metaphorical transformation that aligns race and class is even more intensified and nuanced by Dre's sidekick, Charlie. In true "happy darkie" tradition, Charlie, who also works for the advertising agency, is a "regular" Black person. He is awkward, is socially inept, makes inappropriate jokes, often tries to wheel and deal favors (charming but amoral), and, when given a major contract in a different episode, mismanages it and almost loses the client, until Dre saves him. Charlie is woefully lacking in a work ethic and is a "before" to Dre's "after." Though the episode is rife with examples of how a work ethic and assimilation can turn Black people into upper-middle-class (White) Americans, the basic premise of the episode—that we live in a post-race America where racial discontent is the pastime of those who *choose* to look for it—is specific to a story line where Dre tries to teach Andre Jr. that racism still exists in the United States. On the way to the ski resort, the car driven by Charlie, and which includes Dre, Andre Jr., and Andre's White friend Zach (who is much more knowledgeable about Black history than Junior, much to Dre's chagrin), is pulled over by a White officer. Dre immediately assumes that the officer pulled the car over because it has Black people in it:

> JUNIOR: But we weren't doing anything.
>
> DRE: Exactly, son. We're being pulled over for DWB.
>
> JUNIOR, *pronouncing it as a word*: DWUB?
>
> DRE: Driving While Black, idiot. All right, everybody. This is it. Wallets in hands. No sudden moves. Zach, record this. If anything happens, tell our story. [*hands his cell phone to Zach*]
>
> OFFICER, *knocks on window*: License and registration?
>
> DRE: Yeah, because he doesn't think we have it.
>
> OFFICER: No, just a routine question.

Charlie tries to make excuses for Dre by claiming he's a diabetic. But Dre refuses to back down and continues to challenge the officer: "Like you ask everybody for their license and registration. Asking for license and registration . . ." The good-humored White officer seems unfazed and politely explains that this is what they learn on day one and that the car was pulled over, not because it was filled with Black people, but because of expired tags. And because it's a "holiday weekend," he lets them go with a warning.

Dre's racialized outrage over a valid offense, Charlie's nervousness, Junior's oblivion, and Zach's progressive Whiteness that allows him to enthusiastically videotape this "nonevent" mimic the now extensively documented and circulated videotapes of interactions between (White) police officers and (Black) targets. But, whereas the actual videotapes of such interactions—like those of Sandra Bland (2015) and Eric Garner

(2014)—show the very real aggressions between the largely White police force and the Black populace, *Black-ish* medicates these realities by neutralizing the interaction to "chip-on-the-shoulder" politics of Blacks and police officers who are trained to be kind and genial unless provoked. And here provocation is not verbal aggression but physical—and physical "aggression," whether in defense of life or liberty, such as in the case of Eric Garner, is rendered violent enough for detainment and even death. This perpetuates the myth that violence against Black individuals is justified because *they* turn peaceful interactions into physical altercations.

Dre's desire to teach his children their legacy continues in the lobby of the ski resort. He stages a sit-in because the last adjoining rooms have been given to an elderly White couple. After protesting loudly as his family watches with a mixture of resignation and embarrassment, he's wheeled away on the hotel luggage cart he's occupying. As he's wheeled away, he yells, "Junior, this is for you," to which Junior responds, "I don't want this," and turns to his sister with, "That's our father. Have you ever thought about that? Our father. And he's not going anywhere, either." Zoey responds, while continuing to leaf through possible spa options at the resort, "Nope. He's one of the 'good ones.'" This exchange is humorous and well intentioned: pointing out that Dre is one of the "good ones" is to speak to the stereotypes of Black men as absent fathers and to make public the prejudice of that stereotype. But such a humorous critique is to also predicate on the assumption that the stereotype is accepted *as a stereotype* rather than as an *inherent* characteristic of Black masculinity. And therein lies the paradox of *Black-ish*: even while critiquing the assumptions of Blackness and challenging those stereotypes, it is forced to rely on them to make the show successful. While audiences laugh about the absurdity of Dre's antics, and his delusions of living an "authentic" Black life in a White, upper-middle-class context, the show reinforces anti-Black sentiments as a fiction of the Black community itself. The actual value of *Black-ish*—as a biting commentary on the ways in which mainstream American exceptionalism (White, middle class, educated, wealthy) requires African Americans to conform—is harder to find in the midst of the incessant promotion of the show as a post-race, "everyone is Blackish" comedy.

The Johnsons, much like their predecessors the Huxtables and the

Jeffersons, reinforce the notion that Black success is only possible by emulating particular White values. Even in its critique, *Black-ish*, unintentionally perhaps, contributes to the fiction that absent fathers and welfare mothers—the staples of political and public discourse on African American families—are products of laziness and willful ignorance rather than a legacy of slavery and its more contemporary systemic marginalizations. This fiction is only interrupted toward the end of the episode, when Dre tells Bow, "I know I've been acting a little crazy lately, but I'm worried about Junior.... We've sheltered him so much. What is he gonna do when something real happens?" But moments like this—that give voice to the very real concerns of parents raising Black children today—are fleeting, as the comedy continues to medicate the pathology of racism. As the following section highlights, Dre's concerns are real and their manifestations the rule rather than the exception.

Philippic Truths

It is relatively well documented that the study of race and ethnicity in the Unites States has, for the most part, been shaped by the struggles of African Americans and their relationship to a hegemonic Whiteness. This Black–White spectrum dominated the racial landscape of the United States until the events of September 11, 2001, when brown identities became a locus of race negotiations, couched in terms of security, freedom, and democracy. Within this new(er) reindexing of race usurped by a focus on international terrorism—and then declared dead by the election of President Barack Obama, as the first Black president—ongoing anti-Black racism begs the question of what brown has done to, and for, Blackness.

Though the discussions around Obama's racial identity and postrace culture seem a distant memory (and we are well aware that the exuberance and hope around that election have long dwindled to an exhausted and rather hoarse echo of possibilities), I mention Obama here because his election was pivotally tethered to the formation of brown as discussed throughout this book. Obama's candidacy in 2008 shored up already existing anxieties around brown deviance, while also setting up brown identity as a way to implicitly express anxieties around other historically marginalized communities in the United States. Brown became a straw man, a scapegoat of sorts, through Obama and, by extension, a strategic circumvention of and for anti-Black sentiments. Essentially, brown has, over the last fifteen years, been constructed as the representative deviant: the color to be managed, secured, and contained. As such, it's inherent sociopolitical value as a malleable concept/identity/identification comes from its ability also to be a diversion—a sort of rerouting panacea for the historical race battles that seemed to simmer, until their recent eruption, just below the surface of the securitized nation. Brown as a diversion crystalized for me as I was becoming more fully immersed in this project, which was during the 2008 presidential election. The spectacle that surrounded that election, and the subsequent pseudo-celebration of the first Black president of United States, highlighted the ways in which brown had become a way of deferment. Because this iteration of brown, as I've mapped throughout the book, rests on its "malleability," it had become a way to effectively dodge other discomforts and disconnections around the "interrelations" of race (Ong 2006). Indeed, after 9/11, Black–White racial tensions seemed passé as America obsessed about the *management* of brown as a sociopolitical pastime. The umbrella of nationalism that covered the country seemed to ignore previous racial tensions and histories to come together to protect and nurture the nation as it battled unidentifiable terror.

But, when historical racism and race hierarchies make up the scaffolding of contemporary class and race structures, such diversions come at a cost: the repercussions of America's obsession with brown, for almost a decade and a half after 9/11, publicly reverberated throughout the country starting in 2012. At first, it seemed random and shocking: a young Black boy shot dead by an overzealous neighborhood watch vigilante, whose subsequent acquittal created a public firestorm. For sociohistorical amnesia–prone American publics, who have long forgotten the brutal beating of Rodney King and the LA riots, George Zimmerman's acquittal for the murder of seventeen-year-old Trayvon Martin seemed "isolated." Zimmerman, much like Wade Michael Page and Craig Stephen Hicks, was viewed by his supporters as an individual who acted on the best of intentions—outside of any ideological and racial motive—and was merely an overzealous neighborhood watch captain. For example, as stories about both Martin and Zimmerman gripped national news media, a former neighbor of Zimmerman told the *Los Angeles Times* (Pearce 2012) that

> their parents taught them to treat everybody with respect. . . . I'm tired of hearing about this race thing. It could be an element in it . . . but I never would have thought of him as being a racist. His father was in the Army and was a white American, and his mother was Peruvian. That makes him 50% Peruvian. A lot of stuff I hear, it irks me because people are drawing their own conclusions with very little evidence.

Whatever Zimmerman's own racial makeup was, and whatever role that played in his actions, seems less important now in light of what Martin's assassination brought to the forefront: that Blackness, and the inherent value (or lack thereof) it carries, regardless of how long it is deferred, forms the foundation of racism in American civil (or lack thereof) society. As the case unfolded, and details of Martin's murder emerged, Zimmerman's subsequent acquittal was met with outrage by the general populace, but this outrage did not translate into any real change and was followed by other incidents, ongoing even as I write this.

Among these other events was the August 9, 2014, death of eighteen-year-old Michael Brown. Brown was unarmed when he was shot and killed after a verbal altercation with a police officer in Ferguson, Missouri. The police officer claimed that he "may" have been involved in a robbery and was trying to run away, was aggressive, and was not responding to his call to calm down. Brown's death was marked on August 10 by a peaceful candlelit vigil in the largely Black suburb of St. Louis, Missouri. While a few participants chanted "No justice, no peace," the march itself was a commemoration of Brown's life and a public acknowledgment of his brutal end. Despite its general calm, and in a move that acted as a self-fulfilling prophecy, the march was met by police in riot gear, carrying guns and shields.

Perhaps in keeping with the structures of power long established between the largely White police force and the African American community in St. Louis and surrounding suburbs, little to no thought was given to how those participating in this expression of sorrow and a public and peaceful acknowledgment of injustice would respond to being met with the expectation that they *will* eventually turn violent. Over the next couple of days, the altercations between the police and the protestors would continue to escalate, with police repeatedly breaking up crowds with tear gas and rubber bullets. Fueled by a national news media that focused on angry faces and fire-engulfed buildings, Ferguson was evidence that controlling Black—even while managing brown—was still necessary, and even justified.

In the midst of ongoing anti-Black violence—and voicing the fears and realities of many African Americans—Ta-Nehisi Coates released *Between the World and Me* in July 2015. Coates's beautifully written account of growing up in an impoverished Black neighborhood in Baltimore, and the ways in which Black youths of his generation felt the same fears and repercussions of violence that his ancestors had felt as slaves on White plantations, resonated with many who were witnessing the violence enacted on Black bodies by both vigilantes and those sworn to protect them. Opening the book with "Letter to My Son," Coates writes of the connections between history and contemporary race hierarchies that "the elevation of the belief in being white was not achieved through wine tastings and ice-cream socials, but rather through the pillaging of life, liberty, labor, and land." Coates poignantly documents his son's reaction to the verdict absolving all those involved in the murder of Michael Brown:

> You learned that the killers of Michael Brown would go free. The men who had left his body in the street would never be punished. . . . You were . . . waiting for the announcement of an indictment, and when instead it was announced that there was none . . . I did not tell you that it would be okay, because I have never believed it would be okay. What I told you is what your grandparents tried to tell me: that this is your country, that this is your world, that this is your body, and you must find some way to live within the all of it. (Coates 2015, 11)

Here Coates echoes the contemporary reality of W. E. B. Du Bois (2011), who described the schizophrenic space of navigating the expectation of Blackness *in* history, its current institutionalization, and the managed response to such implicit and explicit control of one's being as "double-consciousness," "this sense of always looking at one's self through the eyes of others, of measuring one's soul by the tape of a world that looks on in amused contempt and pity . . . two warring ideals in one dark body, whose dogged strength alone keeps it from being torn asunder" (2). For Coates's son, very little has changed since Du Bois's time, even though the veneer of "change," and the incessant relativism of progress that is the cacophony of American thinking, makes it seem dramatically different. It is this seeming difference, built on a separation of history and the here and now, that results in the continuous reproduction of immoral Blackness.

Take, for example, Richard Lowry's response to Coates's *Between the World and Me*. On July 24, 2015, Lowry, editor of the conservative *National Review*, wrote a scathing review of Coates's book. Titled "Ta-Nehisi Coates's New Book Betrays a Toxic Worldview," Lowry dismisses Coates's arguments of continuing racism, and White America's slave ideology toward Black Americans, by stating that, subjecting the book "to even minimal critical scrutiny, you will realize that it is profoundly silly at times, and morally blinkered throughout. It is a masterly little memoir wrapped in a toxic little Philippic" (Lowry 2015). Ignoring Coates's lengthy and honest explanation of how fear, containment, and control, that is, the legacy of children of slaves, result in acts that reinforce violence within the community, Lowry instead chooses to focus on Coates's descriptors to reinforce that anti-Black violence stems from a lack of Black commitment to succeed and assimilate. Lowry takes Coates to task for talking about "White America," rhetorically questioning, "What is this white America? Is it Nancy Pelosi or Ted Cruz? Is it Massachusetts or is it Utah? Is it supporters of affirmative action or opponents? Is it teachers who work in the inner city, or gap-toothed yokels who chortle over racist jokes? . . . This white America contains multitudes" (Lowry 2015). But, like many who rely on the myth of an American meritocracy to negate the historical and systemic effects of racism, Lowry defaults to stereotypes of White middle-class aspiration versus Black sloth/apathy to justify the ongoing racial discriminations. For Lowry,

> they, like all Americans, are in a much better position to succeed if they honor certain basic norms: graduate from high school; get a full-time job; don't have a child before age 21 and get married before childbearing. Among the people who do these things . . . about 75 percent attain the middle class, broadly defined.

"They," for Lowry, are *all* Blacks. The same universal assumptions about Whiteness he accuses Coates of, Lowry uses toward an amalgamated Black community. And in that amalgamated essentialism Lowry associates with Black identity, he attributes willful immorality to the communities' continued struggles to succeed. Lowry writes,

> White Americans don't even have the highest incomes of any group in the country that they have allegedly built to serve their interests with malice aforethought. Asians do. They, of course, didn't experience chattel slavery, or the hideous discrimination of the Jim Crow South. But they still encountered prejudice, overcome with relatively intact families and high levels of education.

Here ignoring the well-documented genocidal and slave history of the United States, and relying on purely neoliberal, capitalist economic theory, Lowry flattens complex and convoluted relationships, not only between Blacks and Whites, but also between Whites and other minorities who have long been held up as models for assimilation and strategically uses these groups to manage Black identity and expectations.

Lowry's statement also resonates with the long-held (implicit and explicit) belief that Asians succeed—despite suffering discrimination—because they, unlike African Americans, know their place (Prashad 2000). *They* aspire (even while they fail at various junctures because of securitized racism) to assimilate, to *disappear* in the best possible way by emulating White values through high levels of education and white-collar jobs.[2] In contrast, Lowry, following others before him, blames African Americans for not "trying hard enough" and for relying too heavily on the welfare state to support their apparent immorality, including sexual promiscuity (single-parent families) and violent proclivities (drugs, gang activity). None of this is seen as a product of history, even while it relies on historically racist assumptions about Black communities. It is to emphasize this last point that I discuss Lowry here: his review is an exemplar of the ways in which historical structures are co-opted by neoliberalism, even as it disavows the same systemic structures it relies on to undergird its (real and imagined) political and social supremacy.

Because Black–White race politics in the United States is intertwined with a class spectrum that is bracketed and defined by the visible aspirations of White middle-classdom, it is easier to ignore historical inequalities and/or blame them on the moral failings of an entire class of imagined subjects than it would be to acknowledge the complex and contingent structures that maintain those White, middle-class aspirations. In essence, the ideological worth of Blackness is always tethered to slavery (where slaves are a commodity of labor, not individuals with rights), but as *historical*, which allows it to be made distinct from and peripheral to *contemporary* forms of racism. Now racism, especially anti-Black racism, is presented as a result of an individual's own behaviors rather than arising from practices that are mired in, but presented as untethered to, long-held assumptions about people of color.[3] Consider the response to the statement on the Trayvon Martin ruling made by President Barack Obama on July 19, 2013. Addressing the press, the president stated,

> There are very few African American men in this country who haven't had the experience of being followed when they were shopping in a department store. That includes me. There are very few African American men who haven't had the experience of walking across the street and hearing the locks click on the doors of cars. That happened to me—at least before I was a senator. There are very few African Americans who haven't had the experience of getting on an elevator and a woman clutching her purse nervously and holding her breath until she had a chance to get off. That happens often. And I don't want to exaggerate this, but those sets of experiences inform how the African American community interprets what happened one night in Florida. (Obama 2013)

Although Obama's comments included much more than this personal anecdote of being followed while shopping, these lines were what garnered the most attention from various conservative news commentators, including Fox's Bill O'Reilly. The day after the president's remarks, O'Reilly, on his Fox show *The O'Reilly Factor* (July 23, 2013), addressed Obama's comments in a segment titled "President Obama and the Race Problem." In it, O'Reilly concluded, "The reason there is so much violence and chaos in the Black precincts is the disintegration of the African American family. . . . Raised without much structure, young Black men often reject education and gravitate towards the street culture, drugs, hustling, gangs. Nobody forces them to do that, again, it is a personal decision."

Although O'Reilly's willfully naive analysis of race in the United States is not unusual—he is, after all, well known as one of the most rabidly conservative political commentators in the country—what did cause outrage among the African American community was the support O'Reilly garnered from CNN news commentator Don Lemon, an African American himself. Positioning his comments within the ongoing coverage of Martin's case, as well as President Obama's comments, on July 21, Lemon agreed that O'Reilly "had a point" and that he "doesn't go far enough" in calling out the problem.

Lemon went on to provide a list of five points that he felt were necessary for the Black community to become less victimized within American society. Not surprisingly, all five points required individual change on the part of African Americans, from language to clothing to housekeeping, rather than acknowledging the systemic inequalities in the country against people of color. Lemon's list was met with outrage by much of the African American community. Commentator Darron Smith (2013) noted that "blaming black Americans for failing to subscribe to white norms, values and aesthetics is not good counsel. The black male experience must be situated within a larger historical framework of systemic oppression. In order to make sense out of the struggles black men endure, it will take more than moral platitudes to overcome a racist structure designed to fundamentally exclude men of color."[4]

For Lemon, the negative response to his five-point plan was not a deterrent to sharing even *more* controversial commentary on race. On November 5, 2013—a couple of months after Kal Penn tweeted his own support of New York City's stop-and-frisk policy[5]—Lemon tweeted "Would You Rather Be Politically Correct Or Safe & Alive?," igniting a host of facetious responses from followers, including "#DonLemonOn #12YearsASlave: At least he was working for 12 years straight. That's more than most Black men today can say" and "#DonLemonOn Jim Crow. Would you rather sit in the back of the bus or walk?" The responses, on Twitter and various other social media websites, connected Lemon's five-point plan to his seeming support for the stop-and-frisk policy, essentially calling him an apologist for White racism and likening Lemon to O'Reilly and Rush Limbaugh in his approach to race. Although Lemon's comments were discussed in news forums as political commentary, the fallout took place mainly within more popular contexts, such as blogs and Twitter. Common to all the responses was a strong critique of Lemon's subversion of his own identity—as Black and as gay—and the elevation and celebration of America's "rugged individualism" and its (largely imaginary) meritocracy.

My somewhat lengthy exposition of these two instances is to provide context for a fairly straightforward observation: that Lemon's five-point plan and the Twitter comment were essentially about self-disciplining in the hope of transcending identification. Lemon's implicit belief seemed to be that while skin color could not be changed, performing a form of metaphorical Whiteness in terms of control, clothing, and behavior would protect African Americans from *further* racism, both by the state and by the general (White) populace. Lemon disassociates the anti-Black racist history of the United States from the discourse of "rugged individualism" and the bootstrap mentality, thereby attributing the mythical narratives of an American meritocracy to a form of self-disciplined "White" performance. Because Black bodies have been positioned by political and popular culture as "unruly" for almost three hundred years, the internalization of this form of biopolitical neocolonization is the call to prescribe White social performances as (individualized) remedies for transcending racism in the United States. Here Lemon's support for the policies that explicitly discriminate against him comes from the same internalized sense of self-preservation that also animates Kal Penn's response to stop-and-frisk policies.

This notion of a bizarre (racialized) individual agency that is tied to one's willingness to embrace and reproduce White, middle-class identity and values is validated and reproduced in various contexts, including popular media. Here individuals like prescandal Bill Cosby and Oprah Winfrey, and even fictitious characters like Olivia Pope (*Scandal*, 2012–), are (re)presented as models of Black exceptionalism. Individually, and as a collective group of elites who have correctly mastered assimilation and the American Dream, they are held up not only as aspirational models but also as exemplars of Black individuals who have transcended their collective history. Because these individuals' personal stories are often rags-to-riches narratives, a founding myth of the United States, such success is seen as a collective possibility (over a particular racialized reality), where their success is a "choice" over the "other choices" made by people who end up as welfare mothers and deadbeat dads in Black communities.

Post-race and the "New" Black

On January 17, 2009, Barack Obama, following in the footsteps of Abraham Lincoln, traveled from Chicago, via Philadelphia and Delaware, to Washington, D.C., to take office not only as the forty-fourth president of the United States but also as the first Black president of the country. Cat Stevens's "Peace Train"[6] played in the background on live television, and crowds cheered along the way—even the most cynical among us felt like we were witnessing, if not the possibility of a post-race America, at least a shift in the right direction (even though nothing leading up to, or since, that event has brought that promise to fruition). Of course, history tells us why Obama's election would have so little impact on race politics, or even on reconciliation.

In a country largely built on contradictory narratives of freedom and genocidal slavery—and whitewashed with more contemporary but equally ambiguous terminologies like "democracy" and "patriotism"—the election of a non-White president quickly becomes a symbolic gesture rather than sustained change. But the premature celebration of post-race America that reverberated in 2008 is in keeping with the general approach to race and racism that has marked the last four decades since the civil rights movement in the United States. Barack Obama's candidacy and eventual election reinforced the liberal notion of color-blindness that has long been synonymous with progress following the civil rights movement. In their succinct summary of race in the United States since the 1960s, and providing a context for the concept of color-blindness, Sarah Nilsen and Sarah Turner (2014, 2) note that

> colorblind ideology must be understood as the outcome of a rhetorical strategy deployed in the wake of the modern civil rights movement in the early 1960s. . . . Neoconservative politicians insisted that the passage of the Civil Rights Act of 1964 and the Voting Rights Act of 1965 eradicated any remaining structural barriers to the advancement of the African American community . . . any remaining racial inequalities were the product of individual choice rather than social policy.

This post-1960s "color-blindness"—one that essentially erases inequality by blithely stating that inequality is "unseen" because of the measures in place to hinder racism—was reworked for contemporary culture by Obama's election. Obama himself was careful to present his race politics within the framework of a "fair and just" America. In fact, when, as junior senator for the state of Illinois, Barack Obama gave the keynote speech at the Democratic National Committee annual convention in 2004 in Boston, Massachusetts, he introduced himself to the American public as a representative of the "new" America: one where American exceptionalism and American opportunity were unconstrained by race and the race politics of the past:

> My father was a foreign student, born and raised in a small village in Kenya. . . . Through hard work and perseverance my father got a scholarship to study in a magical place: America which stood as a beacon of freedom and opportunity to so many who had come before. While studying here, my father met my mother. . . . They shared an abiding faith in the possibilities of this nation. They would give me an African name, Barack, or "blessed," believing that in a tolerant America your name is no barrier to success. They imagined me going to the best schools in the land, even though they weren't rich, because in a generous America you don't have to be rich to achieve your potential. . . . I stand here knowing that my story is part of the larger American story, that I owe a debt to all of those who came before me, and that, in no other country on earth, is my story even possible. (Obama 2004)

Such a compelling narrative of bootstrap success, especially by the son of an African immigrant—and Africa as the continent that represents America's deepest shame—was seductive to the American public, largely because of the desire to believe that this was indeed truthful and universal. It also implicitly, and yet significantly, seemed to atone for America's slave history. After all, if the son of a Black man could reach the highest office, "race" was no longer an issue in the United States, and "the broad ideological draw of post-race exhorts Americans to see race but only as a signal of its legacies having been defeated" (Mukherjee 2014, 51).

Here the general American desire for a teleological progress tied to the strategic color-blind machinations of White supremacy from the 1960s, and then effectively severed from ongoing systemic and social inequalities and disadvantages, allowed Barack Obama's election to be declared the end of American racism—a "break" that "now cleared ground for claims about key civil rights protections as unnecessary" (Mukherjee 2014, 49), and the active dismantling of legislative measures that were put into place to allow historically marginalized populations to participate in the democratic processes of the country and its governance. One such example is the recent changes to the aforementioned VRA.

The VRA, signed into effect by President Lyndon Johnson on August 6, 1965, declared that "no voting qualification or prerequisite to voting or standard, practice, or procedure shall be imposed or applied by any State or political subdivision in a manner which results in a denial or abridgement of the right of any citizen of the United States to vote on account of race or color."[7] Consisting of nineteen sections that addressed areas of discrimination, and the legal changes in place to eliminate these discriminations, the act has been one of the most effective means of addressing ongoing issues of representation for minorities in the democratic process. Despite clear evidence for its continued need—and entirely connected to the rapid reinstitutionalization of aforementioned conservative 1960s ideologies that strategically positioned Obama's election as a sign of race reconciliation—in 2013, the U.S. Supreme Court voted 5–4 in favor of changes to the VRA, changes that significantly diminished its legislative value and all but eliminated its core interventions. In calling for these changes, Chief Justice John Roberts, along with Justices Scalia, Kennedy, Thomas, and Alito, declared Section 4 of the Voting Rights Act, which sets the formula that determines which state and local governments must meet the terms of Section 5—which requires states to get federal permission before making any changes to voting laws—"unconstitutional." While acknowledging that the VRA had been enormously effective since its enactment in combatting discrimination, Chief Justice Roberts nonetheless stated that there "is no denying, however, that the conditions that originally justified these measures no longer characterize voting in the covered jurisdictions" (U.S. Supreme Court 2013). According to Roberts and the other presenting justices, by 2009, "the racial gap in voter registration and turnout [was] lower in the States originally covered by §5 than it [was] nationwide." . . . Since that time, Census Bureau data indicate that African-American voter turnout has come to exceed white voter turnout in five of the six States originally covered by §5, with a gap in the sixth State of less than one half of one percent.

Roberts also went on to note that while "problems remain," "there is no denying that, due to the Voting Rights Act, our nation has made great strides." Roberts's equal-but-lesser (Jim Crow) justifications, based in neoliberal relativisms, were not unchallenged by the dissenting judges of the U.S. Supreme Court, nor by other nonpartisan organizations such as the American Civil Liberties Union (ACLU).

In her strong rebuttal to Roberts, Justice Ruth Bader Ginsburg pointed out that

Congress approached the 2006 reauthorization of the VRA with great care and seriousness. The same cannot be said of the Court's opinion today. The Court makes no genuine attempt to engage with the massive legislative record that Congress assembled. Instead, it relies on increases in voter registration and turnout as if that were the whole story. . . . Without even identifying a standard of review, the Court dismissively brushes off arguments based on "data from the record," and declines to enter the "debat[e about] what [the] record shows." . . . One would expect more from an opinion striking at the heart of the Nation's signal piece of civil-rights legislation.

Ginsburg went on to document several recent antivoting practices, including the following two:

In 2001, the mayor and all-White five-member Board of Aldermen of Kilmichael, Mississippi, abruptly canceled the town's election after "an unprecedented number" of African American candidates announced they were running for office. The U.S. Department of Justice required an election, and the town elected its first Black mayor and three Black aldermen.

In 2006, the court found that Texas's attempt to redraw a congressional district to reduce the strength of Latino voters bore "the mark of intentional discrimination that could give rise to an equal protection violation" and ordered the district redrawn in compliance with the VRA. . . . In response, Texas sought to undermine this Court's order by curtailing early voting in the district but was blocked by an action to enforce the Section 5 preclearance requirement.

Despite this rebuttal by Ginsburg, supported by Justices Breyer, Sotomayor, and Kagan, the law was overturned. While Section 5 remains intact, by eliminating Section 4, Section 5 becomes ineffectual and neutralizes one of the most effective legal structures put into place to address systemic inequalities.[8]

Its impact has reverberated throughout the country, especially in southern states where historical racial inequalities give rise to new ones. Such policies are often more subtle than the pre–civil rights voter blocks and, as noted by Ginsburg, are "second-generation barriers" that include "gerrymandering [and] the redrawing of legislative districts in an effort to segregate the races for purposes of voting" (U.S. Supreme Court 2013). Providing even more evidence for these second-generation barriers, the ACLU (2015b) notes that "voter turnout in the 2008 election was the most racially diverse in American history. And in response to this historic moment, lawmakers nationwide have erected more barriers to the ballot box. . . . Poll taxes and literacy tests [of the past] have given way to more modern voter suppression tactics packaged as voter ID laws, restrictions to voter registration and cuts to early voting." Such sweeping legislative restructuring around race, democratic politics, and new strategies for disenfranchisement of historically marginalized populations continues, but it is largely overshadowed by the parallel discourse against containing and neutralizing terrorism, vis-à-vis the brown body.

Fueled by false parallels made between Obama's election and democratic representation, and bolstered by "shared" brown enemies, Black racism has been declared "dead," or at least "minimal," as everyone is "secured" under the umbrella of nationalism. Essentially, under political and judiciary language, *citizenship*, which marks belonging (as mapped in chapter 2), now incorporates Blackness as part of American patriotic identity, thereby simultaneously neutralizing any discourse of disenfranchisement, at the same time as it actively (as with the VRA) continues to erode civil liberties.

The myth of a decline in anti-Black racism runs parallel to discourses of brown enemies, illegal immigration, and terrorism. Though the two discourses never meet (unless Black is incorporated into brown, as I show later), they are nonetheless intertwined. More simply, while Obama's election was significant enough to shift the discourse of race away from systemic inequalities against Black populations, that alone would not have been enough to trigger the ensuing dismantling of institutionalized civil liberties that had been in place for almost five decades. Instead, what strengthened these more recent neoconservative moves is the collective focus on something other than Blackness as disruptive and disorderly. That something was an increased focus on securing the borders, as well as American communities broadly defined, against the threat of a terrorist brown.

Here we see, yet again (as in chapter 3), the ideo-mathematical re-structuring of race and racism to maintain a White supremacist race hierarchy, where Blackness is invited to share in a common enemy. Through this sharing of enmity, both Black and White communities seemed to come together to protect the homeland (Ahmad 2002). That shared commitment, which softened the anti-Black racism—at least on the surface—created social conditions that made Obama's election possible. Simultaneous to this, under the guise of a shared brown enemy (and the need to restrict civil liberties to ensure the protection of the citizenry from this brown enemy), and the resulting sanguinity around Black–White racial tensions, some of the most important legal protections against the disenfranchisement of minority groups have been effectively removed from the political and social landscape of the United States.

Immigrant Obama: Black, White, and Brown

The (re)inscription of Obama within brown has made anti-Black racisms more invisible through a focus on anti-(mainly brown) immigration policies and rhetoric that fuels a collective sense of *constructed* nationalist identity. This is a nationalism that nourishes racism through ignorance and fear rather than through factual knowledge of the conditions and possibilities of immigration. It is also one that uses embodied racism as a form of humorous medication for the pathologized anxieties surrounding color and color politics in the United States. It fuels and maintains the myth of color-blindness. It is one that allows Dean Grose to imagine that his denial of any knowledge of the watermelons as shorthand for the "happy darkie"—who wanted nothing but a sweet treat to keep him working—would actually be an acceptable defense (see chapter 2).

More recently, this kind of shorthand racist humor has been made explicit in the plethora of cartoons depicting Obama as an illegal immigrant, or an illegal immigrant sympathizer, apparently because of his own (immigrant) roots. Certainly over the last two hundred years, cartoons have been used both for humor and for political commentary and as such are not a new phenomenon reflecting contemporary race or global politics. But cartoons dealing with issues of race and racism are especially prolific on the Internet, where there is less censuring of conventional social behaviors, including racism (Weaver 2011, 417).

In keeping with Weaver's assertion, of note here is that many of the images of Internet cartoon humor conflate Obama's Blackness with the aforementioned random brownness that moves across and between Hispanic, South Asian, and terrorist/Muslim—representations that would garner considerable censuring and social dissent (as in the case of Grose) if circulated outside of an Internet context. Take, for example, conservative blog *iowntheworld*'s series of cartoons entirely devoted to the Obamas. In one cartoon—a black-and-white film still—Obama is depicted in the foreground, his face in a maniacal smile, superimposed on a bandito wearing a large sombrero. Hung across his chest is a bandolier, and a speech balloon reads, "Birth Certificates? We don't need no stinkin' birth certificates." The "we" that Obama is referencing are an army of sombrero-wearing men, in the background, who seem to be following him. In this cartoonish representation, humor and horror (at the violent hordes crossing the border) are harnessed to conflate Obama's identity with those who cross the border illegally, fueling and providing supporting evidence for the notion of Obama's own illegality. Essentially reinscribing racism as an issue of national security rather than of xenophobia, when bandito Obama references "we," he is seen as admitting that his mixed-race heritage is, in fact, the same as illegal immigration.

This commitment to security and the discourse of securitization is pivotal in companion cartoons published in 2007 and 2008 by Jerry Breen on his website Newbreen.com. In the first image, headlined "Obama Been Lyin,'" Barack Obama, holding a red marker, stands next to a list of popular assertions about his birth, education, and upbringing as a Muslim that Obama has apparently struck through with the marker. For example, in the first sentence, which reads, "His Kenyan father was a Muslim," "Muslim" has been struck through and replaced with "Atheist." The list goes on to fashion Obama's implied deceit in hiding other aspects of his Muslim (read un-American) upbringing, including schooling, his stepfather, and baptism.

Its companion cartoon is much more explicit in its use of embodied racism and brown deviance. Headlined "Obama Been Lyin' Part 2—'Why Lie'?" and with a subheading that reads "The Secret Identity," Obama is depicted as an Indonesian, wearing the Indonesian national dress, including a *peci* (an Indonesian head cap for men), who turns into a superhero with the Obama campaign logo on his chest. Next to his image as an Indonesian, the text reads, "Meek mild mannered Indonesian citizen Barry Soetoro says the magic incantation and he transforms into OBAMA MAN." A speech balloon helps Soetoro tell us that he has "the power to cloud men's minds," as he shares another speech balloon with Obama Man that shouts, "HOPE! CHANGE!"

Here all the powers of embodied racism—in the form of deceit, magic (clouding minds), the "murkiness" of brown space, and the hierarchies of color and power (foreigner to iconic American hero)—are effortlessly channeled to critique the naïveté of the American public in trusting Obama, while reinforcing his status as an alien.

A similar discourse of American (White) naïveté and its possible repercussions is articulated in a cartoon that uses the quintessential cinematic Christmas extravaganza of *It's a Wonderful Life* (dir. Frank Capra, 1946) as the backdrop for the chaos that Obama will cause. In the image, protagonist George Bailey—who is saved from suicide by his guardian angel and friends who attest to his generosity and love in making the world a better place—stands next to his wife, Mary, holding a baby Obama (Obama's face superimposed on Bailey's daughter Zuzu) in his arms. George and Mary seem to be laughing out loud with joy, as baby Obama declares that "every time a bell rings an illegal alien gets an entitlement check." Over the years, this cinematic classic from 1946 has come to represent the possibilities of America and symbolize the mythos of the American Dream. The Baileys' triumph over destitution, and even death, is a story that resonates with the American public as an iconic narrative representation of both Christianity (a loving God who sends an angel to save George) and (pre–civil rights) American meritocracy. By foregrounding this political commentary within an iconic image of the American Dream, we are meant to recognize that it *is* a wonderful life— not for the legal, hardworking (White) Americans but for the illegal hordes tearing down the borders of the United States. Such policies, the cartoon seems to imply, are only possible because the American public (again, read White) have been duped by a childlike figure who is unable to make rational decisions.

By representing Obama as a Black child (in the 1946 context, pickaninny-like), the cartoon speaks to both the aforementioned pathologized anxieties of the Obama presidency and the use of humor to render him childlike and unthreatening. Here the body—essentially Obama's body as representative of all colored bodies—becomes a source of humorous deviance. Through the broader cultural context and meaning of the image, vis-à-vis the film and its cultural capital, we are expected to laugh at Obama's incongruous representation as Bailey's baby, at the same time that it reinforces his difference, both physically and ideologically. Within this, both Obama and the illegal immigrants he supposedly supports are juxtaposed against the Bailey-esque exceptionalism of American society and validate the Tocquevillian assertion of American exceptionalism. Thus, by positioning Obama as a babe in arms within the post–World War II family—exemplars of the "greatest generation" that ever lived—we are simultaneously expected to understand the core values of American society, at the same time that we recognize the childlike threat of Obama. Concurrently, this racist infantilizing of a powerful Black figure circumvents anti-Black racism altogether and couches it in terms of contemporary narratives of legality (legal resident, illegal alien), where legality—especially birthed, rather than naturalized— is seen as an important indicator for claiming a quintessential and mythologized notion of *American*. But, in keeping with the absurdity of such constructions, these representations are in stark contrast to the popular and public narratives of immigrant success that are part of the American discourses of immigrant and multicultural success, especially within the context of American exceptionalism.

Take this recent example: in 2009, Bobby Jindal, governor of the state of Louisiana, in his response to President Obama's State of the Union Address, began by presenting President Obama's election as some form of redemptive closure to the history of slavery. Jindal posited that "regardless of party, all Americans are moved by the president's personal story, the son of an American mother and a Kenyan father who grew up to become leader of the free world" (Jinbal 2009). He then went on to connect Obama's story to his own success: "Like the president's father, my own parents came to this country from a distant land. When they arrived in Baton Rouge, my mother was already four-and-a-half-months pregnant. . . . To find work, my dad picked up the yellow pages and started calling local businesses." This narrative of seemingly effortless immigrant success—as simple as picking up the Yellow Pages—belies the challenges of gaining legal employment faced by immigrants in the contemporary United States. Jindal continued, "Even after landing a job, he still couldn't afford to pay for my delivery, so he worked out an installment plan with the doctor. Fortunately for me, he never missed a payment." Jindal seemed to be oblivious to the contradictions of his narrative of immigrant success and to the limits of American democracy in providing adequate health care and support for its people as he continued his narrative of immigrant success: "As I grew up, my mom and dad taught me the values that attracted them to this country, and they instilled in me an immigrant's wonder at the greatness of America." The neoliberal wonders of American immigrant success, recounted by Jindal as a pastoral narrative of self, while intended to evoke some kind of celebration around the utopian success of colored bodies in the contemporary United States, nonetheless re-create the post-1960s tensions between African Americans and South Asian Americans (Prashad 2000).

Jindal, as well as fellow politician and second-generation Indian Nikki Haley, represents the uber–model minority success story that is held up as an exemplar for African Americans, *even now.* Responding to these comparisons of success becomes even more challenging for African Americans within the post-racial context, where the *history* of Black becomes an invisible or irrelevant history and the playing field for brown and Black is presented as even. Jindal's comparison of his upbringing to Obama's constructs a linear comparison that obfuscates the complicated relationships with race that both groups have struggled with throughout U.S. history. It also completely ignores Obama's identity as *bi*-racial and his complex and contested relationship with and to *Whiteness*. But such an omission of White should not be too surprising. The notion of White as neutral or without value, and therefore as valuable, has been much debated in Whiteness studies. My intention here is to not get into this larger discussion at this time but to consider the relationship between brown and White, as I have done with Black and brown.

As White as Brown as Black

A few years back, in a class on race and representation, after reading Bayoumi's (2008) *How Does It Feel to Be a Problem?*, an African American male student, who had been completely silent up to that point, raised his hand and said, "While I understand where they are coming from, it makes me so mad that people can think that being Black is no longer a problem." His honest outburst sums up the very real consequences of racial hierarchies that this brown, both metaphorically and somatically, in politics and in popular culture, introduced in a post-9/11 society. The cultural obsession with brown—as terror (political) and commodity (popular)—somehow neutralized, or made irrelevant, the need for continued discussions of Black racial oppression in popular discourse. By focusing on brown as the unidentifiable "new" threat, and introducing racism as part of a national security matrix (which Obama's birth became, and continues to be, part of), unresolved tensions between Black and White seemed to become passé. Because these historical tensions are (seemingly) passé, the new forms of racism introduced through hyper-documentation and routinized systemic discourses of security and terror threats, though serving racialized purposes, become a form of neoliberal securitization rather than *racism*.

This is perhaps most visible in the way that security translated into both social and economic vectors, with privatized prisons and security details flourishing since 9/11. For example, Steve Logan, CEO of the third largest private prison firm in the United States, Cornell Corporation, is widely cited as stating, "I think it's clear that with the events of September 11, there's a heightened focus on detention, both on the borders and within the U.S. [and] more people are gonna get caught. . . . So I would say that's a positive. . . . The federal business is the best business for us. It's the most consistent business for us, and the events of September 11 are increasing that level of business" (Welch 2011, 523). In the immediate aftermath of September 11, tied to the newly refined and wildly extensive powers of the U.S. Department of Justice and the INS, approximately twelve hundred immigrants from the Middle East, or of Middle Eastern descent, were incarcerated (Welch 2011, 385). Because of the nature of the accusations, "unlike people charged criminally, INS detainees are not entitled to government appointed counsel," and many remain without representation, indefinitely detained (Welch 2002, 201–2). Against this general backdrop of 9/11 security measures, the historically consistently higher rate of incarceration of Black and Latino populations has either been largely ignored or incorporated into the war against terror. This is especially true as the notions of illegality and terrorism after 9/11 became, and continue to be, conflated within discourses of immigration and immigration policy, especially around "conventionally" browned bodies. Of incarceration and illegality for the Latino/a population, Lisa Cacho (2012, 101) writes,

> Anxieties of undocumented immigration following September 11 generated a new kind of crisis over "illegal" immigration. Because Latina/o bodies have rendered the status of illegality recognizable, differently racialized unauthorized immigrants unsettled this racial coupling, producing considerable anxiety over not being able to distinguish "illegal" immigrants from "fraudulent" foreigners. These anxieties worked to simultaneously create and legitimate a racially profiled threat to national security.

Such a conflation between historically browned bodies that were largely tied to the southern borders of the United States and the "newly" browned terrorists seeping into the country from other, less secured boundaries created a new kind of racialized system between brown, Black, and White. In fact, shortly after 9/11, Muneer Ahmad (2002, 105) observed that "the events of September 11 have brought blacks and whites closer together," noting that "Arabs, Muslims, and South Asians have assumed the primary position of racial scorn," where "African Americans have become more American at the expense of Arab, Muslim, and South Asian immigrants."[9] Though such an observation is not without merit, and indeed, in the immediate aftermath, the twin discourses of national melancholia and patriotism were able to "bring together" White and Black populations against a terrorizing brown, such affinities were short-lived. More recently, similar to Lisa Cacho's observations around Latino/a populations, Sasha Torres (2013) has noted the ways in which the Black body becomes reinscribed as brown to justify enacting the antiterrorist legislature on their personhood. According to Torres, "African American figures have come to be linked to terrorism via either their association with the US-based Nation of Islam or with a vaguely defined pan-African blackness that, putatively, has insidiously made its way into the United States, bringing Islamic terrorism with it" (171). Here their Blackness is subsumed by the deviant brown, and anti-Black racism becomes justified as antiterrorism vis-à-vis Islam.

Disciplining Practices

These larger disciplining legislative strategies organize daily lives in such a way that the general citizenry also (re)organizes itself to respond to these changes by producing and policing their own (brown) identifications. One of the most powerful visual exemplars of this comes from Applied Autonomy's "Routes of Least Surveillance," included in *An Atlas of Radical Cartography* (Mogel and Bhagat 2007), a 160-page book of ten essays and ten individual maps. Editors Mogel and Bhagat contend that their intent was "for *An Atlas of Radical Cartography* to act as a primer on issues which the maps and essays address: identity, land-use, imprisonment, energy, migration (an-atlas)." By including the map "Routes of Least Surveillance," Mogel and Bhagat provide a context for understanding the process of managed visibility and invisibility after 9/11. The map speaks to how the number of surveillance cameras around Manhattan creates an *interpretation* of identity (essentially, identification) about, and of, people's behavior around the cameras:

> Although born in Brooklyn, Zahid's olive complexion and dark hair makes him unnaturally attractive to surveillance camera operators.

He is particularly careful to avoid CCTV on his way to the market
from his local mosque after evening prayers. (Map 2)

Here Zahid is aware that his olive skin and dark hair, when connected to
the mosque, already place him as a possible "suspect in the city" and that
the technology may categorize him as deviant, based on random nodes
(color, location, activity) that map and produce an identity. This identity
produced through nodes of (deviant) identification also controls and
modifies social behaviors of Whiteness that would otherwise go unnoticed. For example, the map notes that "Ethan is a model Columbia student who maintains a 3.7 average, and is active in student government.
However, his unruly hair and military clothing makes him a target for
video surveillance—which is especially problematic when he's off to
purchase marijuana from the friendly vendors in Tompkins Square Park."
The combination of hair, military jacket, and purchase of marijuana
produces an identity that could possibly be considered "un-American,"
because it contradicts the image of middle-American Whiteness. Such
performances of patriotic American Whiteness are also part of the "you
are with us or against us" rhetoric that George W. Bush established when,
on September 20, 2001, he declared in a speech to a joint session of
Congress and to the American people, "Either you are with us, or you are
with the terrorists" (Bush 2001c). Therefore any activities challenging the
decision of the government—the act of democratic dissent—become a
form of deviant behavior, as in the case of Skye, documented by *An Atlas
of Radical Cartography*: Skye is an antiglobalization activist organizing
an April 29, 2007, antiwar protest march. Knowing that the New York
City Police Department increasingly relies on surveillance footage to bolster activist prosecutions, she is planning a route that avoids as many
cameras as possible. Essentially, through these new forms of technology,
surveillance, and the language of "securitization," post-9/11 acceptance
and tolerance have been redefined within a systematically produced and
managed somatic, where discourses of Black and brown become sub-
merged in murky brown space. Inherent to this submersion in brown
spaces is a restructuring of what *White* means both metaphorically and
somatically in a globalized world. Because what is held against it is unidentifiable and involves political, social, and legal supervision, White
too becomes an increasingly elusive, but very *valuable*, commodity, al-

beit one that is different from the commodification and consumption of brown that this chapter documents. Because Whiteness provides a neutralized freedom—vis-à-vis the Baileys, the "birthers," and birth itself—very different from brown or Black, its construction and management seem *ideological* rather than physical. But Whiteness too has a form that the state and popular culture recognize as legitimate in a way that they do not brown or Black. And it is this elusive legitimacy that both brown and Black seek in the age of Obama.

As this chapter documents, regardless of the celebration of a post-race America in 2008, the election of Barack Hussein Obama as the forty-fourth president of the United States merely reinscribed and, perhaps more importantly, *displaced* conventional nodes of racist discourse. By harnessing race to security, and security to unidentifiable deviant bodies, both politics and popular culture have rearticulated racism within a system of identification rather than identity in its historical fashion.

Conclusion
Wielding Identity to Organize Warfare

> In our world of rampant "individualization," identities are a mixed blessing. They vacillate between a dream and a nightmare, and there is no telling when one will turn into the other.
>
> —ZYGMUNT BAUMAN, *IDENTITY*

It's close to midnight on a random day in April 2014. I am on eBay, looking for dress-up clothes for a five-year-old. I type "broomstick skirt Indian" into the search engine in an effort to find something that is shiny and twirls. One of the first things I see is an advertisement that says "Broomhilda skirt Indian Genie Hindu Design unique chic." There is one image of the product that isn't very clear, and I take the description at face value, vaguely noticing blue figures against a bright orange and red background. I bid on it, even though it doesn't look like it has the obvious markers of "Indo-chic" (Maira 2007): no mirror work or intricate thread work. Although it may not be dress-up worthy from the vantage point of a five-year-old, because of the way it is advertised, the skirt is a research purchase for the ongoing archive (see the introduction), and I want a closer look at the skirt to see what "Hindu" means to the seller. At that moment, both the description and the product are ideal representations of the commoditized neutralizing of brown in contemporary culture: it is both "unique" and "chic," and genies and Hinduism are merged in one spectacular advertisement for brown fashion.

A few days later, the skirt arrives, and it's even more emblematic of the entire premise of this book: that brown is malleable. The "Indian

Genie Hindu" is neither Hindu nor genie, nor even South Indian. Instead, it is a repeated pattern of Pueblo women, with baskets of red chilies, sitting in front of adobe homes. The images are clear and very large, up close. The clothing the women are wearing is obviously Native American, as is their jewelry. The adobe structures behind them signify the American Southwest.

But for the purposes of advertising and selling, *these* brown figures are the same brown figures as Hindu "genies": blue bodies that are not of a previous genocide[1] but of contemporary political and consumer cultural discourses, where Hinduism becomes a corollary of (Middle Eastern) Aladdin (via Disney) and the magic lamp, essentially a baseline of conjectures—blue genies, spices, Hinduism, and brown bodies—that produces an identification of brown. It is an identification that has become increasingly easy to make, that has become more popular and very commonplace, in the last fifteen years.

Throughout the book, I've mapped this theory of brown based on one simple observation: accelerated by the events of 9/11, identity (raced and otherwise) has shifted to identification to maintain a form of social control that benefits those in power and maintains the paradoxical fiction that America is welcoming to all but also discerning of who has the right to its exceptionalism. The practices, both popular and political, of this paradoxical fiction manifest in forms of racist governmentality that are systematically and routinely evoked. Though racism is hardly new in the United States, what makes *this* iteration of brown "newer" is that, tethered as it is to the rapidly changing and institutionalized policies and practices of the neoliberal state, and coupled with popular culture, anyone, at any time, can be discursively produced as a deviant. Roped to historical marginalizations, and formed within contemporary forms of hypernationalisms that arose in the aftermath of September 2001, these identifications feed into a parochial sense of American exceptionalism that increasingly endangers difference (Ahmed 2008).[2] This provincial patriotism was certainly birthed (at least most visibly) in the aftermath of 9/11, but—as I've explained in the preceding chapters—the patriotic virulence is also incubated within more broad sociopolitical and economic shifts for, and in, the United States in recent times.

Essentially, though 9/11 is instrumental as shorthand for producing brown anxieties, these anxieties are also fed by the outsourcing of jobs *to* brown spaces, immigration *from* brown spaces, and economic challenges *by* brown spaces, especially in South Asia. And whereas the materiality of brown, in the form of commodity culture, can freely cross the border for pleasurable consumption, the brown body itself, as it is currently produced, is a site of fear and loathing. Of course, such fear and loathing in contemporary times are predicated and built on past histories and existing tensions between and along color lines.

As such, the preceding chapters map the numerous relationships that shape contemporary notions of brown as a form of identification, simultaneously tethered to and separated from its early somatic identity. It is to map these convoluted processes that I theorize the concept of brown as a form of identification. While acknowledging that identification is linked to historically produced practices of brown somatics, my intent is to provide an alternate framework or map to study identities in contemporary culture.

This map is not definitive, nor is it without contradictions. But the very lack of marked boundaries, as well as the inclusion of contradictory and co-exiting practices of producing race, gestures toward the ways in which identity is wielded. My use of *wield* is deliberate here. Race and identity markers are the foundational weapons organizing warfare, whether it be the cultural politic of producing and commoditizing identity as a form of exchange or consumption or the kind that results in the loss of life and property. While somatically based racism is alive and (sadly) well, deploying other kinds of demonizations and expulsions—such as homophobia and sexism—along the same vectors of racism requires an interrogation of where these notions of deviance converge and how they are distributed.[3] It is important to recognize that subjugated essentialisms, defined early on in this book as an essentialist identity that is produced by and works to justify the actions of those in power, are not produced merely by how someone "looks" but by how someone "acts" and how those actions seem to disrupt a copacetic nationalism.

This notion of nationalism was largely animated by rallying citizens around a marriage between the pastoral homeland, national security, and the surveillance state—and validated by the establishment of the DHS and the USA PATRIOT Act. The very combination of the words *homeland*

and *patriot* was meant to evoke a sense of *amantes patriae* that the citizenry was expected to follow and act upon. Although many understood, and protested, the impact that such administrative institutions would have on civil liberties, more believed that these structures "would rid our country of terrorism" (Egan 2002, 23).[4] The process of "weeding out" and identifying those who are not of the country continues more than a decade after 9/11 and the institutionalization of draconian laws that followed in its immediate aftermath. The rush to prove one's love of country set into motion a continuing cycle of violence against anyone or any group of people who disrupts the "visual" of the American patriot.

As I documented in chapter 2, the ongoing violence of intolerant patriotism extended well into recent times, when we witnessed the rabid response to the first South Indian American Miss America. When Nina Davuluri was called a "terrorist," "Arab," and "Muslim," among other forms of identification, people did so to mark her inauthenticity as an American. Here an imaginary logic creates a chain of identities that produces the identification: brown is Arab, Arab is Muslim, Muslims are terrorists, therefore Davuluri must be a brown terrorist. Through this chain, we see how processes of producing belonging (very narrowly) also produce those who do not belong (very broadly). While the citizenry rally around evicting and eliminating brown from their midst, popular culture in the United States has embraced brown as a form of ethnic chic. The reduction of brown to something "consumable" is part of the symbiotic relationship between the fear of brown and the "control" of brown.

Not So "Hooray, Hooray"

On Thursday, March 6, 2014, E! Online told readers that they *need* to see the newest episode of *The Neighbors*, a sitcom about a family of aliens (from outer space) who, along with their entire community of aliens, take over a gated suburb of New Jersey and become best friends with the human family—Marty and Debbie Weaver and their children, Amber, Max, and Abby—next door.

Much like *Aliens in America*, the series itself abounds with cultural and social mishaps because Larry Bird, his wife, Jackie Joyner-Kersee, and his two children, Reggie Jackson and Dick Butkus—names chosen because of the athletic prowess of the namesakes—are unable to under-

stand American behaviors, which, for the purposes of the show, are generally introduced as "human" behaviors. But when E! informed viewers
not to miss the episode scheduled to air on Friday, March 7, it was for
more than another clash of aliens and humans. It was an invitation to
enjoy the best of brown: a Bollywood musical number, "Balle Balle" (a
Punjabi expression of happiness that loosely translates to "hooray"), that
was going to be an important part of that Friday's episode. In it, Larry
Bird[5] is invited by a coworker to attend the coworker's wedding, which
will be traditionally Indian. Because Bird is an overachiever (like many
"aliens"), he decides that he will give the couple an extraordinary gift that
will mark the occasion: the "gift of Bollywood."

After watching an endless stream of Bollywood films, the family, together with their alien community, choreograph an elaborate dance sequence, including one that requires the dancers to mimic "petting the
dog, and changing the lightbulb." The preparations veer, rather predictably, toward the absurd, with fire-eaters, penguins, and other circus
performances that are meant to mimic India and Bollywood. Although
the Weavers—as sane White Americans who are somewhat uncomfortable with the ostentatious displays of the Orient—are initially reluctant
to join in, they eventually get caught up in the excitement. Even Marty,
the last hold out in the Weaver household (as befitting White patriarchy),
eventually acquiesces when he is asked to "put on his man-dress and
sing" (Fogelman and Weinger 2014).

Much like the premise of *Vijay and I* (see chapter 1), this racist display of brownface is subsumed in the humor and presumed alterity of
the alien characters who are performing the race switch. Furthermore,
the aliens' racist display is negated by the fact that they come from a
planet where race doesn't exist. Their lack of race awareness is represented by Bird being White, Kersee being Black, and, together, the two
being parents to an Asian American child and a White child. Their own
"diverse" family unit distracts from and effectively neutralizes the actual
racism of the "Balle Balle" performance. And when the Weavers finally
join the routine, it is represented as a celebration of multiculturalism
rather than as a form of subjugated essentialism that is produced via a
consumable Bollywood.

This episode—and its multiple discourses[6]—encapsulates the various processes that produce brown. Similar to the strategy used by *Passions* in 2006 (see the preface), *The Neighbors* used brown exotica to bring in viewers—viewers who become armchair anthropologists and lay authorities on what being brown means. The composite of India that the family puts together, *in* the show, from watching Bollywood films—and represented by the dance spectacle—mirrors expectations for the actual audience, where spectacular voyeurism turns brown into an entertainment commodity. The subtle jab at the essentialist representation at the end, when the procession arrives on white horses to find out that it's the "other" kind of Indian ceremony (Native American), is lost in the absurd humor of the genre itself.

Representations like "Balle Balle," produced in contrast to the turbaned terror image that captured the imagination of post-9/11 America, neutralize any latent anxieties about shifting power structures between the United States and brown spaces by producing those spaces as harmless and humorous—spaces that are neither a terrorist nor an economic threat to the United States. Whereas brown as a product is "harmless" and meant to be enjoyed as a commodity, its actual visibility in the United States causes anxieties that are quelled by legal means or that are disciplined and managed under intolerant patriotism.

When "Balle Balle" Meets Brown

This intolerant patriotism is also tied to legal disciplining, as was the case of truck driver Jagjeet Singh. On January 16, 2013, just six months after the brutal deaths at the Wisconsin *gurdwara*—which *should* have alerted the American public to misguided violence against brown bodies—Singh was driving through Pike County, Mississippi, when he was pulled over for a flat tire. When the officers saw the turban on his head and the religious *kirpan* sewn into his waistband, they accused him of being armed and a terrorist. According to the ACLU—which publicized the incident as part of its ongoing efforts to make aware and educate the public around issues of racism against South Asians after 9/11—"contending, wrongly, that his kirpan was illegal, the officers demanded that Mr. Singh remove it. When Mr. Singh explained that he was a Sikh and that the kirpan was a sacred religious article, the officers laughed at him and mocked his religious beliefs. One officer declared that all Sikhs are 'depraved' and 'terrorists'" (Atwood 2013).

In addition to this, the officers "forced Mr. Singh to circle his truck with his hands on his turban while they searched the vehicle. Finally, not content with this humiliation, they arrested him, claiming that Mr. Singh had refused to obey an officer's lawful command" (Atwood 2013). Singh was later released, but the harassment did not end with that. On March 26, Singh appeared in court only to be ordered by the presiding judge, Aubrey Rimes, to remove his turban if he wanted his case heard. When Singh explained that it was against his religion to remove the turban in public, Judge Rimes ordered that the "rag" be removed from his courtroom and threatened to hear Singh's case last. According to the ACLU, "Mr. Singh respectfully declined to remove his turban. As threatened, Judge Rimes forced Mr. Singh and his attorney to wait for several hours until every other litigant had been heard before allowing him into the courtroom" (Atwood 2013).

Singh's experiences, made public by the ACLU and by Sikh organizations around the country, resulted in the Pike County Personnel Policies and Procedures Manual including a new policy against harassment and discrimination that defines "religious discrimination" to include requiring the removal of head coverings.

When the story was published on *Huffington Post*, it garnered a fairly sympathetic response, but among the commentators were also those who felt that the judge had every right to request the removal of the turban because "it's a great place to hide a bomb or a knife made of plastic." This comment on "security," by a regular *Huffington Post* commentator, keyperk, also seamlessly extended to "being American," continuing with, "I'm sorry but if they want to be integrated into American society they'll have to give up certain beliefs and one may be the turban and for some women veils. This is definitely about religious rights but also security of a nation." Keyperk's solution was to "have them enter through a different room and have them unwrap prior to entering in the court room to ensure no dangerous articles hidden." Here even the most "liberal"-seeming commentators, who acknowledge "rights" and "justice," embrace the composite of a turban—regardless of where it comes from or whom it represents—to be a form of brown terrorism. These online commentaries reflect an ideology that has become a form of living in the United States since 9/11: one that says that justice, rights, and even truth are secondary to some abstract notion of security that is tied to expelling people who don't look like "us."

Ten months after the incident in Mississippi, on September 22, Columbia University professor Prabhjot Singh was returning home late one evening when he was brutally attacked in Harlem, New York. With shouts of "get him!" "Osama!" and "terrorist!" Singh was chased, beaten, and left on the street with a broken jaw and other injuries.

Almost as foreshadowing of the inevitable, a year previously, Singh, with coauthor Simran Jeet Singh, had written an op-ed piece for the *New York Times* titled "How Hate Gets Counted." In it, Singh and Singh critiqued the notion of mistaken identity, arguing that every anti-Sikh act of violence was not "just" about being mistaken for Muslim but was actually really about Sikhs and about the "fear and loathing" of others rather than of one particular group. They noted that, starting with the first documented anti-Sikh riots in Bellingham, Washington, in 1907, the legacy of anti-Sikh violence and its contemporary prevalence make it painfully obvious that anti-Sikh violence is often purposeful and targeted. They argued that "the government must begin tracking and counting anti-Sikh hate crimes, just as it must continue to vigorously combat bias and discrimination against all Americans, including Muslims. We must do away with a flawed and incomplete assumption of 'mistaken identity' regarding Sikhs; until we do, we will all be the ones who are mistaken" (Singh and Singh 2012).

"Mistaken identity" has increasingly become one of the most overused and underanalyzed ways of overlooking or dismissing violence against brown bodies. Discourses of mistaken identity also implicitly give credence to "nonmistaken" identities, ones that justify the violence and brutality enacted on them. Here the mistaken identities of brown aren't the funny moments of arriving at a Native American wedding in South Indian clothing; instead, they are the conjecture between life and death.

Conjectures

Around 10:00 P.M. on February 10, 2015, I get a text message from a friend that reads, "So sorry to hear about what happened in Chapel Hill. Hope you are OK." I'm confused by the message, but it prompts me to check online for any news about Chapel Hill, North Carolina. I live twenty minutes away and haven't heard anything from anybody regarding an "incident." As I comb the news, I feel the same dread I felt coming back to the United States after 9/11. It's the slight metallic taste of fear and anger. But it is a fear and anger more intensified, especially now that I have a young child. After reading the little information that is available online at that moment, I check in on my daughter as she sleeps. I look at her face, which is pale in winter but becomes so brown in the summer from days playing outside, and worry that someone will know that she is not entirely White. I think about the families of Razan Mohammad Abu-Salha, Yusor Mohammad Abu-Salha, and Deah Shaddy Barakat.

Yusor Abu-Salha (aged twenty-one) and Razan Abu-Salha (aged nineteen) were sisters, the former married to Barakat six weeks previously. All were from North Carolina, and all three were devout Muslims. Deah was a second-year dental student at University of North Carolina (UNC) School of Dentistry. Yusor was scheduled to start in the same program as Deah in fall 2015, after graduating from North Carolina State University, where Razan was majoring in architecture and environmental design. All three, based on interviews given to news media by friends and family members, were gentle, thoughtful people whose intellectual abilities and social justice efforts were well known.

On the evening of February 10, police responded to two 911 calls reporting gun shots and screaming in the usually quiet neighborhood in which Yusor and Deah lived. Upon arrival, police found three people dead, with a bullet in each of their heads. Shortly after, their neighbor, Craig Stephen Hicks, was arrested and charged with first-degree murder. Acting on long-standing issues between him and various members of the community, including Yusor and Deah, he walked into their apartment, which Razan was also visiting that evening, and gunned all three down. Almost immediately following the shooting, Hicks's wife, Karen, released a statement saying that the shooting "had nothing to do with religion or the victims' faith but, in fact, was related to the long-standing parking disputes that my husband had with the neighbors" (Lamb 2015) and that "he just believed—and I know that's just one of the things I know about him—is everyone is equal" (Kaplan 2015).

Just as with Wade Michael Page and George Zimmerman, the immediate efforts by those close to him were to recharacterize the perpetrator and to declare this a "rupture" in an otherwise "normal" individual. But, as with Page and Zimmerman, a very different picture of Hicks emerged over the days following the shooting. For example, Hicks's "equality" was apparently based in an equal dislike of all religions, including Islam.[7] He was a loner who had moved into the apartment after marrying his current wife seven years previously. Hicks also belonged to the "new atheist movement" that actively and aggressively spoke out against religion, especially Islam and Christianity. According to various news outlets that cited a 2012 posting by Hicks, this atheism was animated after 9/11. The posting, initially attributed to Hicks, is in fact a passage from an essay by prominent atheist Richard Dawkins:

> My respect for the Abrahamic religions went up in the smoke and choking dust of September 11th. . . . The last vestige of respect for the taboo disappeared as I watched the "Day of Prayer" in Washington Cathedral, where people of mutually incompatible faiths united in homage to the very force that caused the problem in the first place: religion. It is time for people of intellect, as opposed to people of faith, to stand up and say "Enough!" Let our tribute to the dead be a new resolve: to respect people for what they individually think, rather than respect groups for what they were collectively brought up to believe. (Dawkins 2001)

This quote is among many antireligious postings on Hicks's Facebook page and provides some context to the way he viewed any symbol of religious affinity. He especially targeted Abu-Salha and Barakat, who mentioned to family and friends that Hicks had threatened them over nonexisting policies around parking spaces.[8] In fact, in an interview immediately after the shooting, Abu-Salha's father, Mohammad Abu-Salha, stated, "Yusor . . . told us on more than two occasions that this man came knocking at the door and fighting about everything with a gun on his belt, more than twice," and also that she thought, "Daddy, I think he hates us for who we are and how we look." When Yusor spoke of how they looked, it was really about the young women's head scarves and their religious beliefs rather than about a racialized or somatic identity. This seems to be supported by the fact that Hicks increased his harassment of the couple once Yusor moved in after the newlyweds returned from their honeymoon. Before that, Deah had shared the apartment with Imad Ahmad, a fellow student at UNC, who has repeatedly stated in interviews that, although Hicks did pick on them more than he did other neighbors, the harassment amped up once he moved out and Yusor started living in the apartment. Ahmad, like many friends and family members of the victims, has repeatedly disputed the parking spot theory. And many of them have stated that the cars belonging to all three victims were parked in their proper locations at the time of their murders.[9]

I share the details of these murders first to acknowledge the tragedy, because the deaths of Yusor, Deah, and Razan touched the community of which I am a part very deeply. I spent days and weeks following the murders talking to students in my classes, some who knew the three victims and were grieving, and others who felt fear, sadness, and a sense of loss about the state of the country and the communities to which they belonged. In the weeks following the murders, and even now, I've often thought of my colleague's incredulity about antibrown racism after 9/11, of which I speak in the introduction, and wondered whether he has gained some insight from the murders. Second, the immediate and even continuing focus on the violence as precipitated by a parking dispute speaks to the ways in which hate crimes and anti-Muslim violence are readily incorporated into a process of "sense making"—similar to the ways in which anti-Sikh violence becomes discussed through the lens of "mistaken identity."

So, rather than call it a hate crime built on an irrational loathing of others—symbolized by a composite brownness of head scarves and Arabic blessings (rather than somatic brown)—the discussion of hate is approached through a more "neutral" and "rational" irrationality. This hate comes not from race/ethnic hate but from a sense of self-loathing and jealousy: many news outlets noted how Hicks was "different" from the upwardly mobile, professionally focused residents of the apartment complex in which he lived[10]—as if to imply that this difference is what drove him to control the parking lots and eventually shoot three of the people who symbolized "that" difference.

In this subtle ideo-mathematical equation (see chapter 3), what is subtracted and equated are American mobilities of class, economics, and meritocracies, as if they are separate from race and ethnic bias. Through this, the central organizing factors of American society—identity and identifications—are left out of the mythologized narratives of a just society.

Even as this book goes to press, the chaos increases and coalesces: on November 13, 2015, a series of coordinated terrorist attacks took place in Paris, killing more than three hundred people. Among the debris, a Syrian passport was found, apparently identifying one those responsible for the attacks. In response to this "evidence," lawmakers across the United States have actively and aggressively started campaigns that discourage or even ban outright (though such bans are symbolic, because state governments do not have the authority to institute such laws) Syrian refugees—those fleeing what is being called the "worst humanitarian crisis of our time" (Ki-Moon 2015)—from settling in the United States. Here, through ideo-mathematical conjectures, for these particular patriots, all of Syria and its people—even young children and infants fleeing from war and genocide—are produced through brown, deviant bodies that are a threat to the securitized state. This is taken up in the rhetoric of the Republican presidential candidate who leads the polls as the nominee for the GOP in November's general elections in 2016. Trump's racist, sexist, homophobic, anti-Islamist language and political stances have resonated with a population that sees the "browning" of America—in its many manifestations—as an active impediment to its own White-bred dreams. Trump's supporters rally for borders, walls, and increased surveillance of other bodies by claiming that their conservative beliefs are under threat. Even as his popularity rises, Trump's own party denounces him as an anomaly and as contrary to the ethical exceptionalism of the GOP and the American public. But in that denunciation of Trump is a willful rewriting of history: to actively argue that Trump rises out of "nothing" and that he is antithetical to American values is to ignore the White supremacist scaffolding that has long been the framework for organizing U.S. political, social, and economic culture.

I map these realities, I also wonder how they continue to exist—and I do so while fully recognizing the naïveté of questioning why history continues to repeat itself. But, although I do not presume to be surprised by the cycle of racial injustice, I continue to be baffled by our complete inability to learn the simplest lessons—our inability to educate ourselves as people who are constantly confronted with the error of our assumptions and still continue to blindly follow them. If the reader wonders why I'm waxing so philosophical and poetic at the end of a book that is entirely about the ways in which racism is systematically and structurally reproduced in popular visual culture and political discourse, it's because I would like to believe that, at some point, we will grow to understand that senseless violence from the past and the recent past (such as the Wisconsin massacre with which I open the book) can educate us about how notions of otherness actually undermine the very foundation of American exceptionalism that (intolerant) patriotism seeks to protect.

Acknowledgments

Although this book is funny at times, it is not on a joyful subject. Therefore I am doubly grateful for the people acknowledged here and for the many forms of joy they bring to my life. Everything good about this work comes from the intellectual and emotional support of the people acknowledged here. All shortcomings are entirely mine.

First, many thanks to Danielle Kasprzak for responding to a random e-mail with a book proposal attached, for her acquisition of my weird little manuscript, and for moving it forward with such enthusiasm and support. Anne Carter at the University of Minnesota Press is editorial assistant extraordinaire. Anne's good humor, kindness, organization, and efficiency should be bottled and distributed across academia.

My parents, Nalini and Percy Silva, and my sister Shyamika and brother-in-law Kevin are the touchstone from which I judge the sanity and well-being of my life. I am who I am because of them, and they are woven into the very fabric of this project. It is good to be surrounded by their love and support, even from thousands of miles away. Kathleen Monje and Greg Smith have lovingly and generously supported me through many journeys, including this one, and I am thankful that they are part of my family.

I am indebted to the people who have shaped and supported my intellectual pursuits and who remain exemplary scholars and mentors: Lisa McLaughlin, Ronald Scott, and David Sholle at Miami University; Carl Bybee, Cheris Kramarae, Julianne Newton, H. Leslie Steeves, Janet Wasko, and Anita Weiss at the University of Oregon; and Norm Denzin, Isabel Molina Guzman, Cameron McCarthy, and Angharad Valdivia at the University of Illinois, Urbana-Champaign, have provided guidance for my academic endeavors at various junctures. I am deeply grateful for their efforts. Lawrence Grossberg—based on a chance meeting and a brief conversation at a national conference—let me guest edit a special issue of the journal *Cultural Studies* on brown. I thank Larry for his generosity and for his support for the project in those early days.

Much of this book was conceived and drafted during my time at Northeastern University. I am especially grateful to the Media Studies faculty—Marcus Breen, Murray Forman, P. David Marshall, David Monje, Joanne Morreale, Craig Robertson, and Vincent Rocchio—for their support during my time there. Also while at Northeastern, I was lucky enough to work with, and to be mentored by, Amilcar Antonio Barreto and Carla Kaplan. I thank them both for their support. As I was completing the book, I joined the faculty in the Department of Communication at the University of North Carolina (UNC) at Chapel Hill. My colleagues in the department set a high standard for rigorous scholarship and collegiality. I am fortunate to be part of this collective. I am grateful for the mentoring of Lawrence Grossberg, Ken Hillis, Steve May, Dennis Mumby, and Patricia Parker in the last few years. In addition, Renee Alexander-Craft, Sarah Dempsey, Christian Lundberg, Michael Palm, Tony Perucci, Sarah Sharma, and Neal Thomas, have supported and fed the intellectual labor of crafting this book. Much of the final versions of these chapters was finessed during a year of leave combing research, supported with a fellowship from the Institute of Arts and Humanities (IAH) at UNC. I am grateful to the university and the IAH for giving me time. A special thank-you to the wonderful cohort of colleagues, from across the campus, who sat at that magic table in the Fellows Room at the IAH.

I am lucky to call the following group of extraordinary people friends, and I thank them for all the many journeys—through multiple geographies—that they have taken (and continue to take) with me: Jon Arakaki, Christobel Asiedu, Gary Bartos, Joe Berkovitz, Vincent Canizaro, Mark Carrato, Bill Cassidy, Tanja Charrier, Samantha Clark, Anne Daniels, Richard Desmond, Susan Desmond, Damnath De Tissera, Tilina Dias, Kevin Dolan, Aisha Durham, Kelly Gates, Nathan Geer,

Dilusha Godamanne, Nuala Goonesekera, Sisira Goonesekera, Asanka Herath, Shaun Kohn, Betsy Kruger, Hillary Lake, Elizabeth Larson, Micky Lee, Marie Leger, Jennifer Lewis, Shoshana Magnet, Jane Marcellus, Jamie McGowan, Joan McWhorter, Jenny Moore, Pavithra Narayanan, Randy Nichols, Jina Park, Sepalika Perera, Christine Quail, Alan Russell, Derek Sanger, Chaamari Senanayake, Kirsten Sherk, Celiany Rivera Velazquez, Neidra Williams, and Wendy Wyatt. Tanja and Randy especially continue to feed my sense of humor and indulge my neuroses from afar.

Edie Shackelford was born during one of the darkest periods of my life. Her birth righted many wrongs, and I want to acknowledge with gratitude her parents, Erin Shackelford and Craig Robertson, for sharing her so generously with us. It allowed me to make peace with a new normal.

Sarah Sharma and Jeremy Packer—whether near or far—show me what is best about the family you choose.

I was fortunate to have David Monje help me think through this entire project—and read through numerous drafts—as I grappled with the idea of brown. His rigorous questioning of the concepts and language has made this book considerably better. That I am surrounded by his love and support is my very good fortune. Through Ruby Monje Silva I see the world as a better place, and I am profoundly grateful for the many gifts she brings to my life, and for reminding me every day that brown girls rule the world. I am proud to be her mother.

This book is dedicated to David and Ruby with so much love and gratitude for all they are.

Notes

Introduction

1　H.Res.775, 113th Congress.

2　Words that asked for *citizens* to *stand with* the Sikh community, which rhetorically reinforced difference.

3　By the evening of August 5, the incident was being referred to as an act of domestic terrorism, and the investigation was handed over from local authorities to the Federal Bureau of Investigations (FBI). The FBI defines *domestic terrorism* as "activities with the following three characteristics: Involve acts dangerous to human life that violate federal or state law; Appear intended (i) to intimidate or coerce a civilian population; (ii) to influence the policy of a government by intimidation or coercion; or (iii) to affect the conduct of a government by mass destruction, assassination or kidnapping; and Occur primarily within the territorial jurisdiction of the U.S."

4　This follows what Sara Ahmed (2011) calls the "fiction of character," where "we might be concerned more with what is behind an action, when this action is not one we are behind" (233). Until then, especially in the case of people like Page, whose racist views and military connections create some kind of existential crises for a pro-military, patriotic Americana, we are happy to ignore the obvious signs that indicate that the "out of character" *is* the character. Ahmed (2014) provides a critical way to understand the connections between will for and against, and the processes that span the space between these two, in *Willful Subjects.*

5　I say "overtly jolly" while acknowledging the significant critiques of American multiculturalism, both from the left and right, that have been documented over the last several decades. Here I follow the critics who point out that the "why can't we all get along" mentality ignores systemic inequalities and resulting social demarcations that seem generally to pervade American culture at large.

6   Consider the continuous call to report suspicious behaviors at public transportation terminals and the number of "Muslim-looking" individuals who have been refused access to flights because other passengers—presumably non-Muslim-looking ones—were uncomfortable.

7   Providing support for this, in *Our Biometric Future: Facial Recognition Technology and the Culture of Surveillance*, Kelly A. Gates (2011, 2) writes how, in November 2001, at a Senate hearing on terrorism and biometrics, Senator Dianne Feinstein asked, "How could a large group of coordinated terrorists operate for more than a year in the United States without being detected and then get on four different airliners in a single morning without being spotted? The answer to this question is that we could not identify them."

8   Starting in 2000, the U.S. Census has allowed respondents to mark more than one race category. In 2010, further amendments were made to distinguish "Hispanic" as an ethnicity rather than as a race. #BlackLivesMatter is an activist movement that began in the aftermath of Trayvon Martin's murder and steadily gained momentum as anti-Black violence and deaths, especially in the hands of law enforcement, became more public.

9   I discuss the murders of Trayvon Martin and Michael Brown in some detail in chapter 4.

10 Eric Garner died on July 17, 2014, in Staten Island, New York. Approached for selling cigarettes without tax stamps, officers tried to arrest him. According to witnesses, Garner slapped Officer Daniel Pantaleo's hand away, asking the officer to please not touch him, because the attempted arrest was unfounded. At that point, according to witnesses, including a friend of Garner's who was videotaping the events on his phone, Pantaleo, who had Garner's arm behind his back, put Garner in a choke hold, bringing Garner to his knees and eventually pushing his face into the sidewalk. Garner, an asthmatic, is repeatedly heard saying on the video that he can't breathe but is ignored by Pantaleo and other officers present, and the handcuffed Garner eventually lost consciousness. By the time the ambulance arrived several minutes later, Garner had been lying unconscious without CPR. He died of a heart attack on the way to the hospital. On August 1, the New York City coroner's office stated that Garner had died from "compression of neck (choke hold), compression of chest and prone positioning during physical restraint by police." Despite the videotaped evidence, and the coroner's report, a grand jury decided not to indict Pantaleo for Garner's death. The lack

of an indictment resulted in mass protests across the nation, including the Millions March NYC in Manhattan on December 12, 2014, where crowds, carrying placards that read "Black Lives Matter" and "We will not be silent," among others, chanted, "I can't breathe." In the months following, "I can't breathe" became a rallying cry among activists and their allies.

11   Andrea Smith herself has, in recent times, become a controversial figure for claiming Cherokee identity when she does not, in fact, have any Native American blood. Her desire to be "of color" speaks to the ways in which race becomes a form of "bartering" power in academia. Although I do not condone her race appropriations, I do recognize here her useful theoretical contribution to understanding how contemporary racisms are predicated on historical structures.

12   On the evening of June 17, 2015, Hurd, Jackson, Lance, Middleton Doctor, Pinckney, Sanders, Simmons, Coleman-Singleton, and Thompson were part of a Bible study group at the historical Emanuel African Methodist Episcopal Church in Charleston, South Carolina. The church is one of the oldest churches in the United States and a site of antislavery and civil rights organization. Among the people attending the study group was twenty-one-year-old Dylann Roof, a newcomer to the weekly meeting. According to eyewitnesses, at some point during the discussion, Roof stood up, took a gun out of his fanny pack, and aimed it at the group. When one member asked him why he was trying to kill churchgoers, Roof responded, "I have to do it. You rape our women and you're taking over our country. And you have to go." By the time Roof was done, he had murdered nine people. Following the shootings, Roof was apprehended in Shelby, North Carolina, and as of the time of writing is currently awaiting trial. Some attention has been paid to the differences in the arrests of Roof and Eric Garner: whereas Garner was put in a choke hold for "possibly" selling cigarettes without a tax stamp, news of Roof being taken to Burger King following his arrest were widely circulated in the news media. (http://www.charlotteobserver.com/news/local/article24952345.html). The Charleston murders initiated a much-needed discussion about race in the southern United States, especially in South Carolina, where the Confederate flag has been flown over the state house for more than half a century. In the weeks following, and even today, the flag remains a symbol of racism, as people rally against and around it in South Carolina as well as in other parts of the nation. As with most acts of violence, there is no closure, and they often lead to more (retaliatory) violence. On August 26, 2015, two television journalists, Alison Parker (aged twenty-four) and Adam Ward (aged twenty-seven), of the CBS affiliate WDBJ-TV in

Roanoke, Virginia, were brutally gunned down on live television by Vester Lee Flanagan, who accused them on a live Twitter upload as he shot them that they had been racist toward him and that the Charleston shootings were "a last straw." The senseless murders of Parker and Ward further added to the Charleston tragedy.

13 Bland (aged twenty-eight) was pulled over by Officer Brian Encinia on July 10, 2015, in Prairie View, Texas, for failing to signal a lane change. The patrol car dashcam video (which the police department released after public pressure, and then rereleased because of "technical glitches," when they were accused of editing the footage) shows the increasingly heated interactions between Bland and Encinia, with Encinia eventually arresting Bland. On July 13, 2015, Bland was found hanging in her cell. Her death added to the already growing number of protests and public calls for investigating anti-Black violence and police brutality.

14 The hashtag was started by feminist blogger Mikki Kendall, in response to the public support for Hugo Schwyzer. Following a public breakdown, on Twitter, Schwyzer, a prominent gender studies professor, admitted that he had had sexual relationships with several of his students and that had used his position as a self-proclaimed and prominent "male feminist" to shame feminists–women of color online. Following his admission, prominent pro-feminist websites and news outlets distanced themselves from Schwyzer. But, as Kendall notes, these sites and their "star" feminist correspondents were also complicit in popularizing Schwyzer's work, even as he openly targeted women of color during his heyday, and that it was not until Schwyzer himself admitted to his transgressions publicly that they started distancing themselves from him. Of this, Kendall writes, "It appeared that these feminists were . . . dismissing women of color (WOC) in favor of a brand of solidarity that centers on the safety and comfort of white women" (Kendall 2013).

1. What Is Brown?

1 Jasbir Puar (2007) argues that the torture of prisoners at Abu Ghraib has been constructed by the U.S. media and political leaders as "exceptional" or contrary to American culture, morals, and politics. She shows how President Bush's statement that the prison guards' "treatment does not reflect the *nature* of the American people" uses U.S. exceptionalism to dissociate the acts of violence and sexual torture performed from the prison guards who performed them. Such dissociation allows for the acts to seem the exception rather than the increasing rule.

2 As Michael Welch (2011) notes, that military order (rather than an executive

order) by George W. Bush to process terror suspects through military tribunals rather than through criminal courts emphasized the militarized aspects of the War on Terror that "reconfigured power" and "put into motion several unusual strategies to detain and prosecute terror suspects" (574–75).

3   Lugo-Lugo and Bloodsworth-Lugo (2010) map the ways in which the language of immigration, political rhetoric, and antigay language and policies were merged and "browned" in a sociopolitical "oven," where "official US rhetoric has created a space within which various categories of people (for example, terrorists, immigrants, and gays and lesbians) have undergone consistent and oftentimes overlapping processes of browning" (252).

4   This connection between popular political discourse and popular culture was beautifully demonstrated in a recent episode of the CBS drama *NCIS*, where, in an attempt to scare a Latino gang into admitting the location of their leader, the Unit *creates* a connection between the gang and al-Qaeda. Also, the USA PATRIOT Act, and the powers that it gives the military to do otherwise illegal interrogations, is evoked throughout the show.

5   *Bend It Like Beckham*, released in Britain in 2002 and in the United States in 2003, was celebrated as a coming-of-age film on both sides of the Atlantic with its tried-and-true formula of Bollywood glitz and Hollywood ending hailing its audience in a predictable manner. Furthermore, as Michael Giardina (2003) explains, the film was released in the weeks leading up to the 2002 FIFA World Cup, and Chadha herself has explained that this was no accident. With a release carefully calculated to coincide with popular sporting interests of that time; evoking Bollywood drama and color through the now ubiquitous Indian wedding scenes; and setting up a proven formula of East versus West, gender discrimination that is overcome, and (seemingly) color-based racial politics that are easy to understand, *Bend It Like Beckham* was destined to succeed. The film tells the story of Jesminder "Jess" Bhamra, an eighteen-year-old of East African–Punjabi parents living in Southall, London—the largest Punjabi neighborhood outside of India. Jess idealizes British soccer star David Beckham, and her idolization, and interest in football, is considered unbefitting to a "good Indian girl" by her orthodox parents. Jess's mother wants her to learn to cook and help organize her sister Pinky's wedding, and her father wants her to focus on her A-levels and become a lawyer. Catching a quick game in the park with the boys in her neighborhood between running errands for her mother is the closest Jess gets to playing the game, until she is spotted by Juliette Paxton, who invites her to join the Hounslow Harriers. Jess is unable to turn away from this opportunity, and the story unfolds as soccer becomes the signifier of the divide

between Jess's British self (read progressive) and her parents' Indian selves (read conservative). She is forced to lie to her family to pursue her dreams, and much drama and many mishaps ensue. The film takes on an added measure of tension when we find out that an American scout from Santa Clara, California, is looking to recruit players. The possibility of moving to a country where a professional soccer league for women already exists becomes first Juliette's dream and, later, Jess's. What keeps the viewer entranced is the way both girls "overcome" the challenges to following their dreams, which are realized by the denouement. If *Bend It Like Beckham,* as Giardina posited, overlooked the racial politics of the United Kingdom and instead celebrated what he calls a "stylish hybridity," it did so partly by transcending the murky politics of the multicultural mayhem of the United Kingdom, moving its celebration of empowerment and possibility to the United States. Hailing America as the ultimate symbol of freedom, the "stylish hybridity" created in Britain finds a home in the United States. The image of America as the land of Mia Hamm, the (now defunct) WUSA, and soccer fields "with corner flags and changing rooms" with limitless potential runs a covert parallel to the overt reality of Jess's and Jules's lives in a sexist and racist Britain. Throughout the film, America is evoked as the "after" to Britain's "before," but this is made most visible through Jess's education in the wonders of American freedom through Jules:

> JULES: I want to play professionally.
>
> JESS: Wow! Can you really do that? I mean like a job?
>
> JULES: Sure! Not really here, but you can in America. They've got a pro league with new stadiums and everything.

As Jess gasps in wonder at the possibilities of America, we are, through this conversation, first introduced to the wonders of the American Dream that has moved beyond the boundaries of the United States. In this conversation, it is not only America but American sports culture that is celebrated as "freedom." This elevation of sporting freedom with American values is not unusual and, indeed, is a staple of U.S. culture. As Roger Rosenblatt (2003) notes, "there probably are countries where the people are as crazy about sports as they are in America, but I doubt that there is any place where the meaning and design of the country is so evident in its games. In many odd ways, America is its sports, central to the country's enthusiasms." Chadha borrows liberally from this belief and sprinkles it throughout the film. The American scout who lingers in the background, unseen, but more present than any physical representation could have possibly achieved, is evoked over and over again and is even used as incentive when Jules begs Jess to play in the final game—"you can't miss the final game, Jess, there's going to be an American scout there." In this instance, sporting values of camaraderie, team loyalty, and "just playing the game" are irrelevant; it becomes instead about moving beyond the miniscule successes of Britain (playing women's soccer in clubs, no professional league) into the larger successes of America (soccer scholarship, professional soccer league). Toward the end of the film, this celebration of American freedom is validated by the ultimate victim of Britain's racism as Mr. Bhamra declares, "When these bloody English cricket players threw me out of their clubs like a dog I never complained. On the contrary, I vowed I would never play again. Who suffered? Me. But I don't want Jessie to suffer. I don't want her to make the same mistakes that her father made of accepting life, accepting situations. I want her to fight and I want her to win." The comparison between cricket and an old Britain and soccer and a new America cannot be overlooked.

6   There are, of course, a number of laws governing immigration to the United States from the early nineteenth and twentieth centuries. Although they are important, the focus here is on more recent laws that deploy brown as a "new" threat to the cultural, religious, and economic stability of the United States.

7   The recent anti-LGBTQ "bathroom bill," known as HB2, passed by the North Carolina Legislature in March 2016, is a good example of this. The bill— passed in response to an antidiscrimination ordinance passed by Charlotte City Council scheduled to go into effect on April 1, 2016—makes it illegal for individuals to use restrooms not matching their birth sex or sex that is on their birth certificate. When passing this in a costly special meeting, the state legislature argued that the bill was to protect women and children from predatory men who would use the Charlotte city ordinance to attack women in restrooms by pretending to be transgendered. The bill also makes it illegal to establish a minimum wage above the state minimum wage and contains language that prevents cities from establishing their own, more progressive antidiscrimination laws. Essentially, this law moves from actual and meta-phorical brown body to brown body to brown body—sexual, economic, and gendered—to define and control the subordinate.

8   Alsultany notes how television series like 24 juxtapose a "terrorist" Muslim with a "good" Muslim who is loyal to America, which exemplifies the myth of the "fair and balanced" coverage of Muslims in popular culture.

9   Edwin McDowell (1990) noted in the New York Times that "the publishing broadsides against Japan coincide with public opinion polls showing that

Americans are reporting increasingly negative feelings toward Japan." As with previous iterations of these economic and political shifts, the cultural and popular representations mirrored these anxieties and gave voice—and credence—to the xenophobia. Speaking to this, Narelle Morris (2001, 58) notes that most works of popular fiction "on Japan" in the early 1990s, with the exception of the pessimistic Rising Sun, complete their narratives with a cathartic downfall of Japan and the Japanese and an equally cathartic ascendancy of the United States or, at the very least, a return to the previous status quo. There is thus an overall fictional vindication of supra-Orientalism: Japan's economic superpower status is very open to interpretation; Japan and the Japanese most likely do have some nefarious intent, but their strategy is not flawless; and a resounding patriotic display of American resourcefulness and tenacity will prevail. Thus multiple and divergent "Truths"— American exceptionalism, Fu Manchu–like Asians, and American tenacity that eventually triumphs—converged with implicit racial biases in both fictive and nonfictive contexts as a response to these fears. In addition, the individuals affected by Japan's economic interventions were implicitly White and working and/or middle class.

10 The Dotbusters was a hate group (made up of Latino men) located in Jersey City, New Jersey. They terrorized and attacked South Asians in fall 1987 with numerous attacks and beatings, including the death of Navroze Mody, who died of wounds inflicted during his beating. The lack of publicity around the attacks could be attributed to the fact that this was "brown-on-brown" violence and therefore not really newsworthy or of interest to a larger audience.

11 This kind of thinking is unwittingly reproduced even within contexts that are attempting to educate or think past this. Case in point is the much-lauded *Beyond Bollywood: Indian Americans Shape the Nation* exhibit at the National Museum of Natural History (of the Smithsonian Institution) in Washington, D.C., which I recently visited. Organized by the Smithsonian Asian Pacific American Center, the exhibit, curated by Masum Momaya, displays a vast array of artifacts and objects to show the contribution that Indians have made to/in American culture since the 1800s. While there is much to be admired about the exhibition, there is also the reproduction of a commodity identity to garner legitimacy. For example, Momaya "wanted a title that people have a reference for, but this is not about Bollywood ... though its color and design draw on Bollywood aesthetics. 'The main wall colors are mango, magenta and bright plum. . . . Our culture is vibrant, so we wanted the gallery to reflect that'" (Parker 2014). A walk around the exhibit

itself reveals a theme of celebratory framed within achievement and success, which belies the realities of more contemporary life. Only one area showcases the post-9/11 realities. Speaking to a section that highlights the "professional" contributions of Indians to American life—walls of doctors, lawyers, and engineers are bookended by replicas of taxicabs and motel entrances—Momaya notes that "we went for the most stereotypical ones with the idea of dismantling the stereotypes." This stereotypical representation is juxtaposed against another stereotype: the ornate glamour of Indian clothing. The central piece of the entire exhibit is the heavily sequined and needleworked dress created by Indian American designer Naeem Khan and worn by Michelle Obama at the 2012 Governors Dinner. According to Momaya, the inclusion of the dress is significant because "Khan comes from a long line of embroiderers and designers, stretching back to the Mughal Courts in India, and this particular gown incorporates embroidery techniques passed down to him on a classic American silhouette. It is literally an example of Indian Americanness being woven into the fabric of the garment" (Smithsonian 2014).

2. Un-American

1 In *Regulating Aversion: Tolerance in the Age of Identity and Empire*, Brown (2006) lays out the ways that tolerance and discourses of tolerance work within a system of a Foucauldian notion governmentality, where "the call for tolerance, the invocation of tolerance, and the attempt to instantiate tolerance are all signs of identity production and identity management in the context of orders of stratification or marginalization in which the production, the management, and the context themselves are disavowed. In short, they are signs of a buried order of politics" (14).

2 I say this because there is no way that there can be a definitive concept of home, or motherland, or any of the notions that we have universal definitions for within various cultures.

3 For example, SikhNet (http://www.sikhnet.com/) has an entire web page of downloadable posters that the organization produced immediately after 9/11, so that Sikhs could either display these posters at their homes or places of business or share them as educational materials. The posters, which feature the American flag, juxtaposed with various images of Sikhs, include lines like "Sikhs from all parts of the world join America in the fight against terrorism. United We Stand" and "Stand Together in Prayer. God Bless America."

4 Espiritu (1992, 10–11) writes that, though "one possible explanation for the development of panethnicity in modern states is the competitive advantage

of large-scale identities," it is also a product of the constructions of ethnic categorizations by the state, where individuals "broaden their identity to conform to the more inclusive ethnic designation," based on shared experiences including oppressions, deprivation, and benefits. What is interesting to note is that what happened among the South Asian and South Asian American community was the "(re)tribalization" or "nationalizing" of their ethnic selves—as American by not being Muslim or Sikh, or being Christian—after 9/11.

5 John Dunham Kelly uses "fast patriotism" to critique the connection between the technologies of flag displays on cars and the metaphorically similar technologies of war that resulted in untold horrors and casualties across the world.

6 Burman (2010, 204) defines affective recircuitry as "a crisis-based realignment of vectors of trust and suspicion in all directions—residents' new psychogeographic mappings, to borrow the Situationists' term—that is nourished by political and media fear-mongering," where each imagines the other as suspicious based on these intersecting anxieties.

7 Ten months into her reign, Vanessa Williams was forced to resign as Miss America when *Penthouse* magazine bought and published nude photos of her. She was replaced by Suzette Charles, who was also African American.

8 Names have been changed.

9 Not his real name.

10 An acronym for "American-born confused Desi."

3. Expulsion and What Is Not

1 Literally: he is currently presenting a bill on the transgender use of restrooms.

2 Franny Tolchuck works together with Justin's guidance counselor to recruit a (White) good-looking European exchange student who will attract friends for the socially awkward Justin—who is number eight on the "list of most bangable girls" in his high school, five spots below his fifteen-year-old sister.

3 Apu has become an increasingly controversial figure among South Asian Americans, largely because Apu, after almost twenty-five years, is the longest-running South Asian brown character in American popular culture and has defined what it means to be Indian *for* America. Apu is voiced by Hank Azaria—a Greek American—who models Apu's voice after the character of Indian Hrundi V. Bakshi from Blake Edwards's *The Party* (1968, starring Peter Sellers) (Rao 2013). Sellers's impersonation of Bakshi, in all his coffee-stained glory, created a lifelong rift between Sellers and award-winning Bengali director Satyajit Ray, who visited the set of *The Party* and was unimpressed by the racist caricature (Lewis 1995). Ironically, Apu is

named after Ray's *Apu Trilogy,* but as comedian Hari Kondabolu notes, "think about Satyajit Ray's work and how beautiful and complicated those characters are. We don't get that from this Apu." In his standup routine, Kondabolu also says of Azaria during a 2012 performance on the FX series *Totally Biased with W. Kamau Bell* that he is "a White guy doing an impression of a White guy making fun of my father"—or, as Manish Vij (2007) notes in *The Guardian,* Azaria, a "Greek-American, is a brown man doing a white man doing a brown man."

4   This is succinctly argued by Aimee Marie Carillo Rowe (2004), who writes in "Whose 'America'? The Politics of Rhetoric and Space in the Formation of U.S. Nationalism" of the abuse of Abner Louima at the hands of the New York City Police Department in 1997 that "the bodily form of Louima's abuse . . . ruptures white Western codes of civility so essential to the hegemony of whiteness. In such moments, the brutality of white hegemony leaks, and the humanitarian basis of white supremacy, on which the U.S. national body is founded, is momentarily called into question. The contradictions that erupt in such cases are contained through a surgical removal of the cancerous cells, so that the larger white body politic may remain intact. The ongoing abuse of black and brown bodies is the unspoken subtext of this white body politic—a set of discursive and material practices designed to keep us in our place: a largely indentured population whose labor sustains the nation, but whose voices, needs, and basic human rights must be subordinated to the needs of U.S. capitalism" (115–16).

5   The ballot was abbreviated as follows for the voters: "This measure amends the State Constitution. It changes a section that deals with the courts of this state. It would amend Article 7, Section 1. It makes courts rely on federal and state law when deciding cases. It forbids courts from considering or using international law. It forbids courts from considering or using Sharia Law. International law is also known as the law of nations. It deals with the conduct of international organizations and independent nations, such as countries, states and tribes. It deals with their relationship with each other. It also deals with some of their relationships with persons. The law of nations is formed by the general assent of civilized nations. Sources of international law also include international agreements, as well as treaties. Sharia Law is Islamic law. It is based on two principal sources, the Koran and the teaching of Mohammed."

6   I define *armchair anthropology* as that condition where audience members become cultural authorities based on their consumption of mediated experiences about "foreign" spaces.

7   A recent cinematic example of this continuum would be *Looking for Comedy*

in the Muslim World, where comedian Albert Brooks (starring as himself) is asked by the U.S. government to visit India and Pakistan on a mission to find out what "makes Muslims laugh." The film takes the viewer, vis-à-vis Brooks, from the boardrooms of American politics to call centers in India, then to Pakistani terror cells, before the U.S. government eventually extracts the hapless Brooks as tensions rise between India and Pakistan because of suspicions around the comedian and his visit.

4. Blackness in Brown Times

1 Long before the rape allegations and scandal that have now become synonymous with Bill Cosby, *The Cosby Show* introduced America to what hardworking African Americans could achieve. The show revolved around the lives of wealthy gynecologist Cliff Huxtable, his lawyer wife, Claire, and their five children, who lived in Brooklyn, New York. *The Cosby Show* was applauded by critics and audiences for showing Black families in a positive light, though academics questioned the role that shows like *Cosby* played/play in perpetuating the myth of meritocracy for historically marginalized populations (e.g., Jhally and Lewis 1992; Gray 1995). Even after the show ended, and continuing until the recent allegations, Bill Cosby continued to make public commentaries about how African Americans needed to start working harder and stop blaming White America for their problems. For example, in 2004, at an event commemorating *Brown v. Board of Education,* Cosby declared that "the lower economic people are not holding up their end in this deal. These people are not parenting. They are buying things for kids—$500 for sneakers for what? And won't spend $200 for 'Hooked on Phonics.'" And later on: "For me there is a time . . . when we have to turn the mirror around. . . . It is almost analgesic to talk about what the white man is doing against us. And it keeps a person frozen in their seat, it keeps you frozen in your hole you're sitting in." Comments like these made Cosby popular among White conservatives who fully believed that enough opportunities had been provided to, and squandered by, the Black population. Because Cosby became by extension Dr. Huxtable, his character's successes were seen as evidence for the accuracy of Cosby's claims of meritocracy and Black idleness. The impact of the show as well as Cosby's comments have been widely discussed (Jhally and Lewis 1991; Gray 1995; Coates 2014), especially in terms of the ways they both flatten complex race issues in the United States. In their book titled *Enlightened Racism: The Cosby Show, Audiences, and the Myth of the American Dream,* Sut Jhally and Justin Lewis (1992) argue that the Huxtable family—successful, wealthy, and reflecting White

social values—while providing nonstereotypical representations of African Americans in the media (who often portrayed/portray people of color as poor, violent, and deviant), nonetheless exculpated White Americans from their role in creating the conditions that continued to marginalize Black Americans in everyday life.

2   As I've noted in chapter 2, such success is also not rewarded. As I've documented throughout, South and East Asians and Asian Americans are often seen as interlopers and a drain on American jobs and opportunities.

3   Zimmerman claimed that Martin was dressed in a hoodie and "looked suspicious"; Michael Brown, according to his shooter, Darren Wilson, looked like a demon: he "had the most aggressive face. That's the only way I can describe it, it looks like a demon, that's how angry he looked," and "when I grabbed him the only way I can describe it is I felt like a 5-year-old holding onto Hulk Hogan" (Wilson is six foot four inches, and Brown was six foot five inches). According to *Slate* contributor Jamelle Bouie (2014), "Wilson describes the 'black brute,' a stock figure of white supremacist rhetoric in the lynching era of the late 19th and early 20th centuries. . . . That image never went away; it lingers in crack-era stories of superpowered addicts and teen-aged superpredators, as well as rhetoric around other victims of police brutality."

4   Darron T. Smith, quoted here, had one of the most thoughtful responses to the controversy. Many just called out Lemon as a self-loathing racist, and many of the online commentaries and responses revolved around a right/wrong answer to the "Black problem." Smith, in his article in the *Huffington Post*, noted the comparisons between Lemon's advice and similar advice from Bill Cosby more than three decades earlier, when Cosby asked Black people to "stop complaining."

5   See chapter 3 for a discussion of Penn and his tweet.

6   I did muse briefly on the irony of hearing Stevens's song as the anthem for this historic moment—the music of an Englishman who is no longer allowed in the United States because he changed his name to Yusuf Islam (and also changed his religion). In 2004, while arriving into the United States for a meeting with Dolly Parton, Islam was detained and returned to the United Kingdom for being on the TSA's "no fly list" for possibly funding terrorist organizations through his philanthropic work in Palestine. Islam denied any wrongdoing and eventually, after diplomatic intervention, and also in response to public outcry, Islam was allowed to reenter the country in 2006.

7   An act to enforce the fifteenth amendment to the Constitution of the United States and for other purposes, August 6, 1965, Enrolled Acts and Resolutions

of Congress, 1789, General Records of the United States Government, Record Group 11, National Archives, http://ourdocuments.gov/doc.php?doc=100.

8   The state of North Carolina signed this into the state constitution by introducing and passing House Bill 589 in 2013. House Bill 589 effectively "shortens the early voting period by a full week, eliminates same-day registration, requires strict forms of voter ID, prevents out-of-precinct ballots from being counted, expands the ability to challenge voters at the polls, and ends a successful pre-registration program for 16- and 17-year-olds" and "has a disproportionate impact on North Carolina's African-American and Latino voters" (advancement project). In July 2015, the bill was contested in *NAACP v. McRory*, with the plaintiffs stating that "this lawsuit seeks to protect and preserve the voting rights of North Carolina citizens—rights imperiled by the passage of new legislation that imposes unjustified and discriminatory electoral burdens on large segments of the state's population and will cause the denial, dilution, and abridgement of African-Americans' fundamental right to vote"; http://b.3cdn.net/advancement/5c1d651b4df32b320a_jtm6bx3u8.pdf. Reverend William Barber, president of the North Carolina chapter of the NAACP and one of the plaintiffs in the case, called the battle over voter registration and the court case "our Selma," referring to the 1965 Selma to Montgomery Voting Rights Marches led by civil rights activists, including Dr. Martin Luther King Jr.

9   Here Ahmad is retriangulating the argument by Toni Morrison that immigrants are not fully American until they learn and practice racism toward African Americans (102). Ahmad argues that after 9/11, African Americans were able to circumvent, at least on the surface, racial subordination by separating their identities from those whose bodies were more "clearly" marked as brown terrorists, such as Arabs and South Asians, or in the case of conflation between brown categories, as Cacho (2012) notes, between brown terrorism and illegal immigration.

Conclusion

1   This case of "mistaken identity" also gestures to the way that Native Americans are almost entirely absent from popular and political culture. In a recent article on the systemic erasure and ongoing practices of the legislative genocide of Native Americans, Angelique Townsend EagleWoman (2015, 424) writes, "For American Indians, real consequences flow from these subjugation myths. . . . As one elementary social studies book summed up, 'Native Americans lost the animals they used for food, lost their land, caught diseases, and were sent to reservations.'" She goes on to state that "by teach-

ing this type of erroneous closed chapter summary to schoolchildren, the present day lives of tribal peoples are absent from the mainstream knowledge base," and that "while mainstream United States citizens believe the chapter was closed and they have little contemporary information on the trust status imposed on American Indians and Alaska Natives, the United States Congress claims and exercises plenary power over tribal peoples and the power is upheld by the United States Supreme Court" (439).

2 Ahmed (2008, 121–37) writes of the ways in which conversations of multiculturalism and happiness are intertwined in the sociopolitical landscape, where political and popular actors predicate happiness on being around homogenous communities (thereby avoiding conflicts of difference); at the same time, there is the call for and the institution of multiculturalism through a shared nationalist ethos. She writes, "We could say that happiness is promised as a return for loyalty to the nation, where loyalty is expressed as 'giving' diversity to the nation through playing its game" (129).

3 For example, brown becomes a way of mapping an identity that produces a corresponding image of terrorist, Muslim, turban, and so on, that justifies the random searches, the deplaning of passengers, and other actions to "protect" nonbrown people. This is similar to the underlying homophobia of the "family values" focus of the George W. Bush administration, where God, country, and family were used as ways to validate certain unions over others.

4 In her discussion of anthrax, Egan (2002, 15–26) notes how biological warfare is introduced as something "new" and "terrifying"—despite that the United States has used biological warfare for years—that can happen to anyone, from political entities to Hollywood stars. Because of the way it's discursively produced, and the corresponding fear it induces in the general public, we accept the administrative structures that are put in place to "protect" us from such dangers.

5 Almost following in the footsteps of Kumar in *Harold and Kumar* (see chapter 3), Larry Bird is a slacker-genius. When Larry's father cuts him off financially (for refusing to return to their home planet), Larry starts working in a coffee shop to support the family, even though he is shown to be a mathematical genius in other episodes, including one where he helps Marty finish a spreadsheet for work to meet a deadline. Aliens, wherever they come from, apparently lack the work ethic the Americans have.

6 Connected to this particular performance around brown is also the general narrative arc for the entire series. The aliens, as hyperintelligent, represent the general notions of overachieving immigrants to the United States, but

the inability of the parents, Larry and Jackie (the former works in a coffee shop, the latter in fast food), to assimilate and therefore live up to their full potential in the promised land neutralizes the anxieties about immigration and aliens (both from outer space and from other countries).

7   Hicks's biological daughter, a devout Christian, who has long been estranged from him, stated that she cut off ties with her father after he became abusive toward her religious beliefs over social media.

8   According to the *New York Times,* Hicks "was undeniably obsessed with parking. Each unit got permits for up to two cars, but only one assigned spot.... The housing association allowed residents to have improperly parked cars towed. But Mr. Hicks abused this power until the housing association asked him to stop" (Katz 2015).

9   http://www.huffingtonpost.com/2015/03/06/unc-shooting-hate-crime_n_6801582.html.

10 On June 22, 2015, Margaret Talbot published an article in *The New Yorker* titled "The Story of a Hate Crime." Months after the murders, and with little public news of Hicks or any conversation of pursuing the events as a hate crime within the legal system, Talbot's article was a reminder for a public that seemed to have forgotten about the horrific loss of lives. In the same article, Talbot also summarized the socioeconomic differences between Hicks and the other residents at the condominiums, which became public news: "Most of the young residents of Finley Forest were on an upward arc in life. Hicks was not. In the mid-aughts, he had been laid off from a job as an auto-parts salesman." At the time of the shooting, "he was taking classes at Durham Tech Community College, in the hope of becoming a paralegal." Despite doing well at school (as the college itself has reported), Talbot also noted the financial troubles that Hicks had experienced: "He'd recently received a summons to appear in court and pay fourteen thousand dollars in child support for his other daughter, who was ten."

Bibliography

Agamben, Giorgio. 1998. *Homo Sacer: Sovereign Power and Bare Life.* Stanford, Calif.: Stanford University Press.

Agnew, Vijay. 2005. *Diaspora, Memory, and Identity: A Search for Home.* Toronto: University of Toronto Press.

Ahmad, Muneer. 2002. "Homeland Insecurities: Racial Violence the Day after September 11." *Social Text,* no. 72: 101–15.

Ahmed, Sara. 2008. "Multiculturalism and the Promise of Happiness." *New Formations* 63, no. 1: 121–37.

———. 2011. "Willful Parts: Problem Characters or the Problem of Character." *New Literary History* 42, no. 2: 231–53.

———. 2014. *Willful Subjects.* Durham, N.C.: Duke University Press.

Alsultany, Evelyn. 2012. *Arabs and Muslims in the Media: Race and Representation after 9/11.* New York: New York University Press.

American Civil Liberties Union. 2013. "Letter to Mississippi Department of Transportation." https://www.aclu.org/sites/default/files/assets/letter_to_dot.pdf.

———. 2015a. "Fix FISA—End Warrantless Wiretapping." https://www.aclu.org/fix-fisa-end-warrantless-wiretapping?redirect=nationalsecurity/fix-fisa-end-warrantless-wiretapping.

———. 2015b. "Voting Rights." http://aclu-nh.org/issues/voting-rights/.

Appadurai, Arjun. 1990. "Disjuncture and Difference in the Global Cultural Economy." *Theory, Culture, and Society* 7, no. 2: 295–310.

Appiah, Anthony Kwame. 2006. *Cosmopolitanism: Ethics in a World of Strangers.* New York: W. W. Norton.

Atwood, Blair. 2013. "Judge to Sikh Man: Remove 'That Rag.'" https://www.aclu.org/blog/judge-sikh-man-remove-rag.

AZNTV. n.d. Homepage. http://www.azntv.com/.

Barreto, Amílcar Antonio, and Richard L. O'Bryant. 2014. *American Identity in the Age of Obama.* New York: Routledge/Taylor and Francis.

Barris, Kenya, and Lindsey Shockley. 2015. "Martin Luther sKiing Day." *Black-ish,* season 1, episode 12. Directed by Stuart McDonald. Aired January 14.

Bauman, Zygmunt. (2004) 2008. *Identity.* Cambridge: Polity Press.

Bayoumi, Moustafa. 2008. *How Does It Feel to Be a Problem? Being Young and Arab in America.* New York: Penguin Press.

———. 2012. "Did Islamophobia Fuel the Oak Creek Massacre?" *The Nation,* August 10. http://www.thenation.com/article/169322/did-islamophobia-fuel-oak-creek-massacre.

BBC. 1999. "World: Americas Six Cubans to Stay in US." http://news.bbc.co.uk/2/hi/americas/381572.stm.

Benedict, Burton. 1983. *The Anthropology of World's Fairs: San Francisco's Panama Pacific International Exposition of 1915.* Berkeley, Calif.: Lowie Museum of Anthropology.

Bhabha, Homi K. 1990. *Nation and Narration.* London: Routledge.

Binder, Matt. 2013. "Racist Americans Whine That First Indian American Miss America is . . . Arab and/or Muslim?" *Public Shaming,* September 15. http://publicshaming.tumblr.com/post/61428932482/racist-americans-whine-that-first-indian-american.

Bloomberg, Michael. 2013. "Michael Bloomberg: 'Stop and Frisk' Keeps New York Safe." *Washington Post,* August 18. https://www.washingtonpost.com/opinions/michael-bloomberg-stop-and-frisk-keeps-new-york-safe/2013/08/18/8d4cd8c4-06cf-11e3-9259-e2aafe5a5f84_story.html.

Borders, William. 1976. "India's Economy Is Heading from Rags to Riches." *New York Times,* December 21.

Bouie, Jamelle. 2014. "Michael Brown Wasn't a Superhuman Demon." *Slate,* November 6. http://www.slate.com/articles/news_and_politics/politics/2014/11/darren_wilson_s_racial_portrayal_of_michael_brown_as_a_superhuman_demon.1.html.

Bourdieu, Pierre. 1991. *Language and Symbolic Power.* Malden, Mass.: Blackwell.

Brewer, Jan. 2011. "Letter to the Secretary of State, Ken Bennett." http://www.azleg.state.az.us/govlettr/50leg/1R/HB2230.pdf.

Brown, Wendy. 2001. *Politics out of History.* Princeton, N.J.: Princeton University Press.

———. 2005. *Edgework: Critical Essays on Knowledge and Politics.* Princeton, N.J.: Princeton University Press.

———. 2006. *Regulating Aversion: Tolerance in the Age of Identity and Empire.* Princeton, N.J.: Princeton University Press.

Buchanan, Ian. 2010. *A Dictionary of Critical Theory.* Oxford: Oxford University Press.

Burman, Jenny. 2010. "Suspects in the City: Browning the 'Not Quite' Canadian Citizen." *Cultural Studies* 24, no. 2: 200–213.

Bush, George W. 2001a. "President Discusses War on Terrorism." http://georgewbush -whitehouse.archives.gov/news/releases/2001/11/20011108-13.html.

———. 2001b. "Remarks by the President to Airline Employees O'Hare International Airport, Chicago, Illinois on September 27, 2001." http://georgewbush -whitehouse.archives.gov/infocus/ramadan/islam.html.

———. 2001c. "Statement by the President in His Address to the Nation." http:// georgewbush-whitehouse.archives.gov/news/releases/2001/09/20010911-16 .html.

———. 2002a. "The Department of Homeland Security." http://www.dhs.gov/ xlibrary/assets/book.pdf.

———. 2002b. "Remarks by President George W. Bush in a Statement to Reporters during a Meeting with U.N. Secretary General Kofi Annan, the Oval Office, Washington, DC, November 13." http://georgewbush-whitehouse.archives .gov/infocus/ramadan/islam.html.

Butler, Judith. 1990. *Gender Trouble: Feminism and the Subversion of Identity.* New York: Routledge.

———. 2004. *Undoing Gender.* New York: Routledge.

Cacho, Lisa Marie. 2012. *Social Death: Racialized Rightlessness and the Criminalization of the Unprotected.* New York: New York University Press.

Chadha, Gurinder, and Guljit Bindra. 2002. *Bend It Like Beckham.* United States: Kintop Pictures.

Chandrasekhar, Charu A. 2003. "Flying While Brown: Federal Civil Rights Remedies to Post-9/11 Airline Racial Profiling of South Asians." *Asian American Law Journal* 10, no. 2: 215–52.

Chitnis, Deepak. 2013. "Two Andhra-Origin Girls in the Finals, One Becomes Miss America." *The American Bazaar,* September 16. http://www.american bazaaronline.com/2013/09/16/two-andhra-origin-girls-finals-one-becomes -miss-america/.

———. 2014. "Balbir Singh Sodhi's Turban on Mannequin at Smithsonian Exhibition Reminder of Discrimination Community Has Faced." *The American Bazaar,* February 26. http://www.americanbazaaronline.com/2014/02/26/balbir-singh -sodhis-turban-mannequin-smithsonian-exhibition-reminder-discrimination -community-faced/.

CNN Wire Staff. 2012. "Military, Music Marked Temple Suspect's Path to Wisconsin." August 7. http://www.cnn.com/2012/08/06/us/wisconsin-shooting -suspect/.

Coates, Ta-Nehisi. 2014. "The Cosby Show." *The Atlantic*, November 19. http://www
.theatlantic.com/entertainment/archive/2014/11/the-cosby-show/382891/.

———. 2015. *Between the World and Me*. New York: Spiegel and Grau.

Conway, Gordan. 1997. *Islamophobia, Its Features and Dangers*. London: Runnymede Trust.

Dave, Shilpa, Pawan Dhingra, Sunaina Maira, Partha Mazumdar, Lavina Dhingra
Shankar, and Jaideep Singh. 2000. "De-privileging Positions: Indian Ameri-
cans, South Asian Americans, and the Politics of Asian American Studies."
Journal of Asian American Studies 3, no. 1: 67–100.

Dawkins, Richard. 2001. *Time to Stand Up*. Madison, Wisc.: Freedom from Religion
Foundation. https://ffrf.org/news/timely-topics/item/14035-time-to-stand-up.

de Certeau, Michel. 1984. *The Practice of Everyday Life*. Berkeley: University of
California Press.

Derrida, Jacques. 1978. *Writing and Difference*. Chicago: University of Chicago
Press.

———. 2002. *Negotiations: Interventions and Interviews, 1971–2001*. Translated by
Elizabeth Rottenberg. Stanford, Calif.: Stanford University Press.

———. 2003. "Autoimmunity: Real and Symbolic Suicides." In *Philosophy in a
Time of Terror: Dialogues with Jürgen Habermas and Jacques Derrida*, edited
by Giovanna Borradori, 85–136. Chicago: University of Chicago Press.

de Tocqueville, Alexander. 1945. *Democracy in America*. New York: Alfred A. Knopf.

Du Bois, Joshua. 2012. "First Lady Michelle Obama Visits Sikh Community in
Wisconsin, August 24." http://www.whitehouse.gov/blog/2012/08/24/first-lady
-michelle-obama-visits-sikh-community-wisconsin.

Du Bois, W. E. B. 2011. *The Sociological Souls of Black Folk: Essays*. Lanham, Md.:
Lexington Books.

Dyer, Richard. 1984. "Stereotyping." In *Gays and Film*. New York: Zoetrope.

———. 2002. *The Matter of Images: Essays on Representations*. London: Routledge.

EagleWoman, Angelique Townsend. 2015. "The Ongoing Traumatic Experience
of Genocide for American Indians and Alaska Natives in the United States:
The Call to Recognize Full Human Rights as Set Forth in the UN Declaration
on the Rights of Indigenous Peoples." *American Indian Law Journal* 3, no. 2:
424–51.

Egan, R. Danielle. 2002. "Anthrax." In *Collateral Language: A User's Guide to
America's New War*, edited by John Collins, 15–26. New York: New York University Press.

Elias, Marilyn. 2012. "Sikh Temple Killer Wade Michael Page Radicalized in Army."
Intelligence Report, no. 148. http://www.splcenter.org/get-informed/intelligence
-report/browse-all-issues/2012/winter/massacre-in-wisconsin.

Ernst, Carl W. 2013. *Islamophobia in America: The Anatomy of Intolerance.* New York: Palgrave Macmillan.

Espiritu, Yen Le. 1992. *Asian American Panethnicity: Bridging Institutions and Identities.* Philadelphia: Temple University Press.

Esposito, Roberto. 2008. *Bíos: Biopolitics and Philosophy.* Minneapolis: University of Minnesota Press.

Federal Bureau of Investigation. 2002. "Unified Crime Report." https://www2.fbi.gov/ucr/01hate.pdf.

Feldman, Alan. 2001. "Philoctetes Revisited: White Public Space and the Political Geography of Public Safety." *Social Text* 19, no. 3: 57–89.

Fogelman, Dan, and Scott Weinger. 2014. "Balle Balle." *The Neighbors,* season 2, episode 17. Directed by John Fortenberry. Aired March 7.

Foucault, Michel. 1979. *Discipline and Punish: The Birth of the Prison.* New York: Vintage Books.

Foucault, Michel, and Paul Rabinow. 1984. *The Foucault Reader.* New York: Pantheon Books.

Gandhi, Lakshmi. 2013. "Kal Penn Tweets in Support of Stop and Frisk and We Become Really Sad." *The Aerogram,* August 14. http://theaerogram.com/kal-penn-tweets-in-support-of-stop-and-frisk-and-we-become-really-sad/.

Garfield, Bob. 2007. "7-Eleven's Simpsons Movie Stunt: Brilliant Cross Promotion in Advertising Age." *Advertising Age,* July 9. http://adage.com/article/ad-review/7-eleven-s-simpsons-movie-stunt-brilliant-cross-promotion/119062/.

Gates, Kelly. 2011. *Our Biometric Future: Facial Recognition Technology and the Culture of Surveillance.* New York: New York University Press.

Giardina, Michael. 2003. "'Bending It Like Beckham' in the Global Popular: Stylish Hybridity, Performativity, and the Politics of Representation." *Journal of Sport and Social Issues* 27, no. 1: 65–82.

Gilbert, James. 1994. "World's Fairs as Historical Events." In *Fair Representations: World's Fairs and the Modern World,* edited by Robert W. Rydell and Nancy Gwinn, 13–27. Amsterdam: VU University Press.

Gilroy, Paul. 1993. *The Black Atlantic: Modernity and Double Consciousness.* Cambridge, Mass.: Harvard University Press.

———. 2004. *After Empire: Multiculture or Postcolonial Melancholia.* Abingdon, U.K.: Routledge.

Goffman, Erving. 1990. *The Presentation of Self in Everyday Life.* New York: Doubleday.

Gorman, Steve. 2011. "Jewish Prayer Ritual Alarms Alaska Airlines Crew." http://www.reuters.com/article/2011/03/13/us-security-plane-prayers-idUSTRE72C3NX20110313.

Gottschalk, Peter, and Gabriel Greenberg. 2013. "Islamophobia and American History: Religious Stereotyping and Out-grouping of Muslims in the United States." In *Islamophobia in America: The Anatomy of Intolerance,* edited by C. W. Ernst, 21–52. New York: Palgrave Macmillan.

Gray, Herman. 1995. *Watching Race: Television and the Struggle for Blackness.* Minneapolis: University of Minnesota Press.

Grewal, Inderpal. 2003. "Transnational America: Race, Gender, and Citizenship after 9/11." *Social Identities: Journal for the Study of Race, Nation, and Culture* 9, no. 4: 535–61.

Grossberg, Lawrence. 1996. "Identity and Cultural Studies." In *Questions of Cultural Identity,* edited by Stuart Hall and Paul du Gay, 87–107. London: Sage.

———. 1997. *Bringing It All Back Home: Essays on Cultural Studies.* Durham, N.C.: Duke University Press.

Grout, Pam. 2013. "Miss America's Sgt. Theresa Vail Is First Contestant to Expose Tattoos." *People Magazine,* September 10. http://www.people.com/people/article/0,,20732653,00.html.

Gutel, Renee. 2006. "Arizona's Sept. 11 Memorial Called Offensive." National Public Radio. http://m.npr.org/story/6648907.

Hafiz, Yasmine. 2013. "Nina Davuluri's Miss America 2014 Win Prompts Twitter Backlash against Indians, Muslims." *The Huffington Post,* September 16. http://www.huffingtonpost.com/2013/09/16/nina-davuluri-miss-america-religion_n_3934428.html.

Hall, Stuart. 1990. "Cultural Identity and Diaspora." In *Identity: Community, Culture, Difference,* edited by Jonathan Rutherford. London: Lawrence and Wishart.

———. 1992a. "The Question of Cultural Identity." In *Modernity and Its Futures,* edited by Stuart Hall, David Held, and Anthony McGrew, 274–316. Cambridge: Polity Press in association with the Open University.

———. 1992b. "What Is This 'Black' in Black Popular Culture?" In *Black Popular Culture,* edited by Gina Dent, 21–33. Seattle, Wash.: Bay Press.

———. 2000. "Who Needs 'Identity'?" In *Questions of Cultural Identity,* edited by Stuart Hall and Paul du Guy, 1–17. Thousand Oaks, Calif.: Sage.

———. 2007. "Living with Difference." *Soundings* 37 (Winter): 148–58.

Harewood, Susan. 2010. "Tings Brown!" *Cultural Studies* 24, no. 2: 167–82.

Harvey, David. 2005. *A Brief History of Neoliberalism.* Oxford: Oxford University Press.

Hebshi, Shoshana. 2011. "Some Real Shock and Awe: Racially Profiled and Cuffed in Detroit." https://shebshi.wordpress.com/2011/09/12/some-real-shock-and-awe-racially-profiled-and-cuffed-in-detroit/.

Heim, Joe. 2012. "Wade Michael Page Was Steeped in Neo-Nazi 'Hate Music' Movement." *Washington Post,* August 7. http://www.washingtonpost.com/ lifestyle/style/wade-michael-page-was-steeped-in-neo-nazi-hate-music -movement/2012/08/07/b879451e-dfe8–11e1-a19c-fcfa365396c8_story.html.

Hinsley, Curtis M. 1991. "The World as Marketplace: Commodification of the Exotic at the World's Columbian Exposition Chicago, 1893." In *Exhibiting Cultures: The Poetics and Politics of Museum Display,* edited by Ivan Karp and Steve D. Lavine, 344–65. Washington, D.C.: Smithsonian Institution Press.

hooks, bell. 1994. *Teaching to Transgress: Education as the Practice of Freedom.* New York: Routledge.

Hopkins, W. W. 1991. "Flag Desecration as Seditious Libel." *Journalism Quarterly* 66: 814–22.

Huffington Post. 2012. "Obama Calls Indian Prime Minister Manmohan Singh over Wisconsin Shooting." August 8. http://www.huffingtonpost.com/2012/ 08/08/obama-singh-wisconsin-shooting_n_1756584.html.

Hull, J. 2003. "Executive Order No. 2003-02 [i.e. 2003-02]: Establishing the Governor's 9-11 Memorial Commission." http://azmemory.azlibrary.gov/cdm/ref/ collection/execorders/id/410.

Ignatiev, Noel. 1996. *How the Irish Became White.* New York: Routledge.

Jeong, Michael. 2013. "An Exclusive Interview: Miss California 2013, Crystal Lee." *AsianWeek,* November 18. http://www.asianweek.com/2013/11/18/an-exclusive -interview-miss-california-2013-crystal-lee/.

Jhally, Sut, and Justin Lewis. 1992. *Enlightened Racism:* The Cosby Show, *Audiences, and the Myth of the American Dream.* Boulder, Colo.: Westview Press.

Jindal, Bobby. 2009. "The Republican Response." *New York Times,* February 24. http://www.nytimes.com/2009/02/24/us/politics/24jindal-text.html?scp =2&sq=jindal&st=cse.

Kaplan, Amy. 2004. "Violent Belongings and the Question of Empire Today: Presidential Address to the American Studies Association, Hartford, Connecticut, October 17, 2003." *American Quarterly* 56, no. 1: 1–18.

Kaplan, Sarah. 2015. "Suspect in Chapel Hill Killings Described as Troublemaker, Obsessed with Parking." *Washington Post,* February 12. https://www.washington post.com/news/morning-mix/wp/2015/02/12/alleged-chapel-hill -killer-described-as-neighborhood-bully-obsessed-with-parking-and-noise/.

Katz, Jonathan M. 2015. "In Chapel Hill, Suspect's Rage Went beyond a Parking Dispute." *New York Times,* March 3. http://www.nytimes.com/2015/03/04/us/ chapel-hill-muslim-student-shootings-north-carolina.html.

Kelly, John Dunham. 2003. "U.S. Power, after 9/11 and before It: If Not an Empire, Then What?" *Public Culture* 15, no. 2: 347–69.

Kendall, Mikki. 2013. "#SolidarityIsForWhiteWomen: Women of Color's Issue with Digital Feminism." *The Guardian*, August 14. http://www.theguardian.com/commentisfree/2013/aug/14/solidarityisforwhitewomen-hashtag-feminism.

Ki-Moon, Ban. 2015. "Secretary-General's Opening Remarks at Humanitarian Pledging." Conference for Syria, Kuwait City, March 31. http://www.un.org/sg/statements/index.asp?nid=8505.

Kotkin, Joel. 2011. "India Conquers the World." *Newsweek*, July 25. http://www.newsweek.com/indias-most-important-exports-brains-and-talent-68395.

Kumar, Amitava. 2000. *Passport Photos.* California: University of California Press.

Kurien, Prema A. 2003. "To Be or Not to Be South Asian: Contemporary Indian American Politics." *Journal of Asian American Studies* 6, no. 3: 261–88.

Laclau, Ernesto. 1994. *The Making of Political Identities.* London: Verso.

Laclau, Ernesto, and Chantal Mouffe. 1985. *Hegemony and Socialist Strategy.* New York: Verso Press.

Laguerre, Michael. 1999. *Minoritized Space: An Inquiry into the Spatial Order of Things.* Berkeley, Calif.: Institute of Governmental Studies Press.

Lamb, Amanda. 2015. "Wife of Triple-Shooting Suspect Said Crime Not Motivated by Bias." WRAL. http://www.wral.com/wife-of-triple-shooting-suspect-said-crime-not-motivated-by-bias/14440671/#tKTv5xgkZ3BotCCl.99.

Lee, Michelle Ye Hee. 2015. "Donald Trump's False Comments Connecting Mexican Immigrants and Crime." *Washington Post*, July 8. https://www.washingtonpost.com/news/fact-checker/wp/2015/07/08/donald-trumps-false-comments-connecting-mexican-immigrants-and-crime/.

Lee, Robert G. 1999. *Orientals: Asian Americans in Popular Culture.* Philadelphia: Temple University Press.

Lehman, Christopher P. 2007. *The Colored Cartoon: Black Presentation in American Animated Short Films, 1907–1954.* Amherst: University of Massachusetts Press.

Leonard, Karen. 1997. *South Asian Americans.* Westport Conn.: Greenwood Press.

Lewis, Roger. 1995. *The Life and Death of Peter Sellers.* London: Arrow Books.

López, Alfred J. 2005. *Postcolonial Whiteness: A Critical Reader on Race and Empire.* Albany: State University of New York Press.

Lowe, Lisa. 1996. *Immigrant Acts: On Asian American Cultural Politics.* Durham, N.C.: Duke University Press.

Lowry, Rich. 2015. "Ta-Nehisi Coates's New Book Betrays a Toxic Worldview." *National Review*, July 24. http://www.nationalreview.com/article/421543/ta-nehisi-coatess-new-book-betrays-toxic-worldview-rich-lowry.

Maira, Sunaina. 2007. "Indo-Chic: Late Capitalist Orientalism and Imperial Culture." In *Alien Encounters: Popular Culture in Asian America*, edited by Mimi

Thi Nguyen and Thuy Linh Nguyen Tu, 221–43. Durham, N.C.: Duke University Press.

———. 2009. *Missing: Youth, Citizenship, and Empire after 9/11.* Durham, N.C.: Duke University Press.

Mani, Bakirathi. 2012. *Aspiring to Home: South Asians in America.* Stanford, Calif.: Stanford University Press.

Mannur, Anita. 2010. *Culinary Fictions: Food in South Asian Diasporic Culture.* Philadelphia: Temple University Press.

Marchetti, Gina. 1993. *Romance and the "Yellow Peril": Race, Sex, and Discursive Strategies in Hollywood Fiction.* Berkeley: University of California Press.

Márquez, John D. 2013. *Black–Brown Solidarity: Racial Politics in the New Gulf South.* Austin: University of Texas Press.

Martinot, Steve. 2010. *The Machinery of Whiteness: Studies in the Structure of Racialization.* Philadelphia: Temple University Press.

Mbembe, J.-A. 2003. "Necropolitics." *Public Culture* 15, no. 1: 11–40.

McDowell, Edwin. 1990. "After the Cold War, the Land of the Rising Threat." *New York Times,* June 18, C13.

Mendible, Myra. 2007. *From Bananas to Buttocks: The Latina Body in Popular Film and Culture.* Austin: University of Texas Press.

Miller, Toby. 2007. *Cultural Citizenship: Cosmopolitanism, Consumerism, and Television in a Neoliberal Age.* Philadelphia: Temple University Press.

Mogel, Lize, and Alexis Bhagat, eds. 2007. *An Atlas of Radical Cartography.* Los Angeles: Journal of Aesthetics and Protest Press.

Mohan, Anand. 1980. "Acculturation, Assimilation and Political Adaptation." In *The New Ethnics,* edited by Pratama Saran and Edwin Eames, 272–93. New York: Praeger.

Molina-Guzmán, Isabel. 2010. *Dangerous Curves: Latina Bodies in the Media.* New York: New York University Press.

Morely, David. 1999. "Bounded Realms: Household, Family, Community, and Nation." In *Home, Exile, Homeland,* edited by Hamid Naficy, 151–68. New York: Routledge.

———. 2007. *Home Territories: Media, Mobility, and Identity.* London: Routledge.

Morley, David, and Kuan-Hsing Chen. 1996. *Stuart Hall: Critical Dialogues in Cultural Studies.* London: Routledge.

Morris, Narelle. 2001. "Paradigm Paranoia: Images of Japan and the Japanese in American Popular Fiction of the Early 1990s." *Japanese Studies* 21, no. 1: 45–59.

Mukerjee, Aditya. 2013. "Don't Fly during Ramadan: The Chilling Story of a New

York Man Detained and Interrogated for Hours by TSA, FBI, NYPD and JetBlue." http://www.alternet.org/civil-liberties/dont-fly-during-ramadan.

Mukherjee, Roopali. 2006. *The Racial Order of Things: Cultural Imaginaries of the Post-soul Era.* Minneapolis: University of Minnesota Press.

———. 2014. "Rhyme and Reason: 'Post-race' and the Politics of Colorblind Racism." In *The Colorblind Screen,* edited by Sarah Nilsen and Sarah E. Turner, 39–56. New York: New York University Press.

Muñoz, José Esteban. 1999. *Disidentifications: Queers of Color and the Performance of Politics.* Minneapolis: University of Minnesota Press.

Munsil, Lee. 2006. "Lee Munsil's Comments on the Arizona 9-11 Memorial." September 25. http://votesmart.org/public-statement/215207/len-munsils -comments-on-the-arizona-9–11-memorial#.VeYzidNViko.

Naficy, Hamid. 1998. *Home, Exile, Homeland: Film, Media, and the Politics of Place.* New York: Routledge.

Nakayama, Thomas K., and Robert L. Krizek. 1995. "Whiteness: A Strategic Rhetoric." *Quarterly Journal of Speech* 81, no. 3: 291–309.

Newsmax. 2012. "Clinton Tries to Calm India's Anger over Wisconsin Attack." August 6. http://www.newsmax.com/Newsfront/wisconsin-shooting-sikh-temple/ 2012/08/06/id/447749#ixzz35f0PQFqp.

New York Civil Liberties Union. n.d. "Stop-and-Frisk Data." http://www.nyclu.org/ content/stop-and-frisk-data.

Nilsen, Sarah, and Sarah E. Turner, eds. 2014. *The Colorblind Screen: Television in Post-racial America.* New York: New York University Press.

Obama, Barack H. 2004. "Transcript: Illinois Senate Candidate Barack Obama." *Washington Post.* http://www.washingtonpost.com/wp-dyn/articles/A19751 -2004Jul27.html.

———. 2013. "Obama, Barack. Remarks by the President on Trayvon Martin." July 19. https://www.whitehouse.gov/the-press-office/2013/07/19/remarks-president -trayvon-martin.

Ong, Aihwa. 2006. *Neoliberalism as Exception.* Durham, N.C.: Duke University Press.

Ono, Kent A., and Vincent Pham. 2009. *Asian Americans and the Media.* Cambridge, Mass.: Polity.

Ono, Kent A., and John M. Sloop. 2002. *Shifting Borders: Rhetoric, Immigration, and California's Proposition 187.* Philadelphia: Temple University Press.

Parker, Lonnae O'Neal. 2014. "Spring Preview Museums: 'Beyond Bollywood' Passage to American." *Washington Post,* January 31. https://www.washington post.com/entertainment/museums/spring-preview-museums-beyond

-bollywood-passage-to-america/2014/01/31/ff308aa4-822f-11e3-bbe5
-6a2a3141e3a9_story.html.

Pearce, Matt. 2012. "George Zimmerman Calls Show He Has Support—but from Whom?" *Los Angeles Times,* June 18. http://articles.latimes.com/2012/jun/18/nation/la-na-nn-who-are-george-zimmermans-supporters-20120618.

Prashad, Vijay. 2000. *Karma of Brown Folk.* Minneapolis: University of Minnesota Press.

Puar, Jasbir K. 2007. *Terrorist Assemblages: Homonationalism in Queer Times.* Durham, N.C.: Duke University Press.

Quijano, Anibal. 2007. "Coloniality and Modernity/Rationality." *Cultural Studies* 21, nos. 2–3: 168–78.

Quinones, Sam. 2008. "Officials Plead for Tolerance as 9/11 Anniversary Nears." *Los Angeles Times,* September 8. http://articles.latimes.com/2006/sep/08/local/me-islam8.

Raghavan, Gautam, and Paul Monteiro. 2012. "Honoring the Victims of the Oak Creek Tragedy. August 14." https://www.whitehouse.gov/blog/2012/08/14/honoring-victims-oak-creek-tragedy.

Rana, Junaid Akram. 2011. *Terrifying Muslims: Race and Labor in the South Asian Diaspora.* Durham, N.C.: Duke University Press.

Rao, Malika. 2013. "Is It Time to Retire Apu?" *Huffington Post,* September 20. http://www.huffingtonpost.com/2013/09/20/the-simpsons-apu-racist_n_3956603.html.

Reddi, Rishi. 2007. *Karma and Other Stories.* New York: HarperCollins.

Riker, David. 1998. *La Ciudad.* United States: Journeyman Pictures.

Robertson, Craig. 2010. *The Passport in America: The History of a Document.* New York: Oxford University Press.

Rodriguez, Richard. 2002. *Brown: The Last Discovery of America.* New York: Penguin Books.

Roediger, David R. 1991. *The Wages of Whiteness: Race and the Making of the American Working Class.* London: Verso.

———. 2005. *Working toward Whiteness: How American Immigrants Became White.* New York: Basic Books.

Rosenblatt, Roger. 2003. "Why We Play the Game." *U.S. Society and Values* 8, no. 2. http://www.4uth.gov.ua/usa/english/society/ijse1203/rosenblatt.htm.

Rowe, Aimee Marie Carillo. 2004. "Whose 'America'? The Politics of Rhetoric and Space in the Formation of U.S. Nationalism." *Radical History Review* 89: 115–34.

Rybczynski, Witold. 1987. *Home: A Short History of an Idea.* East Rutherford, N.J.: Penguin.

Rydell, Robert W. 1984. *All the World's a Fair: Visions of Empire at American International Expositions, 1876–1916.* Chicago: University of Chicago Press.

Said, Edward W. 1979. *Orientalism.* 1st Vintage Books ed. New York: Vintage Books.

———. 1993. *Culture and Imperialism.* New York: Random House.

Santa Ana, Otto. 2002. *Brown Tide Rising: Metaphors of Latinos in Contemporary American Public Discourse.* 1st ed. Austin: University of Texas Press.

Sara, P. 1985. *The Asian Indian Experience in the United States.* Cambridge, Mass.: Schneckman.

Scott, Robert T. 2009. "Gov. Bobby Jindal Takes Center Stage in '60 Minutes' Profile." *Times-Picayune, New Orleans,* March 1. http://www.nola.com/news/index.ssf/2009/03/cbs_60_minutes_scrutinizes_lou.html.

Sen, Rinku, and Deepa Iyer. 2013. "Stop and Frisk, South Asians, and Kal Penn's Tweets." *ColorLines,* August 16. http://www.colorlines.com/articles/stop-and-frisk-south-asians-and-kal-penns-tweets.

Shah, Ridi. 2012. "Sikh Temple Shooting: Why Do the Media Care Less about This Attack?" *Huffington Post,* October 6. http://www.huffingtonpost.com/riddhi-shah/sikh-temple-shooting_b_1749866.html.

Sharma, Sarah. 2010. "Taxi Cab Publics and the Production of Brown Space after 9/11." *Cultural Studies* 24, no. 2: 183–99.

Sibley, David. 1995. *Geographies of Exclusion.* London: Routledge.

Siegel, Joel. 2010. "Islamic Sharia Law to Be Banned in, ah, Oklahoma." ABC News, June 14. http://abcnews.go.com/US/Media/oklahoma-pass-laws-prohibiting-islamic-sharia-laws-apply/story?id=10908521.

Silva, Kumarini. 2010. "Brown: From Identity to Identification." *Cultural Studies* 24, no. 2: 167–82.

———. 2014. "Global Nationalisms and Pastoral Identities: Association for India's Development Negotiates Transnational Activism." In *Transnational Feminism and Global Advocacy,* edited by Gita Rajan and Jigna Desai, 55–63. New York: Routledge.

Singh, Simran Jeet, and Pabhjot Singh. 2012. "How Hate Gets Counted." *New York Times,* August 24. http://www.nytimes.com/2012/08/24/opinion/do-american-sikhs-count.html?_r=0.

Smith, Andrea. 2006. "Heteropatriarchy and the Three Pillars of White Supremacy: Rethinking Women of Color Organizing." In *Incite! Women of Color against Violence,* 66–73. Cambridge, Mass.: South End Press.

Smith, Darron T. 2013. "Echoes of Cosby in Don Lemon's Call for Blacks to Clean Up Their Act." *Huffington Post,* October 5. http://www.huffingtonpost.com/darron-t-smith-phd/cosby-don-lemon_b_3695673.html.

Smithsonian. 2014. "Beyond Bollywood: Immigration, Culture, and the Indian American Experience." *Smithsonian Folklife Festival* (blog), February 18. http://www.festival.si.edu/blog/2014/beyond-bollywood-indian-american-experience/.

Smolko, Joanna R. 2012. "Southern Fried Foster: Representing Race and Place through Music in Looney Tunes Cartoons." *American Music* 30, no. 3: 344–72.

South Asian Americans Leading Together. 2001. "American Backlash." Special report. http://saalt.org/wp-content/uploads/2012/09/American-Backlash-report.pdf.

Spigel, Lynn. 2004. "Entertainment Wars: Television Culture after 9/11." *American Quarterly* 56, no. 2: 235–70.

Spivak, Gayatri Chakravorty. 1987. *In Other Worlds: Essays in Cultural Politics.* New York: Methuen.

———. 1988. "Can the Subaltern Speak?" In *Marxism and the Interpretation of Culture,* edited by Cary Nelson and Lawrence Grossberg, 271–313. Urbana: University of Illinois Press.

Stanford Peace Innovation Lab and Sikh American Legal Defense and Education Fund. 2013. *Turban Myths: The Opportunities and Challenges for Reframing Sikh American Identity in Post-9/11 America.* Washington, D.C.: SALDEF. https://issuu.com/saldefmedia/docs/turbanmyths_121113.

Starnes, Todd. 2013. "The Liberal Miss America Judges Won't Say This—but Miss Kansas Lost because She Actually Represented American Values." September 15. https://twitter.com/toddstarnes/statuses/379437735980711936.

Takaki, Ronald T. 1993. *A Different Mirror: A History of Multicultural America.* 1st paperback ed. Boston: Little, Brown.

———. 1998. *Strangers from a Different Shore: A History of Asian Americans.* Updated and rev. ed., 1st Back Bay pbk. ed. Boston: Little, Brown.

Talbot, Margaret. 2015. "The Story of a Hate Crime: What Led to the Murder of Three Muslim Students in Chapel Hill?" *The New Yorker,* June 22. http://www.newyorker.com/magazine/2015/06/22/the-story-of-a-hate-crime.

Talking Point Memo. 2015. "5 Points to Know about Craig Hicks, Man Accused of Killing 3 Muslim Students." http://talkingpointsmemo.com/fivepoints/craig-stephen-hicks-guns-anti-theism.

Torres, Sasha. 2013. "Black (Counter)Terrorism." *American Quarterly* 65, no. 1: 171–76.

U.S. Supreme Court. 2013. *Shelby County, Alabama v. Holder, Attorney General, et. al.* No. 12-96. http://caselaw.findlaw.com/us-supreme-court/12-96.html#sthash.HP6Pg2CN.dpuf.

Valdivia, Angharad N. 2000. *A Latina in the Land of Hollywood and Other Essays on Media Culture.* Tucson: University of Arizona Press.

———. 2008. *Latina/o Communication Studies Today.* New York: Peter Lang.

Vij, Manish. 2007. "The Apu Travesty." *The Guardian,* July 16. http://www.the guardian.com/commentisfree/2007/jul/16/theaputragedy.

Walsh, Jim. 2011a. "Mesa Family of Man Slain after 9/11 Get Apology from Lawmaker." *Arizona Republic,* April 27. http://www.azcentral.com/community/mesa/articles/2011/04/27/20110427arizona-9-11-memorial-ruling-reversed.html.

———. 2011b. "Mesa Man Pushes to Keep Brother's Name on Sept. 11 Memorial." *Arizona Republic,* April 26. http://archive.azcentral.com/arizonarepublic/local/articles/2011/04/26/20110426mesa-man-sept-11-memorial-fight.html.

Weaver, Simon. 2011. "Jokes, Rhetoric, and Embodied Racism: A Rhetorical Discourse Analysis of the Logics of Racist Jokes on the Internet." *Ethnicities* 11, no. 4: 413–35.

Welch, Michael. 2002. *Detained: Immigration Laws and Expanding INS Jail Complex.* Philadelphia: Temple University Press.

———. 2011. *Corrections: A Critical Approach.* 3rd ed. Milton Park, U.K.: Routledge.

West, Cornel. 1993. *Race Matters.* Boston: Beacon Press.

Williams, Raymond. 1961. *The Long Revolution.* New York: Columbia University Press.

Index

KUMARINI SILVA is assistant professor of communication at the University of North Carolina at Chapel Hill. She is the coeditor of *Feminist Erasures: Challenging Backlash Culture.*